DATE DUE

NO 10 '94			
NO 24 '95			
MR 29 '99			
AP 24 00			

DEMCO 38-296

Critical praise for a ground-breaking work

"Brother to Brother is a monument not only to what has been lost but to the incredible hope and creativity now present. This anthology speaks not only brother to brother but to everyone who applauds the ability of a personal and artistic vision to rise above repression and imprint itself."

—*Philadelphia Inquirer*

❁

"This is not a book to read through quickly, but a delicacy to linger over and savor. All the poems, essays, interviews, and short fiction in the book are powerful and well chosen." —*The Advocate*

❁

"Brother to Brother is a book to cuddle with, dream with, dance with, and celebrate with. It heals. Its words jump from the page and find their way to places in the soul that have hurt for far too long." —*BMSN Network*

❁

"A truly inclusive anthology that provides something to satisfy everyone's literary taste, as well as providing a vision of community and hopes for a positive future." —*New York Native*

❁

"Brother to Brother is a worthy addition to a growing body of work that illuminates the African-American gay male experience. I cannot recommend it highly enough for black and non-black readers alike."

—*Bay Area Reporter*

❁

"Apart from being excellent reading, *Brother to Brother* constitues another milestone in black gay literature, filling gaps, adding further visibility, creating its own traditions and identity." —*San Francisco Sentinel*

❁

"The anthology includes poems and stories just as fierce, just as astonishing — and just as sexy and funny — as Hemphill's own writing."

—*Lambda Book Report*

❁

"Brother to Brother is a learning experience for white gay men, a self-affirming, refreshing experience for black gay men." —*Just Out*

❁

"Ranging in tone and pitch from the mournful to the celebratory, the collection's value lies in its ability to express not only the diversity of the black gay community but the empowerment that comes from knowing the self. *Brother to Brother* is so powerful and so successful it would take volumes just to comment on the range of emotions that it brings forward."

—*Washington Blade*

BROTHER TO BROTHER

New Writings by Black Gay Men

EDITED BY ESSEX HEMPHILL
CONCEIVED BY JOSEPH FAIRCHILD BEAM
PROJECT MANAGED BY DOROTHY BEAM

Boston • Alyson Publications, Inc.

This is a trade paperback original from Alyson Publications, Inc.,
40 Plympton St., Boston, Mass. 02118.
Distributed in England by GMP Publishers, P.O. Box 247, London N17 9QR England.

First edition, second printing: November 1991   5 4 3 2

ISBN 1-55583-146-X

Library of Congress card catalog number: 91-71186

PERMISSIONS

"A First Affair," copyright © 1989 Charles R.P. Pouncy, from *Pyramid Periodical*, Winter 1990.

"At the Club," copyright © 1989 Alan Miller, from *At the Club*, Oakland, Calif.: Grand Entrances Press, 1989.

"Aunt Ida Pieces a Quilt," copyright © 1989 Melvin Dixon, from *Ploughshares*, December 1989.

"Brother Can You Spare Some Time?" copyright © 1985 Joseph Beam, from *Au Courant*, vol. 3, no. 33 (1989).

"Brothers Loving Brothers," copyright © Vega, from *Men of Color*, Sicklerville, N.J.: Vega Press, 1989.

"Couch Poem," "Prescription," and "What Do I Do about You," copyright © 1989 Donald Woods, from *The Space*, New York: Vexation Press, 1989.

"Hooked for Life," copyright © 1987 Assoto Saint, from *Tongues Untied*, London: Gay Men's Press, 1987.

"An Infected Planet," copyright © 1989 Wrath, from *The Horrors of Humanity*, Philadelphia: Heartfelt Press, 1989.

"Interview with Isaac Julien," copyright © 1989 Essex Hemphill, from *Black Film Review*, vol. 5, no. 3 (1989).

"In the Darkness, Fuck Me Now," copyright © 1977 Adrian Stanford, from Black and Queer, Boston: Good Gay Poets Press, 1977.

"Introduction," copyright © 1990 Essex Hemphill. Excerpts and adaptations from the introduction have appeared in the following: "The Imperfect Moments," *High Performance*, vol. 13, no. 2 (Summer 1990); "Does Your Mama Know About Me?" *Gay Community News*, vol. 17, no. 36 (1990); "Loyalty," *Men and Intimacy*, Crossing Press, 1990; "Three Voices Closer to Home,"*Lambda Book Report*, vol. 2, no. 1 (1989); "Loyalty," *Pyramid Periodical*, Summer 1989; "Loyalty," *Gay Community News*, vol. 17, no. 10 (1989).

"It Happened to Me," copyright © 1989 Roger V. Pamplin, Jr., from *BLK*, June 1989.

"James Baldwin: Not a Bad Legacy, Brother," copyright © 1987 Joseph Beam, from *Au Courant*, vol. 6, no. 6 (1987).

"Letter to Gregory," copyright © 1984 Alan Miller, from *Black American Literature Forum*, Spring 1984.

"Making Ourselves from Scratch," copyright © 1987 Joseph Beam, from *Au Courant*, vol. 6, no. 13 (1987).

"Names and Sorrows," copyright © 1989 D. Rubin Green, from *Changing Men*, no. 21 (Winter/Spring 1990).

"Non, Je Ne Regrette Rien," copyright © 1989 David Frechette, from *PWA Coalition Newsline*, no. 56 (June 1990).

"Obi's Story," copyright © 1989 Cary Alan Johnson, from *Tribe: An American Gay Journal*, vol. 1, no. 1 (1989).

"Psalm for the Ghetto," "Remembrance of Rittenhouse Square," and "Sacrifice," copyright © 1977 Adrian Stanford, from *Black and Queer*, Boston: Good Gay Poets Press, 1977.

"Safe Harbour," copyright © 1988 David Frechette, from *Pyramid Periodical*, Fall 1988.

"The Tomb of Sorrow," copyright © 1989 Essex Hemphill, from *Bastard Review*, no. 3/4 (1990).

"True Confessions: A Discourse on Images of Black Male Sexuality," copyright © 1986 Isaac Julien and Kobena Mercer, from *Ten-8*, no. 22 (1986).

"When My Brother Fell," copyright © 1989 Essex Hemphill, from *Gay Community News*, vol. 17, no. 10 (1989).

Black men loving Black men is a call to action, an acknowledgement of responsibility. We take care of our own kind when the night grows cold and silent. These days the nights are cold-blooded and the silence echoes with complicity.

— JOSEPH BEAM
"Brother to Brother:
Words from the Heart"

Joseph Fairchild Beam
December 30, 1954 – December 27, 1988

JOSEPH BEAM was the editor of the ground-breaking anthology of black gay literature, *In the Life*. Published in 1986 by Alyson Publications, it provided a generation of black gay men with affirmations for their sexual identities and desires.

In the Introduction to *In the Life* he wrote, "There are many reasons for Black gay invisibility. Hard words come to mind: power, racism, conspiracy, oppression, and privilege — each deserving of a full-fledged discussion in gay history books yet unwritten."

Joe challenged the prevailing silence surrounding the lives of black gay men. "We have always existed in the African-American community. We have been ministers, hairdressers, entertainers, sales clerks, civil rights activists, teachers, playwrights, trash collectors, dancers, government officials, choirmasters, and dishwashers. You name it; we've done it — most often with scant recognition. We have mediated family disputes, cared for and reared our siblings, and housed our sick. We have performed many and varied important roles within our community."

Joseph Beam died of AIDS-related causes at the age of thirty-three in Philadelphia. Prior to his death he had begun editing *Brother to Brother*. While a board member of the National Coalition of Black Lesbians and Gays, he became the founding editor of the organization's *Black/Out* magazine. His commitment to ending the silence surrounding the lives of black gay men has been a most empowering legacy. He was a cultural and political activist dedicated to ending racism, homophobia, heterosexism, and the debilitating oppressions spawned by patriarchy.

In his essay "Making Ourselves from Scratch," he writes, "It was imperative for my survival that I did not attend to or believe the images that were presented of black people or gay people. Perhaps that was the beginning of my passage from passivism to activism, that I needed to create my reality, that I needed to create images by which I, and other black gay men to follow, could live this life."

Joseph Beam was a respected and important figure in the gay and lesbian world. He actively contributed to the empowerment of black gay men. His pro-feminism made him well informed of women's issues and a staunch supporter of women's literature. Reverend Renee McCoy, former executive director of the National Coalition of Black Lesbians and Gays and a good friend of Joe's, noted in an *Au Courant* tribute to him that his work enriched the community on multiple levels. "Joe left behind a legacy of who we are as black lesbians and gays. His work is a resounding affirmation of our lives." *The Philadelphia Inquirer* wrote that "Mr. Beam developed a national reputation as an articulate, sensitive voice for the black gay community." But he was also a man who cared deeply about "black men loving black men."

"The bottom line is this," he said. "We are Black men who are proudly gay. What we offer is our lives, our love, our visions ... We are coming home with our heads held up high."

CONTENTS

ACKNOWLEDGMENTS

Mrs. Dorothy Beam cannot be overly praised for her willingness to ensure that this anthology would be successfully completed. She has provided an example of strength and faith that could wisely inform other parents of gay men and lesbians. Although the loss of her son could have been a debilitating grief, she deliberately worked to ensure that Joe's words and vision would not be lost or forgotten.

The experience of working with Barbara Smith has been invaluable beyond praise. Barbara provided me with excellent information regarding the technical aspects of this book, including suggestions of material to research and authors to contact, the proper way to assemble a manuscript of this size and nature, and much positive encouragement. From questions of copyright to questions of copyediting, Barbara never failed to avail herself to answering my queries. I have received an invaluable education from a person I respect not only for her accomplishments with Kitchen Table: Women of Color Press, but also for her insistence on integrity and excellence, and her insistence that there be a commitment of faith to one's work and politics.

Though some men in the black gay community resented and questioned Barbara's involvement in the project, I stood by my decision to maintain her input. The number of years of independent literary publishing experience she possesses was a priceless resource to draw from, a resource that is not presently equalled by any black gay man, with the exception of a few who are in the closet and would not have worked on a project such as this. I need not say that Joe respected Barbara's work and loved her as a dear friend and comrade. Joe was a pro-feminist black gay man, and none of us should forget that in our haste to complain.

For Mrs. Beam, Barbara Smith, and truly for me, *Brother to Brother* is a labor of love as much as it is a tool for the continuing empowerment of black gay men. But there were others whose input and assistance must be acknowledged and praised to clearly understand how this book was nurtured by a lot of love and support. *Brother to Brother* is a reality because of the faith and courage of its contributors. I thank all of them. I thank the following individuals and organizations in no particular order: Marlon Riggs, Michelle Parkerson, Wayson Jones, Dottie Green, Frank Broderick (*Au Courant*), Ed Hermance (Giovanni's Room), Mike Hargust, Sun Beam, Rita Addessa (Philadelphia Lesbian and Gay Task Force), Jim Bennett (Lambda Rising Bookstore), Dr. C.A.

Caceres, Jane Troxell and Rose Fennell (*Lambda Book Report*), Donald Woods, Charley Shively (*Gay Community News*), Sharon Farmer, Vernon Rosario, Derrick Thomas (*BLK*), Dr. Thomas Martin, Alan Bell (*BLK*), Isaac Julien, Audre Lorde, Jewelle Gomez, Damballah, Amy Schoulder, Gay Men of African Descent, Black Gay Men United, Unity Inc., Tede Matthews (Modern Times Bookstore), Colin Robinson, the Painted Bride Art Center, the Kitchen, Larry Duckette, the Philadelphia Public Library, Jacquie Jones (*Black Film Review*), Smart Place, BJP's, Eric Gutierrez (*High Performance*), John Cunningham, Dr. J. Brooks Dendy, Sandra Calhoun, Tommi Avicolli (*Philadelphia Gay News*), James Charles Roberts, Arleen Olshan, Assoto Saint, my parents and family, and the many friends and supporters affirmed and inspired by the work of Joseph Beam.

A special praise is necessary for two men, Ron Simmons and Charles Harpe, who served as unofficial readers and advisors. They availed themselves to this project and helped me in many important ways. Ron recommended several of the authors in this collection and provided me with historical information which aided me in writing the Introduction. Charles assisted me in proofreading and assembling the manuscript, and has committed himself to helping to promote the book. Ron and Charles are owed much more than my gratitude and friendship for the many selfless ways in which they have assisted this project. Thank you, brothers and sisters, named and unnamed. Let us all take care of our blessings...

Essex Hemphill
August 1990
Philadelphia

INTRODUCTION

I. Mask maker, mask maker, make me a mask

If I had read a book like *In the Life* when I was fifteen or sixteen, there might have been one less mask for me to put aside later in life.

I approached the swirling vortex of my adolescent sexuality as a wide-eyed, scrawny teenager, intensely feeling the power of a budding sexual drive unchecked by any legitimate information at home or on the streets. I had nothing to guide me except the pointer of my early morning erection, but I was not inclined to run away from home to see where it would lead. I couldn't shame my family with behavior unbecoming to an eldest son. I had the responsibility of setting an example for my younger siblings, though I would have preferred an older brother to carry out that task, or a father to be at home.

There would have been one less mask for me to create when long ago it became apparent that what I was or what I was becoming — in spite of myself — could be ridiculed, harassed, and even murdered with impunity. The male code of the streets where I grew up made this very clear: Sissies, punks, and faggots were not "cool" with the boys. Come out at your own risk was the prevailing code for boys like myself who knew we were different, but we didn't dare challenge the prescribed norms regarding sexuality for fear of the consequences we would suffer.

I searched the card catalogue at the local library and discovered there were books about homosexuality in the "adult" section. I wasn't allowed to check out books from that section because I was only in sixth grade, but I could read them in the library, which I did, avidly, stopping in almost every day after school for several hours, and continuing this practice until I had devoured everything. What was there for me to read in 1969 was in no way affirming of the sexual identity germinating within me. The material regarding homosexuality considered it to be an illness or an affliction, and at worst, a sin against God and nature. I knew what masturbation was before I learned to masturbate. The books were very informative about the practice, but not very instructional. The books made no references to black men that I can recall, nor were there black case studies for me to examine, and in the few pictures of men identified as homosexual, not one was black.

Nothing in those books said that men could truly love one another. Nothing said that masturbation would be comforting. Nothing celebrated the genius and creativity of homosexual men or even suggested that such men could lead ordinary lives. Nothing encouraged me to love black men — I learned to do that on my own.

When I finished my month-long reading marathon, I put away the last book knowing only that I had homosexual tendencies and desires, but beyond that awareness I didn't recognize myself in any of the material I had so exhaustively read. If anything, I could have ignorantly concluded that homosexuality was peculiar to white people, and my conclusion would have been supported by the deliberate lack of evidence concerning black men and homosexual desire.

There would have been one less mask to tolerate had I not invested time trying to disinherit myself from the sweet knowledge about myself. I tried to separate my sexuality from my Negritude only to discover, in my particular instance, that they are inextricably woven together. If I was clear about no other identity, I knew, year by year, that I was becoming a "homo." A *black* homo. My outward denial consisted of heterosexual dating which served to lower suspicions about my soft-spoken nature. But the girls I dated will tell you I was barely interested in overcoming our mutual virginity.

Had there been the option of reading *In the Life* when I was a pubescent homosexual, I might have found time to dream of becoming a damn good carpenter, a piano player, a gardener, or a brain surgeon, but instead, a part of my life has been spent making strong, durable masks, and another part has been spent removing them, destroying them whenever possible.

Had *In the Life* been there when I was sneaking around the library looking for my reflection, I would have discovered the affirmations lacking for me in the otherwise strong black novels I was also reading. The modern Negro texts of protest and the black writings of the 1960s never acknowledge homosexuals except as negative, tragic, or comedic characters.

Surely it is one kind of pain that a man reckons with when he *feels* and he *knows* he is not welcome, wanted, or appreciated in his homeland. But the pain I believe to be most tragic and critical is not the pain of invisibility he suffers in his homeland, but the compounded pain and invisibility he endures in his own home, among family and friends. This occurs when he cannot honestly occupy the spaces of family and friendship because he has adopted — out of insecurity, defense, and fear — the mask of the invisible man.

Had there been *In the Life* when I began to have erotic dreams about boys in school, had it been there when I began to steal glances at boys in the showers, I might have spared the girls I pretended to love the difficulty of trying to understand a guy who was merely fence-sitting, waiting for the wind to blow him north or south. I might have spared myself the humiliations of pretense and denial. I might have had the courage to stand up for myself when confronted as a faggot.

I was such a good mask maker. The last one I am now removing was perhaps my most deceptive, my most prized of all. Once it is off my face, I imagine nailing it to the wall like the head of some game, tracked and killed for the sport of it. But this isn't sport. This is my life — not game. Had there been *In the Life* when I needed a father, a brother, a lover, a friend; had it been there when I needed to say no instead of yes and yes when I knew no was cowardly; had it been there to affirm my compounded identity when I was reading Ralph Ellison's *Invisible Man* or Richard Wright's *Native Son*, then perhaps a more whole picture of the black male might have formed in my consciousness. *In the Life* might have mitigated and nurtured my germinating sexual identity, or at the very least I would not have spent part of my life becoming an expert but useless mask maker.

II. Does your mama know about me? Does she know just what I am?

Throughout the 1980s, many of us grieved the loss of friends, lovers, and relatives who were one moment strong, healthy, and able-bodied, but then in an instant became thin-framed, emaciated, hacking and wheezing, their bodies wracked with horrible pain. Sometimes brave souls would return to the family roost to disclose their sexuality and ask permission to die in familiar surroundings. Too often, families were discovering for the first time that the dear brother, the favorite uncle, the secretive son was a homosexual, a black gay man, and the unfortunate victim of the killer virus, AIDS. Some parents had always known and some had never suspected that their son was a black gay man, a sissy, a queer, a faggot. For some families this shocking discovery and grief expressed itself as shame and anger; it compelled them to disown their flesh and blood, denying dying men the love and support that friends often provided as extended family. In other instances families were very understanding and bravely stood by their brethren through their final days.

Joseph Beam, in his powerful essay "Brother to Brother: Words from the Heart," defined *home* as being larger, more complex and encompassing than one's living room:

> When I speak of home, I mean not only the familial constellation from which I grew, but the entire Black community: the Black press, the Black church, Black academicians, the Black literati, and the Black left. Where is my reflection? I am most often rendered invisible, perceived as a threat to the family, or I am tolerated if I am silent and inconspicuous. I cannot go home as who I am and that hurts me deeply.[1]

Beam articulated one of the primary issues black gay men are faced with when our relationships with our families and communities are examined. We cannot afford to be disconnected from these institutions, yet it would seem that we are willing to create and accept dysfunctional roles in them, roles of caricature, silence, and illusion. In truth, we are often forced into these roles to survive. This critical dilemma causes some of us to engage in dishonest relationships with our kin. It can foster apathy between us and the communities of home that we need and that need our presence. The contradictions of "home" are amplified and become more complex when black gay men's relationships with the white gay community are also examined.

The post-Stonewall white gay community of the 1980s was not seriously concerned with the existence of black gay men except as sexual objects. In media and art the black male was given little representation except as a big, black dick. This aspect of the white gay sensibility is strikingly revealed in the photographs of black males by the late Robert Mapplethorpe. Though his images may be technically and esthetically well composed, his work *artistically* perpetuates racial stereotypes constructed around sexuality and desire. In many of his images, black males are only shown as parts of the anatomy — genitals, chests, buttocks — close-up and close-cropped to elicit desire. Mapplethorpe's eye pays special attention to the penis at the expense of showing us the subject's face, and thus, a whole person. The penis becomes *the* identity of the black male which is the classic racist stereotype re-created and presented as "art" in the context of a gay vision.

Mapplethorpe's "Man in a Polyester Suit," for example, presents a black man without a head, wearing a business suit, his trousers unzipped, and his fat, long penis dangling down, a penis that is not erect. It can be assumed that many viewers who appreciate Mapplethorpe's work, and who construct sexual fantasies from it, probably wondered *first* how much larger the penis would become during erection, as opposed to wondering *who* the man in the photo is or *why* his head is missing. What is insulting and endangering to black men is Mapplethorpe's *conscious* determination that the faces, the heads, and by extension, the minds and experiences of some of his black subjects are not as important as close-up shots of their cocks.

It is virtually impossible while viewing Mapplethorpe's photos of black males to avoid confronting issues of objectification.[2] Additionally, black gay men are not immune to the desire elicited by his photos. We, too, are drawn to the inherent eroticism. In "True Confessions: A Discourse on Images of Black Male Sexuality," Isaac Julien and Kobena Mercer accurately identify this dichotomy when they observe that Mapplethorpe's images of black males reiterate "the terms of colonial fantasy" and "service the expectations of white desire." They then ask the most critical question of all: "What do [Mapplethorpe's images] say to our wants and desires as black gay men?"[3]

It has not fully dawned on white gay men that racist conditioning has rendered many of them no different from their heterosexual brothers in the eyes of black gays and lesbians. Coming out of the closet to confront sexual oppression has not necessarily given white males the motivation or insight to transcend their racist conditioning. This failure (or reluctance) is costing the gay and lesbian community the opportunity to become a powerful force for creating *real* social changes that reach beyond issues of sexuality. It has fostered much of the distrust that permeates the relations between the black and white communities. And finally, it erodes the possibility of forming meaningful, powerful coalitions.

When black gay men approached the gay community to participate in the struggle for acceptance and to forge bonds of brotherhood, bonds so loftily proclaimed as *the vision* of the best gay minds of my generation, we discovered that the beautiful rhetoric was empty. The disparity between words and actions was as wide as the Atlantic Ocean and deeper than Dante's hell. There was no gay community for black men to come home to in the 1980s. The community we found was as mythical and distant from the realities of black men as was Oz from Kansas.

At the baths, certain bars, in bookstores and cruising zones, black men were welcome because these constructions of pleasure allowed the races to mutually explore sexual fantasies and, after all, the black man engaging in such a construction only needed to whip out a penis of almost any size to obtain the rapt attention withheld from him in other social and political structures of the gay community. These sites of pleasure were more tolerant of black men because they enhanced the sexual ambiance, but that same tolerance did not always continue once the sun began to rise.

Open fraternizing at a level suggesting companionship or love between the races was not tolerated in the light of day. Terms such as "dinge queen," for white men who prefer black men, and "snow queen," for black men who prefer white men, were created by a gay community that obviously could not be trusted to believe its own rhetoric concerning brotherhood, fellowship, and dignity. Only an *entire* community's silence is capable of reinforcing these conditions.

Some of the best minds of my generation would have us believe that AIDS has brought the gay and lesbian community closer and infused it with a more democratic mandate. That is only a partial truth that further underscores the fact that the gay community still operates from a one-eyed, one-gender, one-color perception of "community" that is most likely to recognize blond before black, but seldom the two together.

Some of the best minds of my generation believe AIDS has made the gay community a more responsible social construction, but what AIDS really manages to do is clearly point out how significant are the cultural and economic differences between us; differences so extreme that black men suffer a disproportionate number of AIDS deaths in communities with very sophisticated gay health care services.

The best gay minds of my generation believe that we speak as one voice and dream one dream, but we are not monolithic. We are not even respectful of each other's differences. We are a long way from that, Dorothy. I tell you Kansas is closer.

We are communities engaged in a fragile coexistence if we are anything at all. Our most significant coalitions have been created in the realm of sex. What is most clear for black gay men is this: We have to do for ourselves *now*, and for each other *now*, what no one has ever done for us. We have to be there for one another and trust less the adhesions of kisses and semen to bind us. Our only sure guarantee of survival is that which we create from our own self-determination. White gay men may only be able to understand and respond to oppression as it relates to their ability to obtain orgasm without intrusion from the church or state. White gay men are only "other" in this society when they choose to come out of the closet. But all black men are treated as "other" regardless of whether we sleep with men or women — our black skin automatically marks us as "other."

Look around, brothers. There is rampant killing in *our* communities. Drug addiction and drug trafficking overwhelm us. The blood of young black men runs curbside in a steady flow. The bodies of black infants crave crack, not the warmth of a mother's love. The nation's prisons are reservations and shelters for black men. An entire generation of black youths is being destroyed before our eyes. We cannot witness this in silence and apathy and claim our hands are bloodless. We are a wandering tribe that needs to go home before home is gone. We should not continue standing in line to be admitted into spaces that don't want us there. We cannot continue to exist without clinics, political organizations, human services, and cultural institutions that *we* create to support, sustain, and affirm us.

Our mothers and fathers are waiting for us. Our sisters and brothers are waiting. Our communities are waiting for us to come home. They need our love, our talents and skills, and we need theirs. They may not understand everything about us, but they will remain ignorant, misinformed, and lonely for us, and we for them, for as long as we stay away hiding in communities that have never really welcomed us or the gifts we bring.

I ask you brother: Does your mama *really* know about you? Does she *really* know what I am? Does she know I want to love her son, care for him, nurture and celebrate him? Do you think she'll understand? I hope so, because *I am* coming home. There is no place else to go that will be worth so much effort and love.

III. The evidence of being

At the beginning of the 1980s, creating poetry from a black gay experience was a lonely, trying occupation. No network of black gay writers existed to offer support, critical commentary, or the necessary fellowship and affirmation.

I had read requisite portions of James Baldwin's works, but I still hungered for voices closer to home to speak to me directly and immediately about the contemporary black gay experience. I wanted reflection. To compensate, I read all I could by gay poets such as C.S. Cavafy, Walt Whitman, Paolo Pasolini, and Jean Genet, but my hunger for self-recognition continued. I began reading lesbian poets such as Audre Lorde, Adrienne Rich, Pat Parker, and Sappho, but my hunger, only somewhat appeased, persisted.

As I approached the mid-1980s, I began to wonder if gay men of African descent existed in literature at all, beyond the works of Baldwin and Bruce Nugent, or the closeted works of writers of the Harlem Renaissance, such as Countee Cullen, Claude McKay, Langston Hughes, Alain Locke, and Wallace Thurman. Baldwin's voice was post–Harlem Renaissance: eloquent, crafted, impassioned; he created some of the most significant works to be presented by an "acknowledged" black gay man in this century. It is not my intention to overlook his broader significance in the context of African American and world literature, where works of his are ranked among the very best this century of writers has created. However, in the specific context of black gay literature, Baldwin's special legacy serves as role model, as source, as inspiration pointing toward the possibility of being *and* excellence. The legacy he leaves us to draw from is a precious gift for us to hold tight as we persevere.

My search for evidence of things not seen, evidence of black gay experiences on record, evidence of "being" to contradict the pervasive invisibility of black gay men, at times proved futile. I was often frustrated by codes of secrecy, obstructed by pretenses of discretion, or led astray by constructions of silence, constructions fabricated of illusions and perhaps cowardice. But I persevered. I continued to seek affirmation, reflection, and identity. I continued seeking the *necessary* historical references for my desires.

In terms of my heritage of Negritude, I found an abundance of literary texts to reinforce a positive black cultural identity, but as a black gay man there was, except for Baldwin, little to nurture me. Unbeknownst to me, Adrian Stanford's *Black and Queer* had been published by the Good Gay Poets of Boston in 1977. I would not be introduced to Stanford's work until 1985. Joseph Beam owned two copies of Stanford's *Black and Queer* and gave me one for my collection. I have treasured this gift since receiving it from Joe, who also told me Stanford was murdered in Philadelphia in 1981. In the poem "Yeah Baby," the late poet tells us:

> i've had them roll up in
>   chauffeured limousines,
> swing open the door and beg
>   "please get in."
>
> i've been approached, followed,
>   waited for, hung onto
> and groped by all those staid
>   white queens that
> don't like *colored boys*.[4]

For me, the evidence of black gay men creating *overt* homoerotic poetry begins with that small, powerful book. What I am suggesting is that black gay men have been publishing *overt* homoerotic verse since 1977, a mere thirteen years as of this writing.

For the homosexuals of the Harlem Renaissance engaged in the creation of literature, it would have been *inappropriate* to "come out" of whatever closets they had constructed for personal survival. The effort to uplift the race and prove the Negro worthy of respect precluded issues of sexuality, reducing such concerns to the sentiment of the popular urban blues song — "Ain't Nobody's Business If I Do." The defeat of racism was far too important to risk compromising such a struggle by raising issues of homosexuality.

For an individual to have declared himself homosexual, no matter how brilliant he was, would have brought immediate censure from what Zora Neale Hurston wickedly called the "Niggerati,"[5] the up-and-coming literary, cultural, and intellectual leaders of the Negro community. However, the work of Locke, Cullen, Hughes, and other Harlem Renaissance men of bisexual or homosexual identities is not to be dismissed in the quest for an African American gay tradition simply because it fails to reveal their homosexual desires. The works that these men created are critically important contributions and challenging legacies in the total picture of African American literature and cultural struggle. But because the mission to uplift the race predominated, there is little homoerotic evidence from the Harlem Renaissance except for selections of work by Richard Bruce Nugent. His work was considerably more daring, judged by the standards of his day, than were those of his more closeted Renaissance contemporaries, none of whom dared risk publishing homoerotic literature for fear of falling from grace.

The evidence of Nugent's daring is best exemplified by his beautiful short story, "Smoke, Lilies and Jade," considered to be the first work by a black writer to examine homosexual desire. The story appeared in the short-lived and very controversial *Fire!!* (published November 1926),[6] a journal created by Thurman, Nugent, Hurston, Hughes, and others of their circle. (Over five decades later, "Smoke, Lilies and Jade" appeared in the controversial gay anthology *Black Men/White Men* (1983),[7] and a little over six decades later it was part of the narrative script for the film *Looking for Langston* (1988).)[8] *Fire!!* was intended to be a black arts quarterly, but only one issue appeared. "The sales of *Fire!!* were very disappointing," writes Faith Berry, in the biography, *Langston Hughes: Before and Beyond Harlem*. Copies of the issue were stored in a cellar in Harlem, but "in an irony like no other, a fire reportedly destroyed them all, leaving the sponsors with a printer's debt of more than a thousand dollars."[9]

Fire!! also contained writing by Hughes, Cullen, Hurston, and Arna Bontemps, and artwork by Aaron Douglas, to name but a few of its contributors. In Charles Michael Smith's "Bruce Nugent: Bohemian of the Harlem Renaissance," we are told that *Fire!!* "created a firestorm of protest, particularly from the black bourgeoisie. The critic for the Baltimore *Afro-American*, for example, wrote acidly: 'I have just tossed the first issue of *Fire!!* into the fire!'"[10]

Continuing this journey through African American literature, we find no evidence of black gay men openly participating in the 1960s Black Arts Movement with the exception of Baldwin, and even he was attacked because of his sexuality by Eldridge Cleaver in *Soul on Ice*, and by writer Ishmael Reed who crudely insulted Baldwin by calling him a "cocksucker,"[11] in an apparent attempt to diminish Baldwin's brilliance.

The evidence of black gay men that exists from this period is mostly created from the perspective of a black nationalist sensibility in that this literature most often condemns homosexuality, ridicules gays, lesbians, dykes, faggots, bulldaggers, and homos, and positions homosexuality as a major threat to the black family and black masculinity. Such a sensibility also considered homosexuality to be caused by white racism (or by exposure to white values), and overlooked the possibility of natural variance in the expression of human sexuality.

Perhaps the only "black revolutionary" spokesperson remotely sympathetic to the struggles of homosexuals and women was Huey P. Newton, Supreme Commander of the Black Panther Party. In "A Letter from Huey to the Revolutionary Brothers and Sisters About the Women's Liberation and Gay Liberation Movements," Newton urged black men and women to align themselves with these movements in order to form powerful coalitions. He writes:

> Whatever your personal opinion and your insecurities about homosexuality and the various liberation movements among homosexuals and women (and I speak of the homosexuals and women as oppressed groups), we should try to unite with them in a revolutionary fashion.
>
> ...I don't remember us ever constituting any value that said that a

revolutionary must say offensive things toward homosexuals or that a revolutionary would make sure that women do not speak out about their own particular oppression.

...[T]here is nothing to say that a homosexual can not also be a revolutionary... Quite the contrary, maybe a homosexual could be the *most* revolutionary.

We should be willing to discuss the insecurities that many people have about homosexuality. When I say, "insecurities" I mean the fear that there is some kind of threat to our manhood. I can understand this fear... [B]ut homosexuals are not enemies of the people.[12]

Aside from Newton and Baldwin, there was no other black male leadership, self-appointed or otherwise, attempting to see heterosexist oppression as being akin to and stemming from the same source responsible for perpetuating oppressions of race, gender, class, and economics.

Many factors have contributed to this *lack of witness*, this lack of participation by black gay men in creating literature that reflects our experiences. The long-standing constructions of fear, denial, invisibility, and racism perpetuated much of the silence that has prevailed.

Black gay men can consider the 1980s to have been a critically important decade for our literature. Literary journals, periodicals, and self-published works were sporadically produced and voraciously consumed. The 1980s gave us *Blacklight, Habari-Daftari, Yemonja* (which later became *Blackheart*), *Black/Out, BLK, Moja: Black and Gay, BGM,* the *Pyramid Periodical*, the *Real Read*, and a promising selection of self-published chapbooks and portfolios that, taken as a whole, suggests that an important period of fermentation and development in black gay literature has been occurring since the release of Stanford's *Black and Queer*. In addition, two significant collections of black gay literature — the ground-breaking *In the Life*, edited by Joseph Beam and published by Alyson Publications (1986), and the poetry anthology *Tongues Untied*, published in London by Gay Men's Press (1987) — served notice that a generation of black gay writers are at work dismantling the silence.

Against stifling odds and breaking rank from historic constructions of repression, black gay men are developing meaningful and significant literary voices through workshops and brotherly encouragement. The most obvious example of this nurturing is the Other Countries Collective based in New York City. Through a process of workshops, collective members critique one another's writings. The workshops are designed to reinforce and stimulate, affirm and encourage. The collective published its first *Other Countries Journal* in 1988, and plans to publish others in the '90s. They also present public readings, some for audiences of primarily black heterosexuals.

By the close of the 1980s, *BLK*, a Los Angeles-based black gay news magazine, was consistently publishing, month after month, and was available nationally. This was accomplished under the leadership of its editor and publisher, Alan Bell. The New York–based literary journal the *Pyramid Poetry Periodical*, founded in 1986 by Roy Gonsalves as a triannual publication, had also achieved the distinction of consistently publishing in its present quarterly format as the *Pyramid Periodical*, and obtained national distribution under the guidance of editor Charles Pouncy. Self-published chapbooks and volumes of verse were produced by Donald Woods (*The Space*), Alan Miller (At the Club), Assoto Saint (*Stations*), Philip Robinson (*Secret Passages*), Roy Gonsalves (*Evening Sunshine*), and Lloyd "Vega" Jeffress (*Men of Color*). The phenomena of black gay men self-publishing, including my own self-published works, *Earth Life* and *Conditions*, surely challenges the insidious racism and homophobia that prevail in the offices of mainstream, small press, and university publishing houses. For what other reasons would so many black gay men take on the task? If there is to be evidence of our experiences, we learned by the close of the 1980s that our own self-sufficiency must ensure it, so that future generations of black gay men will have references for their desires.

And finally, perhaps our most compelling literary achievements were documented in two films as the decade came to its close. Isaac Julien's controversial *Looking for Langston*, and Marlon Riggs's documentary *Tongues Untied*, both splendidly utilized the poetry and writings of black gay men in bold presentations of the black gay experience.

Looking for Langston, which Julien created as a "meditation" on Hughes and the Harlem Renaissance, examines issues of race, sexuality, and the role of the Negro artist during that period. Julien created a beautifully stylized rendering of desire and its many implications. His use of texts created by black gay men is complemented by the scores "Blues for Langston" and "Beautiful Black Man," composed and performed by Blackberri, an Oakland-based black gay singer, songwriter and musician. "Beautiful Black Man," a particularly soul-stirring, jazzy plea for black gay men to love themselves, is superbly performed by Blackberri. Additional music is provided by Wayson Jones, and texts by Hilton Als, Nugent, Hughes, Baldwin, and selections of my own work give the film its poetic voice and conscience.

The film was primarily shot in London, where British-born Julien is based and is a member of Sankofa, a black film and video collective. Unfortunately, the sensuous vision Julien unleashes in his forty-minute black-and-white work was not welcomed in America by the Hughes estate. They legally forced Julien to remove three of Hughes's poems because they objected to Hughes being presented in a homosexual context. As a result of these legal obstructions, two film versions of *Looking for Langston* exist. The original, which can be shown all over the world except in the U.S., and the alternate edited version, created to appease the homophobic censors of the estate.

What is ironic about the estate's efforts to block the film is that selections of Hughes's poetry (including some used in the film) have appeared in two gay anthologies: *Black Men/White Men* and *Gay and Lesbian Poetry in Our Time*.[13] If it was the estate's intention to prevent Hughes from appearing in a homosexual context, why was permission given to print his work in these anthologies?

In the late fall of 1989, Riggs premiered *Tongues Untied*, a black gay documentary which takes its name from the black gay poetry anthology. The work is grounded in personal testimony from Riggs about his life as a black gay man. His experiences are validated and elaborated on through the poetry of Craig Harris, Donald Woods, Reginald Jackson, Steve Langley, Alan Miller, myself, and his own narrative writings. His examination of black gay life is the most affirming document we have yet seen from the film and video community. Riggs, an Oakland-based, Emmy Award–winning documentarist, has created an historic work that captures black gay men in many states of "being." *Tongues Untied* is a social and cultural work that brilliantly articulates itself through the poetry and personal testimonies of black gay men.

The 1990s promise to be a decade of fruition and continuing significance for black gay literature. Novelists such as Randal Kenan (*A Visitation of Spirits*) and Melvin Dixon (*Trouble the Water*) released first works as we neared the close of the '80s. Larry Duplechan released three novels in the eighties (*Eight Days A Week, Blackbird,* and *Tangled in Blue*). Award-winning science-fiction writer Samuel Delany's autobiography *The Motion of Light in Water,* and writer Mickey C. Fleming's *About Courage* were also added to the ever-growing pantheon of black gay literature. Other writers are planning to produce self-published collections of verse, more novels are being written, theater collectives are being formed such as Reginald Jackson's Rainbow Repertory Theater in New York City, and new films and documentaries are being planned and created as this anthology goes to press.

The late 1980s also witnessed the emergence of black gay men's groups such as Gay Men of African Descent (New York), Adodi (Philadelphia), Unity (Philadelphia), and Black Gay Men United (Oakland). These organizations structure themselves around social, cultural, and political issues. In many instances they provide emotional and spiritual support for their members: workshops covering a broad range of issues; retreats and cultural programming; and lectures by guest speakers on subjects ranging from AIDS and health care to developing personal financial resources. The existence of these groups continues the necessary work of affirming us.

What we must do now, more than ever, is nurture one another whenever and wherever possible. Attend the readings of black gay writers, buy their works, invite them to college campuses and community centers to speak and conduct workshops, and subscribe to black gay publications created in order that the necessary nurturing can continue.

Much of the evidence that emerged in the 1980s is only the surface of what is yet to be revealed. We *must* focus our attention around issues of craft and discipline in order to create our very best literature. We must demand this of ourselves. There is a need to look closely at revealing the full extent to which black gay men have *always* participated in positive and nurturing roles in the structures of family within the African American community. There is a need to look closely at intimacy and the constructions of our desire and bring forth from these realms the knowledge that we are capable of loving one another in committed, long-standing, productive relationships. In our fiction, prose, and poetry there is a need to reveal more of our beauty in all its diversity. We need more honest pictures of ourselves that are not the stereotypical six-foot, dark-skinned man with a big dick.

We must begin to identify what a black gay sensibility is; identify its esthetic qualities and components; identify specific constructions and uses of language suitable for the task of presenting our experiences in the context of literature; and then determine how this sensibility and esthetic relates to and differs from African American literature as a whole.

Ours should be a vision willing to exceed all that attempts to confine and intimidate us. We must be willing to embrace and explore the duality of community that we exist in as black *and* gay men. We would be wise to develop strong, powerful voices that can range over the entire landscape of human experience and condition.

Perhaps the second Renaissance in African American literature occurred when black women claimed their *own* voices from the post-sixties, male-dominated realm of the "black experience," a realm that at times resembled a boxing ring restricting black women to the roles of mere spectators. What black women, especially out black lesbians, bravely did was break the silence surrounding their experiences. No longer would black men, as the sole interpreters of race and culture, presume to speak for (or ignore) women's experiences. Black women opened up new dialogues and explored uncharted territories surrounding race, sexuality, gender relations, family, history, and eroticism. In the process, they angered some black male writers who felt they were being culturally castrated and usurped, but out of necessity, black women realized they would have to speak for themselves — and do so honestly. As a result of their courage, black women also inspired many of the black gay men writing today to seek our own voices so we can tell our truths. Thus, we are at the beginning of completing a total picture of the African American experience. Black gay men will no longer exist in a realm of invisibility.

Our immediate task, as black gay men creating our own literary tradition, is to work diligently and to utilize honesty and discipline as our allies. If we commit ourselves to strive for excellence and nothing less, we will create the *evidence of being* powerful enough to transform the very nature of our existence. And the silence and invisibility that we self-imposed, or often accepted will give way to the realization of just how fierce *and* necessary we really are. SNAP!

IV. Loyalty — A prelude to coming home

For my so-called sins against nature and the race, I gain the burdensome knowledge of carnal secrets. It rivals rituals of sacrifice and worship, and conjures the same glassy-eyed results — with less bloodshed. A knowledge disquieting and liberating inhabits my soul. It often comforts me, or at times, is miserably intoxicating with requisite hangovers and regrets. At other moments it is sacred communion, causing me to moan and tremble and cuss as the Holy Ghost fucks me. It is a knowledge of fire and beauty that I will carry beyond the grave. When I sit in God's final judgment, I will wager this knowledge against my entrance into the Holy Kingdom. There was no other way for me to know the beauty of Earth except through the sexual love of men, men who were often more terrified than I, even as they posed before me, behind flimsy constructions of manhood, mocking me with muscles, erections, and wives.

I discovered any man can be seduced — even if the price is humiliation or death for the seducer. Late nights and desperate hours teach us to approach loneliness unarmed, or we risk provoking it to torture us with endless living sorrows we believe only the dead can endure.

But who are these dead, able to withstand the constant attack of merciless loneliness with its intense weapons, its clever trickery and deceit? Many of them are men like me, born of common stock, ordinary dreamers. Men who vaguely answer to "American," or exhibit visible apprehension when American is defined and celebrated to their exclusion. Men who more often than not are simply ignored.

We constitute the invisible brothers in our communities, those of us who live "in the life"; the choirboys harboring secrets, the uncle living in an impeccable flat with a roommate who sleeps down the hall when family visits; men of power and humble peasantry, reduced to silence and invisibility for the safety they procure from these constructions. Men emasculated in the complicity of not speaking out, rendered mute by the middle-class aspirations of a people trying hard to forget the shame and cruelties of slavery and ghettos. Through denials and abbreviated histories riddled with omissions, the middle class sets about whitewashing and fixing up the race to impress each other *and* the racists who don't give a damn.

I speak for thousands, perhaps hundreds of thousands of men who live and die in the shadows of secrets, unable to speak of the love that helps them endure and contribute to the race. Their ordinary kisses, stolen or shared behind façades of heroic achievement, their kisses of sweet spit and loyalty are scrubbed away by the propaganda makers of the race, the "Talented Tenth" who would just as soon have us believe black people can fly, rather than reveal that black men have been longing to kiss one another, and have done so, for centuries.

The black homosexual is hard-pressed to gain audience among his heterosexual brothers; even if he *is* more talented, he is inhibited by his silence or his admissions. This is what the race has depended on in being able to erase homosexuality from our recorded history. The "chosen" history. But these sacred constructions of silence are futile exercises in denial. We will not go away with our issues of sexuality. We are coming home.

It is not enough to tell us that one was a brilliant poet, scientist, educator, or rebel. Who did he love? It makes a difference. I can't become a whole man simply on what is fed to me: watered-down versions of black life in America. I need the ass-splitting truth to be told, so I will have something pure to emulate, a reason to remain loyal.

V. When the silence is exhumed

Joseph Beam died in December of 1988, after beginning to compile material for this book. He would be pleased to know that his bravery is of the same quality that has helped his parents endure their grief. Dorothy and Sun Beam have supported the completion of *Brother to Brother* with an unyielding encouragement and bravery. Let history show that they kept Joe's dream alive. Mrs. Beam's tireless energy assisted in maintaining the communication with contributors that was so necessary as the responsibility for this book changed hands. Mr. Beam frequently went to the post office in Center City to pick up manuscripts. Mrs. Beam would photocopy each one, then mail it to me in Washington, D.C. When I finally realized I would need to finish this anthology in Philadelphia, at the source of its conception, Mr. and Mrs. Beam kindly allowed me to stay at their home where I worked without interruption, except for occasional plates of Mr. Beam's delicious fried chicken, and conversations with Mrs. Beam about Joe, *Brother to Brother*, homosexuality, black life, and other topics of interest and concern to us both. Their participation in this project makes it a very special "family affair," and significant in the context of black gay men and our relationships to our families. *Brother to Brother* is evidence that we can love, accept, and support one another in our constructions of family. It's an effort that cannot be left out of the survival strategies of the African American community for to do so is to beckon cultural destruction. *Brother to Brother* would not be a reality if it were not for the active involvement of Joe's parents, particularly the unyielding faith and love of Mrs. Beam.

In continuing the work on the anthology, I entered this project not sure of what I would find. Joe had not left notes to be followed. The work he had begun to receive bore no markings as to his intentions. Ultimately, I selected material from a pool of roughly 140 manuscripts. What is here represents a diverse mixture of personal opinions, testimony, and experiences.

Much of the beauty of the black gay community is in its diversity of expression and coping. Some of us vogue, some are butch, some give buppie, some give girl, some give fever; diva is an aspiration, darling is a friend; and there are the boys who will be boys and the men who will be men no matter how the pants fall. It would be impossible to say there is one type of black gay male for all seasons. We haven't yet, nor do we need to, become clones.

Brother to Brother is a community of voices that would have been disjointed had I not formally sectioned this book into thematic groupings. I have not tried to assemble a politically correct book inasmuch as I know a book of this type is inherently political by merely being assembled and distributed as literature by black gay men. It is to Sasha Alyson's credit to have continued his commitment to publish this project, but perhaps we will see a day when black gay men will bring forth anthologies and literature published and distributed by companies we have created and own.

There are areas that this anthology, in a formal fashion, does not speak to, such as narratives from older black gay men and black gay couples; spiritual concepts and beliefs; career experiences; community and political activism; historical and biographical reconstructions; health care issues beyond AIDS; interracial relationships; our relationships with women; and numerous other subjects. The density of the silence surrounding our lives does not make it easy to gain this information. Future anthologies will hopefully structure themselves around specifically addressing these subjects and many others.

What *Brother to Brother* tells is a story that laughs and cries and sings and celebrates; it's a quartet of saxophones blowing red-blue squalls; it's a sextet of *a capella* voices searching out notes under a smoky light; it's a conversation intimate friends share for hours. These are truly words mined syllable by syllable from the hearts of black gay men. You're invited to listen in because you're family, and these aren't secrets — not to us, so why should they be secrets to you? Just listen. Your brother is speaking. Yes, that is your father/cousin/uncle/son sitting amongst us; he, too, has a story to tell. I have heard it before. It so gently begins —

"I loved my friend."[14]

Essex Hemphill
January 1990
Philadelphia

Notes

1. Joseph Beam, "Brother to Brother: Words from the Heart," in *In the Life: A Black Gay Anthology*, ed. Joseph Beam (Boston: Alyson Publications, 1986), p. 231.

2. For additional consideration of my charge that Mapplethorpe's images of black males are primarily images of objectification, his catalog, *Black Males* (Amsterdam: Galerie Jurka, 1980), contains the following images listed by page number: 9, 15, 18, 19, 37, 39, 45, 47, 48, and 49. The images cited all depict headless men presented as sexual objects. Further justification for my charges can also be found in Mapplethorpe's *The Black Book* (New York: St. Martin's, 1986). The "Man in a Polyester Suit" is specifically cited because that image of a black male is one of his most well known. It might have been more appropriate to title it "Black Dick in a Polyester Suit," since the emphasis is hardly on the suit or the man.

3. Isaac Julien and Kobena Mercer, "True Confessions: A Discourse on Images of Black Male Sexuality," *Ten-8*, No. 22 (1986), p. 6.

4. Adrian Stanford, *Black and Queer* (Boston: Good Gay Poets Press, 1977), p. 9.

5. Arnold Rampersad, *The Life of Langston Hughes: Volume I: 1902–1941* (New York: Oxford University Press, 1986), p. 132.

6. Wallace Thurman et al. *Fire!!*, vol. 1, no. 1 (New York: Fire Press, 1926). Note: Facsimile edition reprinted in 1983 by Fire!! Press, P.O. Box 327, Metuchen, NJ 08840.

7. Michael J. Smith, *Black Men/White Men* (San Francisco: Gay Sunshine Press, 1983).

8. Isaac Julien, director, *Looking for Langston* (London: Sankofa Film & Video, 1988).

9. Faith Berry, *Langston Hughes: Before and Beyond Harlem* (Connecticut: Lawrence Hill, 1983), p. 83.

10. Charles Michael Smith, "Bruce Nugent: Bohemian of the Harlem Renaissance," in *In the Life: A Black Gay Anthology*, ed. Joseph Beam (Boston: Alyson Publications, 1986), p. 214.

11. Quincy Troupe, *James Baldwin: The Legacy* (New York: Simon & Schuster, 1989), p. 202.

12. Huey P. Newton, "A Letter from Huey to the Revolutionary Brothers and Sisters About the Women's Liberation and Gay Liberation Movements," (Gay Flames Pamphlet No. 7, 1970).

13. Joan Larkin and Carl Morse, *Gay and Lesbian Poetry in Our Time* (New York: St. Martin's, 1988).

14. Langston Hughes, "I Loved My Friend," in *Black Men/White Men*, ed. Michael J. Smith (San Francisco: Gay Sunshine Press, 1983), p. 30.

I. When I think of home

ADRIAN STANFORD

Sacrifice

had my father known
when he cast forth his offering
to the sea of my mother's womb
what creation their joy would bring
would he have welcomed the man/she child in its birth
heralding my duality as natures zenith (in human form)
and blessed the son he held for all to see
keeping my sister/self obscured, until
i understood my second destiny—
or would he have shuddered at the fate his loins possessed
and retracting from those clashing thighs,
let the seeds that bore such strains
meet their end upon the ground

CHARLES HENRY FULLER

The jazz singer

The attic was my one refuge. There, among near-forgotten clothes and furniture, I was free to be whatever I wanted. No script had been prepared for me, no one would become embarrassed when I mangled my lines, and most importantly, no one waited to correct me. In this very special place, far away from my family and those who might be called friends, an eleven-year-old boy with a too-large head and too-thin arms played at creation.

Washed only in the faint glow of the solitary bulb above the staircase and whatever light managed to come through the grimy windows, I looked for a truer vision of myself in my parents' collection of dusty, yellowing photographs. In that wonderfully secluded spot, I found bits of my lost self in each face and frozen attitude which had been laid to rest there. Desperate to be valued and cared for, I breathed new life into the musty clothing which had been packed away in the attic. The rough, manly wool coats and the tattered, wafer-thin dresses fired my imagination with the words and rhythms of black folks doing what they had to do in other, more exciting times than my own.

The sepia-and-gray world of 1960s Tillery faded away as I pranced before the old mirrors, jiving and laughing, acting as low-down or high-tone as I pleased. While I was growing up, the happiest hours of each day were spent in that attic. There my halting speech and imperfect skin could be set aside. I was released from the confining roles of family misfit and neighborhood oddity. Within those magical sloping walls I became the people anybody would be proud to know: I was in touch, in control and remade, thoroughly whole. One particular afternoon I was lost in my rendering of "The Jazz Singer." My parents lived on jazz and blues records in those days. I still know all the old standards inside out. Anyway, The Jazz Singer was my favorite impersonation because with each change of song she became whatever I wanted her to be: she slipped from bopping, good time Ella to ol' dirty blues Bessie with little effort. Though I suspected Billie was much too puffy-looking for my mood that afternoon, I remember having a terrible time deciding whether I felt more like Lena Horne or Sarah. I finally conceded that my voice wasn't deep enough to do Miss Vaughan justice. "Stormy Weather" or that song from *Showboat* that Mom liked so much was the next decision. Choices, choices. That's what I was like up there in that attic — in a world of my own.

The heat from the lights felt terrific on The Jazz Singer's exposed back as she turned away from her audience, seductively adjusting the strap of her gown for the boys in the band. She hummed the interlude with the woodwinds and winked at The Count seated at the piano. Oh, she was a flirt, all right, tapping her foot and rolling those big eyes of hers. When she was ready to bring the last sixteen bars home, she threw her head back, laughed deep down in her throat, and turned ever so slowly into the spotlight. Her arms, growing more elegant every minute, were stretched out as if she were embracing every fan in the audience. The Jazz Singer knew just how to please them.

"What are you doing up here? Dressed like that?" my father spat out from the top of the stairs.

If he'd slapped me in the face, I couldn't have been more startled. Oh God, I thought, oh dear God. I tried to speak, but my stammering was so bad the words were incoherent gibberish.

"Your mother said you were up here play-acting again. You were making so much noise I guess you didn't hear..."

His voice dropped first to a whisper and then, losing conviction altogether, fell silent. My dad looked at the outfit I was wearing — a sloppy wig, old nylons, and open-toed heels which were way too small. The same pained look of disappointment that followed me from morning till night was spread all over his face. I wanted to die. I prayed that God would just come down and carry me away. But my dad's sorrowful look didn't last long. It never did. I watched as his lips curled into a sneer.

"Daddy, I can explain."

"No, you can't," he cut me off. "There ain't no way on God's green earth that you can explain why you're dressed up like that. Don't even bother to put some story together, because I don't want to hear it. Just take all that stuff off and come down to dinner. Everybody's waiting."

I remember that he avoided looking directly at me. Instead, he dragged the toe of his shoe back and forth across a bit of unravelling carpet at the top of the stairs. I felt as though I were going to be sick to my stomach. I tried to figure my chances of making it past him to the bathroom downstairs. Man, I felt bad.

"Are you deaf?" he shouted, rushing at me. "I said take this shit off!"

He snatched the wig off so quickly, I felt my heart jump in my chest. The air was cool as it licked the back of my neck and head where the wig had been. I put my hand up to cover my — what — shame? My dad read this as a sign of protest and struck me with such force that I slammed into a box of clothing. I wanted to disappear, to be somewhere, anywhere else. I slid down the side of the boxes and tried to make myself as small as possible on the floor.

I clutched my cheek and stared at him, more confused than rageful. Why did all our disagreements have to end like this? He wasn't a violent man, not really, but somehow he never missed an opportunity to take a swipe at me. I was an embarrassment to him. On some level I knew that, even then. He'd never be proud of me, not in the way he was proud of Gabriel. Though he and my brother never said it in so many words, neither ever let me forget what a disappointment I was.

My father was a big man. Though he never hit me more than once or twice at a time, I suddenly felt menaced by him, so I called out: "Daddy, I'm sorry. Please don't hit me anymore. I'm sorry."

He looked down at me, this scrawny kid, all arms and legs, homely and clumsy to boot. I'm sure he felt I never seemed to be doing the right thing — always off in some corner, hiding from the world, dreaming my life away. I read in his eyes a singular sense of defeat. What had he ever done to deserve such a son?

"Christopher, I'm sorry." His voice was so awkward and soft, it pained me to hear it. "I thought we'd been all through this dress-up nonsense a couple of months ago. I don't care what your mother or that damn speech therapist says, you're getting too old to be playing this kind of game. Now change your clothes and come to the table."

At that moment, hearing the concern in his voice, I wanted him to understand how it was with me. It didn't matter who I pretended to be. He was never around when Billy Eckstine and Joe Williams were there. Like Bessie and Lena and Sarah, those men were cool in ways I would never be. There was a music in all of their souls I could feel, could touch, a music that made me less afraid of life.

"I don't just wear women's clothes," I mumbled.

"Will you shut up about that!" he said through gritted teeth. "I don't want to hear any of your shit about why you wear women's clothes. If you acted more like a boy's supposed to, instead of being such a goddamned sissy all the time, you'd be able to hang onto some friends. That's all there is to it! Now get dressed." Disgusted, he picked up some of my clothes and threw them at me. "Boy, why you so funny-acting?"

That question. How much a part of my life that question had already become. I wanted to answer him. I wanted to shout all I felt inside but couldn't. My mouth opened and closed, soundlessly, again and again, until a thread of saliva streamed down and caught in the folds of the dress. I didn't wipe it away. My dad, seeing this, knelt down very close beside me and dabbed at it with his dinner napkin. He steadied himself on my shoulder and then withdrew his hand quickly, as if gentleness between us held some danger.

"Everybody's got something they want to change about themselves," he began. "Me, I fly off the handle before I think of what I'm doing. I know that's wrong and I'm working on it. But Christopher, you've got to know when you can do something about a thing and when you're just spitting in the wind. There are things in this world a man can do and there are things a man would be better off dead than ever getting caught up in — especially a black man." He scooped up the wig, felt the texture of the hair, and smiled sadly, remembering some happier moment. After a while, he dropped the wig in my lap. "Do you understand what I'm telling you?"

What could I say? Poor Dad. I nodded and watched as he walked to the top of the stairs. He turned around and we looked at each other. His expression had become hard again, his voice, dark and unwavering.

"If I ever catch you dressed like this again, I'll beat all the black off you, so help me God. You got that, Mister?"

"I hear you, Daddy," I said softly and watched the light bulb at the head of the stairs until I heard the door close at the second-floor landing.

The Jazz Singer would have apologized to the audience, but embarrassed by this tasteless show of domestic violence, her audience and band had long since disappeared. She and yours truly sat for a short time, each rubbing our cheeks, confused by the harshness of the world and its *real* men. I rose first, pulled off the gown, the shoes, the nylons, and lazily scratched my kinky hair. The Jazz Singer carefully folded the clothes and put them away. When she finished, she drew me close to her. She wanted to go backstage to see if anyone in the band would take her back to her hotel. She simply couldn't manage a late supper with all those noisy Negroes tonight, she laughed. Until the next time, she smiled. I watched as her delicate figure was absorbed into the darkening theater wings. I remember how much I, too, wanted to be folded up in that illusory blackness. Her perfume was still strong in the air. Smelling it, I knew I would find so little beauty, so little acceptance or peace of mind until she returned.

RORY BUCHANAN

Daddy lied

my daddy taught me
i must be perfect
i was weak if i cried
i had to know everything
that feelings only get in my way

my daddy told me
white men don't like me
then he drank until i knew
he didn't like himself either

my daddy pushed me
to be better than everyone else
forgetting to tell me
i could set my own standards
instead of working toward theirs

my daddy talked to me
but never told me how he felt
never seemed to care what i felt
he only talked about what interested him
and told me to look the rest up in a book

my daddy showed me
that being a man meant being aloof
catering to white man dreams
raising kids that didn't understand you

until they were thirty
and then didn't want to

my daddy lied to me
but i forgive him
he lied to himself too
his daddy taught him how

CHARLES R.P. POUNCY

A first affair

I was running across the schoolyard of George Washington Carver Junior High. The buzzer would sound any minute now. I had to get to the spot where my homeroom class was supposed to line up. I couldn't afford to be late again.

"*Maricón!*" As soon as I heard that word, every other sound in the schoolyard became muffled, overpowered by a droning background static. There were black and brown kids running everywhere, playing box-ball and Chinese handball against the school wall. Seconds before it had seemed very noisy, as though we were using the impact of our voices and feet against the ground, the concrete, trying to hold back the minutes before the buzzer summoned us into a gray metal-and-glass building bounded on two sides by vacant garbage-strewn lots. But all I heard was the ripple that the sound of that word made on the world around me. I wanted to look back, to see if that word had been thrown at me, but I was soon to learn that the aim had been much more reckless.

"Who you calling a Mighty Cong?" I turned around and there, a few yards behind me was Stacy, one hand on his hip and the other grasping something tightly in his jacket pocket. Stacy took two steps closer to the boy who had made the offending remark — an average-looking boy with a forehead like the back of a shovel.

"You muthafuckin' greasy cross-eyed monkey!" With every word Stacy's head bobbed, angled, and virtually twirled on his long neck. His eyes narrowed until they were as sharp as knives. "You better take that shit back on that fuckin' banana boat 'cause, bitch, I'll kill your tired ass and pay it no mind!" Stacy had taken his hand off his hip and was ripping the air in front of the boy's face with a long, perfectly straight finger. The boy was shocked, totally unprepared for, and apparently offended by, Stacy's reaction.

That was the first time I became aware of Stacy as a person. Before that I knew him only by sight and by bad reputation. A tall, thin, yellow boy with a huge afro and buckteeth, he was older than most of the other kids because he had been held back a couple of times. He was decidedly sissified, though I was aware of no one, until now, who would risk saying that to his face. For it was known that he would cut anybody for almost any affront, no matter how slight, or even on "GP" (general principle). The boy who had made the mistake of calling Stacy *maricón* still hadn't noticed that Stacy was now playfully fingering something in his pocket. Instead, the boy foolishly took a step forward, trying to jump in Stacy's face. His friends tried to hold him back, but they were too slow. I heard—

"What, leggo. I nah 'fraid a dat!"

"Nah, man. He's loca, man." I had become part of a steadily growing crowd of kids assembled spontaneously by the smell of a fight. I saw Stacy step in toward the boy but I didn't see what happened next, just the boy as he doubled over clutching his groin. Then I heard a sharp crack and saw the back of Stacy's fist hit the corner of the boy's chin. Instantly the boy collapsed and he was on the ground rocking, his hands holding his head. His friends tried to lift him up, shaking their heads.

"I told you he's loca, man!" one of the boy's friends yelled. Stacy laughed and spat, "Tell her next time I'll cut her fuckin' balls off!" He picked up his books from where he had tossed them, bending at the knee, and turned to walk away, the crowd parting on cue. He stopped for a second and looked in my direction. I was sure he had seen me staring at him. He raised his eyebrows at me, but continued walking.

The bell rang and the teachers came out of George Washington Carver Junior High School to escort the students in. I found my class and we coalesced around our assigned places in the schoolyard and began our largely silent movement into another world. I followed the other kids in my homeroom, but kept glancing around looking for Stacy. As we entered the school I kept saying to myself, over and over, "Try that again, bitch, and I'll cut your fuckin' balls off."

A few weeks later Stacy and I ended up having detention together after school. Me, for being habitually late, and him, for calling Mrs. Klein a muthafucka. We were the only two kids in the detention room that afternoon and we weren't supposed to talk, but the aide had left us alone. The room was like most in the relatively new building. It was dirty, some of the bulbs in the light fixtures needed replacing, and there were a number of broken windows which had not been repaired but simply had a sheet of plastic pasted over them. I was reading, intently, intensely. I read that way to put myself inside the book and forget what

I had come to view as the limitations of my reality. Stacy had said something to me, but I was concentrating on my book.

"Yo! You, over there — glamour girl, you think you too good to talk or something?" I was startled, and instantly became aware of my green chinos and green plaid shirt. I spent a few seconds wondering how those clothes could possibly label me a "glamour girl," until I realized that I was probably being too literal again.

"Are you talking to me?" I managed, almost looking in his direction. He was wearing a skin-tight purple pullover with purple-and-white plaid bell-bottoms. His eyebrows were raised and he was staring at me in a very haughty manner.

"No, I was talking to the Holy Ghost. Shit! Who you think I'm talking to?"

"Oh, I didn't hear you. What did you say?" I had wanted to ask him what he had meant by calling me "glamour girl," but his taking the name of the Holy Spirit in vain was altogether too scary. I had decided that most of that church stuff was just stuff, but I had seen what could happen to people when the Holy Ghost got ahold of them. I mumbled something that passed for an assent to conversation before glancing outside to make sure it wasn't raining fire or something.

We talked about teachers, or more accurately, he talked to me about teachers, or as he referred to them, "pricks," "bitches," and "cunts." I was trying hard not to seem affected by some of his word choices. I had seen most of those words before on walled-up buildings, subway cars, and the sidewalk outside of school. But some I had never heard spoken before. I was still trying to remember if taking the name of the Lord thy God in vain was a sin for which there was no forgiveness. Stacy was talking about how Mrs. Klein had said, "That's highly improbable," when he had called her a "muthafucka." Then he went on about how Mrs. Cammepello and Mr. Osterwick were "doing it" in the supply closet behind the science lab. I sat there listening to all of this as best I could while trying to figure out why he was talking to me. I heard my mother's voice, "You just know he's up to no good — a boy like that." Yes, a boy like that.

It was becoming clear that the aide wasn't coming back anytime soon. Then he asked me—

"How long you been gay?"

"Been what?" I stammered, nearly spitting out the gum in my mouth.

"Honey, please. You want to go to a party?"

"A what?"

"Chil', you awful slow for somebody supposed to be college material." He pronounced "college" as if there were a "ch" at the end of it. Stacy put a pencil in his mouth and pulled out a strand of the bright pink bubble gum he was chewing, twirling it around the eraser before putting it back in his mouth. I wanted to say something about germs but decided against it. I tried to calm myself, wondering how I would describe this event in my diary. *In a flash the disparate particles of my life, charged by energy from this strange, new, wonderful creature, assumed a clear and shining order.*

"Yes, a party, Saturday night. Do you want to go?" Stacy wasn't looking at me as he spoke, but at his nails. Looking at them, in fact, the wrong way, with his hand stretched out in front of him.

"What kind of party?" I thought that was both a safe and important question.

"What you mean, what kind of party?" Stacy turned his head to stare at me, his head starting a slight back-and-forth flutter like a rhetorical question mark. I just sort of looked back, wondering if my eyes were bugging out as I had been told they had a tendency to do. I wasn't sure how to be more clear.

"Well, there won't be any fish there, if that's what you mean. At least not *real* girls."

"Fish?" I knew Shakespeare had used that term that way, but I had never heard anyone else use it to describe girls. And if there weren't going to be any "real" girls — now I was breaking out into a heavy sweat even though it was November and rather cool in the room.

"Chil', is you sweating or did you eat them greasy french fries for lunch?"

I rubbed my sleeve across my forehead.

"I can't go to parties," I said, with a sigh tinged with something like relief, my head descending.

"What do you mean, 'I can't go to parties?'" Stacy mocked me with a voice that was somewhere between a pout and a moan.

I took a deep breath. "My family is very religious. They don't believe in parties." Stacy shook his head and looked at me as if I were a puppy whose master had just been killed.

"That's too sad," he sighed. I started to protest. It wasn't that sad. I mean, it wasn't like famine or pestilence or something. But instead, thinking out loud, I asked, "Where's this party gonna be at, anyway?"

"Right around the corner from where you live, at Willie's house." I wondered how he knew where I lived before I realized the implication of what he had said.

"Willie James's house? Willie the—"

"Yeah, Willie-the-Woman. Mother Nature herself." Well, at least now I knew it was hopeless. Willie was a boy who carried a purse and wore a scarf around his head in the wintertime. Once, my father and I were sitting on the stoop as Willie walked by. My father continually shook his head, smiling, as Willie approached, but he didn't say anything. After Willie was about a half a block away, Daddy turned to me, looked me directly in the eye, and said, "All that ain't even necessary, you hear!" My eyes remained locked to his. I was shocked and felt hurt and naked in the streets. I was relieved when he refocused his attention toward the passing cars.

I couldn't possibly be seen going into Willie-the-Woman's house. And besides, how could I get away from home on a Saturday night? And anyway, did I really want to go? And if I did, what would be going on at a party, a party like that? This was too much to deal with.

"So, how do you know where I live?"

"Oh, I know your song, line by line, sweetheart. All about you and Egghead in the basement, while you supposed to be washing clothes. Yeah, she tells all her business." At that moment the aide returned, looking flushed. Stacy's latest statement had left me reeling. I wondered if I looked as stupid as I felt.

"She just had herself a taste," Stacy whispered.

"No talking," the aide slurred. I pretended to read my book. Thank God that Egghead had moved to Philly. My eyes were glued to one word, one page, for what seemed like hours. Without really intending to, I started running every plot through my mind that I could imagine to get me to that party on Saturday night. I started thinking about the hundreds of episodes of "I Love Lucy" that I must have watched since shortly after my birth.

✪

"What were you doing walking down the street with that boy with all that hair?" The question jolted me, coming as it did the minute I entered our apartment. My mother was mixing something in a large bowl. I figured she must have just dashed back from staring out of the window. She liked to appear omniscient.

"Good evening, Mother." Instantly her eyes narrowed and she banged the wooden spoon on the edge of the steel bowl.

"Don't call yourself getting smart with me, Stanley, 'cause I'll slap the wine out of you in a minute! Who was that?" I took a deep breath. Why couldn't I have television parents? I never heard June threatening to slap the wine out of the Beaver.

"Just some boy I had detention with. He lives across the bridge, so we were walking the same way."

"Across the bridge in the projects? I thought I told you about hangin' out with those kids from the projects."

"We were just walking home. I barely know him."

"Well, I should hope not. I been working all my life trying to keep y'all away from that element. Besides, that boy just don't look right, no way. All that hair, walking 'round like some woolly beast!" Something snapped inside me. Suddenly my voice engaged, sounding like Bing Crosby in a priest suit.

"But, Mother, what would Jesus have said about that 'element'?" I heard the words. I felt the sound of my voice, but I could not believe they were coming from me. It was at that point in my life that I began to seriously consider the possibility of demonic possession.

My mother was livid. Her left eye was wide open, but her right had narrowed to a slit. Her nostrils were flaring and she was breathing with a force I had never seen before. I knew I was in trouble, but I didn't realize I had committed one of the unpardonables.

"You gonna stand there and 'spute *my* word?"

I looked for someplace to run, someplace to hide. I had seen this happen once before when I watched, terrified, as my mother stalked my older brother with a baseball bat, fully intent on doing him grievous bodily harm.

"Boy, you think you gonna raise up Jesus in my face like that! I'll beat the black offa you!" I knew there was an offense that the children of southern blacks dared not commit and that it was called "'sputing their word." However, at that time I did not know what "'spute" was, or how I had only seconds before accomplished just such a crime. Later I would learn that "'spute" was short for *dispute*, but that didn't help at the time.

"Mommy, I didn't mean it that way!"

"Yes, you did, Mr. Man. Well, when I get through with your hard head we'll see how grown you are!"

"But, Momma—" I was saved by the sound of the telephone ringing. Although she was closer to the phone than I was, I dashed over and grabbed the receiver. She couldn't beat me while I was on the phone. It might be one of the saints from church. Not that she was concerned that they might find out that she beats us, no, indeed. She was always on the phone talking about "spare the rod and spoil the child." But I was sure she wouldn't want to sound like she had just been beating me.

"Momma, it's Sister Jones." My mother's eyes were drawn so tight I wasn't sure she could see the receiver I was handing her. She put her hand over the mouthpiece.

"You ain't got away, you just got by, 'cause when I get you, I'm gonna pay you for the old and the new." She then turned her attention to the phone. "Hello, Baby, how you?"

Life is so strange. Only moments before I was on the verge of having a real life. Now, I was just glad to be alive. There was no point thinking about that party. This was an omen. I hobbled into my room past Jesus' plastic eyes, eyes like the ones in the toys in the Cracker Jack box, eyes that followed me from where His portrait hung over the kitchen table. I took off my jacket and threw my books on the bed. I was shaking and my heart was still jumping. I knew my parents wouldn't actually kill us, though they often expressed their inherent right to do so. I also knew that they probably loved us in some way that only sanctified people can love their children. But getting beat with a broomstick or an electric cord was no laughing matter. I knew!

My head felt like a sieve. As soon as anything entered it, it rushed out again. I sat there, vacant. At some point I realized that most of the sounds coming out of the kitchen were laughter. My mother could easily fall into a rage, but she couldn't sustain it for very long. It was time to test the waters. I went back into the kitchen as she was finishing her conversation. I looked in the refrigerator for a soda but settled for some cherry Hi-C, pouring myself a glass before sitting at the table. I tried to look completely dejected; if nothing else I might get away with inflicting a little guilt. My mother squinted at me for a second and then started.

"You know, they announced at church last night that there's going to be a tarry service this coming Saturday." She spoke largely to herself, but knew that I couldn't avoid listening. "I don't care much for these citified tarry meetings. Just seems like an excuse to stay up all night, just like the heathen. But maybe this time you can finally get yourself saved. Chil', it's past time you had yourself some religion."

"Saturday?"

"Yes, what's wrong with Saturday? You ain't got no plans or nothing?"

"No," I whined, feeling a lie rush from my brain to my lips — and a good lie at that. "No, but I was planning to write my term paper for Social Studies on Saturday night." I breathed deeply and tried to look sincere. "The only afternoon the library is open late is tomorrow, and I'm supposed to go to the youth program at church on Friday night. I was counting on having Saturday free to finish my research and write the paper." I hoped she wouldn't remember that it's far too early in the semester for term papers.

"Well, maybe you need to work on that paper on Friday night, 'cause you needs to get saved. And there ain't no way you gonna get saved watching some movie about some half-nekked Africans." I suppressed a frown. The youth programs sponsored by the Missionary Society were one of the few things I liked about church. I hadn't known that the upcoming film had scantily dressed men (they rarely showed women), and thought I would give up the Africans for the party, but I would not give up both the Africans and the party. But, surprisingly, she continued.

"Okay. You can stay home by yourself on Saturday night, but I'll take Jimmy with me, 'cause I don't want to get home and see y'all done wrecked the place."

I couldn't believe what had just happened. The Negro drive for education did have unexpected advantages. My father worked every Saturday night and Mommy and Jimmy would be at church praying right through breakfast Sunday morning. It was almost as if the Lord wanted me to go to this party. Well, at least I hoped it was the Lord.

I spent all of Saturday afternoon and early evening in my room, pretending to read. I was too excited to withstand close scrutiny. I avoided everyone, claiming to be working on my paper. As soon as my mother and Jimmy left for church I broke into a panic. I couldn't possibly go to a party. A party with — all boys! What might happen? Who might find out? What if somebody got shot? I shook myself and waited for my mind to settle down. I was going to go! The worst thing that might possibly happen would be that everyone in the neighborhood would find out, my father would beat me viciously, and I would be sent to Cheraw, South Carolina, to live with my Aunt Gert. Was all of that worth one little party?

"Of course, sweetheart," I reassured myself with a flourish. I went to my closet and started pulling out clothes left and right. I really didn't have anything to wear to a party. I had school clothes, church clothes, and play clothes, but no party clothes. I would have to be creative. I looked through some of the clothes my older brother, Lucius, had left when he went into the Army. I finally settled on my white turtleneck, the pants to my good blue suit, and a blue satin cowboy shirt that belonged to Lucius. The shirt was studded with clear but highly reflective beads of various shapes and sizes. The beads made the shirt very heavy, and it was already far too large. I would wear it over my turtleneck and outside my pants to make a fashion statement. I was determined not to be loud, but I wanted to be clear. I ran into the kitchen and ironed the shirt feverishly. I got dressed and put on the blue marshmallow shoes I had convinced my father were sneakers. I was ready. I looked in the full-length mirror on the bathroom door and grimaced. I just looked like a kid wearing flashy clothes that were too big for him. I looked again. No, the clothes were fine. It was my hair. I had to do something with my hair.

I ran to the utility closet and pulled out an old straightening comb. Not my mother's good one, of course, but an old one. I turned on an eye on the stove, put the straightening comb on it, and ran to the bathroom for a towel to drape over my shoulders. Sure, I had never done this before, but how hard could it be? When the comb started smoking I took it off the stove and plunged it into my head. A full inch of my hair went up in smoke as I caught the scream in my throat when I felt my skin sizzle. "The wages of sin is death," I thought as I ran into the bathroom, jumping up and down to control the pain. Finally, it occurred to me to put a cool damp cloth on my head. The pain intensified but gradually subsided. Luckily, the burn wasn't serious. I looked at the clock. It was nearly 7:30. Stacy was going to ring my bell at a quarter to eight.

"A hat!" That's what Mother would do. I ran to the closet and started rummaging through Lucius's headwear. The only thing in blue was a denim cap that looked like the top of an overgrown pumpkin.

"What choice do you have?" Just then the bell rang. I went to the intercom. "Who is it?"

"Stanley, it's me." I threw the cap on my head and told myself that I probably looked like Michael Jackson. When I got downstairs I realized it wasn't as dark as I had hoped it would be. It was all those streetlights. Who needed all those streetlights in Brooklyn? I was grateful for my gray Sunday coat. All that anyone could see were the blue shoes and the cap, from which they should be able to conclude no more than poor taste. Stacy was another matter. I tried not to stare, but I was instantly convinced that Stacy had some Puerto Rican in him somewhere. That coat! It had to have been someone's rug in another life. And loud! Well, it was dark; I'd keep my head down and walk fast.

"Where are you running to? Ain't you gonna let me see what you have on?"

I was already on the sidewalk. I answered with a "come along" gesture and kept walking. There were a few neighborhood guys hangin' out at the corner. As we walked by, one of them said, "Hello, girls." I was sure Stacy was going to pull out a razor and I would also get to experience jail before I got beat and sent South. But Stacy just turned and gave them a smile. The guys giggled a little but didn't say anything else. I tried to bury my head in my jacket, hoping none of them recognized me. Just down the street and around the corner and the worst would be over.

Stacy talked continually as we walked, but I couldn't concentrate on anything he said. All I could think about was attending the most important social event of my life, and how I looked like an overdressed cowboy from Gary, Indiana. As we approached Willie's front door, breathing became very difficult. What was behind that door? Stacy rang the bell.

The door opened. Oh my God, it was Willie's mother.

"Hey there, Beaufort, who that you got with you?" I had assumed that Willie's mother would be out of town or something. It never occurred to me that she would know about the party or, much less, be there.

"Aunt Liz, this is Stanley Lanier, from down the street." I shuddered. Why did he have to give my last name?

"Who? Stanley? Boy, your momma know where you are tonight?" I nodded my head up and down, hoping my gestures would be more convincing than my voice.

"Well, all right, you boys come on in." Just inside the front door was a closet where another woman stood offering us hangers.

As I slowly peeled off my coat I asked Stacy, "Beaufort?" The look he shot me silenced that question forever. Aunt Liz smiled with genuine amusement as she reviewed my ensemble, despite the fact that she was wearing a loud yellow jumpsuit with a neckline so low that under other circumstances I might have been embarrassed for her. I was ready to go home. When she turned to Stacy she became as radiant as he in fact was. Stacy was dressed in white double-knit pants and a matching white shirt with a collar that looked like two dog ears flapping halfway down his chest. But you couldn't tell him nothing. I raised a proper eyebrow. Even I knew one did not wear white in the winter.

Aunt Liz giggled. "Chil', you sho' a mess, ain't you? All dressed in white. You ain't supposed to be no bride now, is you?" I felt myself slowly shrinking into the background, wondering what I had gotten myself into. These folks were strange!

We began to move forward down a narrow hall. Just ahead, I could hear voices — too many voices. Pulled along by Stacy's glow and Aunt Liz's big hands, I found myself in a living room with ten or twelve other boys, all looking older and much more interestingly dressed. Everyone glanced in our general direction, but fortunately somebody put on a record and almost everyone started dancing.

I inched my way over to the sofa and sat down. The back of my shirt crinkled with static electricity as it made contact with the clear plastic slipcover. Aunt Liz and the other woman were surveying the scene. The boys, for the most part, weren't really coupled off as they danced. They just sort of all danced in various ad hoc groupings. I felt like I had been captured by some hostile tribe and was going to be eaten at any minute. Why on earth had I thought this party was a good idea? I saw Aunt Liz motioning to me with her finger. I got up and went over to where she was standing.

"Baby, you can't sit in my house with no hat on." My face fell. I could feel myself trembling.

"But, but I sort of had an accident — with my hair."

"An accident? Let me see," she said, snatching off my cap, still seeming very amused. "Uh huh! Come on with me." Then, turning to the other woman, "Janie, you watch those chicken wings for a minute, you hear?"

"Sure, Liz," the other woman answered. She also seemed amused. I was sure they must have been talking about me. Aunt Liz led me by the hand into the bathroom. She closed the door and plugged in a hand-held hair dryer. It had a comb attachment and she combed it gently through my hair for several minutes. Then she picked it out, patted it a little here, pushed it a little there, and I found myself with a short, but respectable-looking afro.

"Now, Baby, don't take this the wrong way, but where did you git that shirt? You just gonna be all hot in that, and, besides, that thing's so bright it hurts my eyes." I looked at her like she was crazy. Here she was dressed in something even Aretha Franklin wouldn't wear, trying to tell *me* how to dress! I was fuming, but she started laughing.

"Wait, wait in here for a minute." When she returned she pinned a small rhinestone brooch to the neck of my turtleneck before taking my brother's shirt off my back.

"Now, that should give you all the flash you need. Just remember not to walk out my door with my pin on!" I looked in the mirror and was not displeased.

"When you finish admirin' yourself, wipe some of that shine off your face and come back to the party."

"Thank you," I mumbled as she left me in the bathroom, taking my shirt with her. She turned, laughed, and went back toward the kitchen. I closed the door. I couldn't get over the change. I looked good, but how was I going to drag myself out of that bathroom? Just then the door opened.

"Oh, are you finished?" I nodded yes to the very tall brown-skinned boy who looked like a horse in the face. I left him in the bathroom and walked slowly back into the living room. As I entered, I heard someone whisper, "Cinderella has returned." Suddenly Stacy, who had disappeared almost as soon as we got there, was at my side.

"Don't you jump grand, Miss Thing, not with my dearest friend." His dearest friend? Stacy then proceeded to introduce me around the room. I was the youngest. Most of the other guys were sixteen or seventeen. I was only fourteen. Fortunately, I was tall for my age, so I tried to cast a worldly air about myself, not being quite sure what a worldly air was. But I was beginning to feel better. And once all of these strange people had names, they seemed more human, less alien. Stacy started dancing and since I was standing next to him, I started dancing, too. When the song ended, Stacy was off again, so I sat. This wasn't so bad after all. Someone sitting next to me named Milt started talking to me, something about Diana Ross, and I was talking back, something about Gladys Knight.

There were guys there I had seen around the neighborhood or at school but had never talked to before. I felt as if I were grown. Willie was being the grand host, or hostess, or whatever, decked out in a black satin suit that he wore without a shirt, and a pair of black patent leather loafers. He slowly sauntered toward me.

"Stanley dear, I'm so pleased you were able to attend my little soirée." *Soirée?* I refused to believe that Willie could possibly be using a word I had never heard before.

"Thanks for having me," I replied.

"Having you! Darling, please, my husband is in the next room." I thought that Daddy was right, all that couldn't be necessary.

The music had slowed down and people were wandering into the kitchen and wandering out balancing paper plates of chicken and potato salad against paper cups filled with Kool-Aid. I felt myself smiling so hard that my ears were beginning to ache.

"Hi." Someone was standing in front of me with two plates in his hands, saying something.

"Aunt Liz told me to give this to you."

"Thanks," I replied, trying to sound nonchalant and sophisticated. He handed me a plate and sat down between me and Milt. The guy was tall, like me, and dressed very simply in dark pants and a sky-blue sweater. He shrugged his shoulders and rocked his head in a goofy sort of way. Through his gold-rimmed glasses I could see that he was slightly cross-eyed.

"Hi," he said again, "my name is Paul. You probably don't remember me, but we were in the same gym class last year." There were 150 people in that class, and he was right, I didn't remember him. "I go to Erasmus now," he continued.

"I'm planning to go to Erasmus next year."

"Oh, yeah, well you'll like it," he said into his lap. We were both spending a lot of time staring at our food. "It's a great school and there are a lot of 'the children' there." *The children*, I thought, *hmm*.

He spoke slowly, choosing his words carefully and speaking television English like my parents tried to force us to speak at home. I found myself thinking, "He's cute," recognizing that I had never let such a thought take such definite form before. Although he was trying hard to make conversation, and I was helping, at least a little, he would only look at me in tentative, fleeting glances. It was as if he expected me to say "get lost" at any minute.

"You know, everybody thought Stacy was kidding when he said you were coming to this party. Since your family is so sanctified and proper and all. Oh, maybe I shouldn't have said that." I sat and nodded, gradually becoming aware of how smooth and pleasing his voice was.

"You don't talk much, do you?" He laughed a little. I became afraid that maybe I really wasn't talking enough.

"No, not really," I shrugged. "But then I guess I'm sort of nervous." I lowered my voice a little. "This is my first party."

"You mean your first all-boy party?"

"No, my first party of ... of any kind." I had started to say "of any denomination," but that seemed a bit much. Paul seemed shocked.

"Not even a birthday party?"

"No, not since I was eight or nine."

"Wow!"

"Yeah," I nodded, beginning to recognize how deprived I had been.

We ate in silence until we had cleaned our plates. When the music picked up again he asked, "Do you want to dance?" I was glad I had spent so much time watching "Soul Train" on TV (with the sound turned down, of course). I wasn't doing the same steps that most of the other kids were doing, but at least I was doing something. I didn't feel as foolish as I thought I would. I didn't feel strange at all. Here I was in Willie-the-Woman's house, dancing with a boy like it was right. I thought, "Honey, this ain't nothing but the truth." I began laughing out loud as we danced. I knew why people chose to hang out in beer gardens and dance halls instead of waiting on the Lord. This was a lot more fun than waiting on anything, no matter how divine.

"But what of your eternal soul that you are condemning to the pit with Satan and his minions?" My mother's stern voice slid through my head. But I remembered that Lucius had found some place in the Bible where it said, "If your conscience don't condemn you neither will I," and right now my conscience was saying, "If it feels good, it's all right." I started laughing again and Paul smiled broadly in response.

Paul and I continued talking off and on for the rest of the evening. We talked about our favorite TV shows, about our favorite subjects at school. This was the first time I had spoken to another boy who admitted that he really liked school. He talked about different colleges he might want to attend. I now wished I had skipped a grade last year when I had the chance; then maybe we would be in the same high school now. Maybe we'd be planning to go to the same college in a couple of years. But then maybe I would have never been invited to this party. I was becoming more relaxed, but still found myself sounding like Sammy Davis, Jr., from time to time.

About a quarter to eleven Aunt Liz turned the music down and we all knew it was time to go home. Stacy, whom I had barely seen after he announced the depth of our friendship, found me and said that he was spending the night at Aunt Liz's, but that he would walk me home.

"That's okay. I'm going that way. I'll walk with Stanley." I heard the words, but I didn't believe Paul or any other human being was speaking them. They sounded as if they had come from on high. I had to be hallucinating or this was a dream. He was smiling at me and I was smiling back. We should have been on TV.

"Okay. You boys git home safe," Aunt Liz said, giving me a hug and whispering, "You can bring my pin by tomorrow." Putting on my coat, I found Lucius's shirt stuffed in a sleeve.

We walked slowly, kicking pebbles and bottle caps before us, bumping into each other every couple of steps or so.

"You know, Stanley, I want to say something, but I think you'll think I'm stupid." I tried to frame a reassuring response, but before I could Paul continued. "I don't know any other guys who — well — I don't have a lot of friends, or I don't have a lot of good friends. You know? I really don't know any other guys I can talk to about school and stuff, and who also have to go to church every Sunday." We continued walking, my eyes glued to the sidewalk in front of me, my heart racing like a subway train. "You know, I don't know a lot of gay people and all, but a lot of the ones I know are sort of strange. You know what I mean?" His voice shot up with "You know what I mean?" and he seemed so sincere. He continued.

"I'm really glad I ran into you tonight. It's sort of hard not knowing people you have things in common with, and trying to be — gay. You know what I mean?" His voice dropped with the word "gay." I nodded, trying to keep up with time, which had become strangely fluid; trying not to get stuck on his every word; trying not to anticipate how wonderful I was going to feel when I got home and convinced myself that all of this had really happened — had really happened to me.

"Maybe sometime we could go to the movies, or go to the library. I mean, assuming you would want to, you know?"

I thought for a minute that I was going to pee on myself, and stopped for a second to take a deep breath.

Paul paused. "Are you okay?"

"Oh, yeah, just a little cramp." I wondered if that was what love felt like. I tried to talk. "Yeah, you know what you said, it sounds like a good idea to me. I mean if you would want to." I sounded like I was three years old. I tried again. "What I mean, Paul, is I would like it very much if we could become good friends." We turned, walking up the stairs to my house. I took out my key and opened the first door. We stepped inside.

"Are you going to be around tomorrow?" he asked. "Maybe I could come by after church and we could talk some more?"

"Sure, in the afternoon, maybe about five-thirty or six o'clock."

"Okay." We both stood with our hands in our pockets, bobbing around like we were much colder than we actually were. Sort of looking at each other, but not too hard, not too long.

"Okay, so I'll see you tomorrow, Stanley." Before I could nod out another okay, Paul's head turned sharply toward me and he gave me a little peck on the lips. We both sort of laughed until—

"Jimmy, who is that down there in that hall?" Paul's eyes swelled and then contracted at the sound of my mother's voice. He said, "See you," and was out the door.

"I don't know, Momma," my brother yelled back. "It looked like Stanley was kissing some man."

GUY-MARK FOSTER

The Book of Luke

I am alone in the showers with an older white boy. He has the same bandaid-colored complexion as the painting of Jesus Christ hung in my momma's house. His naked back faces me. Oh, I'm naked too, but he's more naked, because I'm watching him slap soap between his reddened hindparts, on the backs of his thighs, and over his heart-shaped calves. When I'm in the showers nothing matters but the other boy I'm watching and the water hitting my head. I come here lots of times. After my swim, I take extra long washing my whole body three or four times: ears, throat, under the arms, chest, stomach, and down below. This way I can see more boys.

It's these ninth-graders with shoulder-length, wavy hair that I like best. Maybe I should not think it, but when I watch them it's like that painting's come to life. The thing is: I don't have religion like Momma. Oh, I want it sometimes, but it's not there. This is the reason we left my old man, she tells me — he doesn't feel the Holy Spirit squirming in the dark of his soul, and he laughs too often for no sure reason. But I rode atop his big shoulders when I was little and I'd wave at the other kids to make them jealous because my father was always happy. Their own daddies were drunk or off in the arms of glassy-eyed, wig-wearing ho'es. My father never drank until Momma said she hated him and was taking me away from his bad influence. He drank a whole fifth of JB Scotch that night and sat on the front stoop outside our building.

When he came back inside Momma cussed the day she ever married him. She cussed her government job with D.O.T. She cussed the pink silk dress he brought back from the war, with the pearl buttons and the white silk pants underneath. She cussed all her TV programs, even "The Flip Wilson Show." They were all bad for the race, she said. No, worse;

they were losers. And my daddy was the biggest loser, because he was the cleanup nigger at D.C. General Hospital. According to her she was not a lucky woman. A person had to be born into good luck. You could not acquire it like red hair or a Lerner's credit card. This was something in the blood like the trait for slanted eyes and pretty feet. Parents with pretty feet have begot children with pretty feet every day the world over for generations. It was the same with luck. The Rockefellers had it, and the Vanderbilts. Lord knows Rose and Joe Kennedy had the lion's share of it, until lately. But Momma did not have one drop in her veins, it seemed, nor did anybody she was "acquainted" with. This was humiliation itself. She said all this to my father.

I sat listening in their bedroom, the volume turned down on "Police Woman." I thought Angie Dickinson was beautiful. I especially liked the easy curving of her index finger around the trigger of her shiny black revolver. It always gave me a small thrill when she would take it out, point it at the accused, and shoot: "Bang, bang, bang!" My parents continued to argue in the room the Christ painting hung in. This was before Momma moved it to where we live now, near the Olympic-sized public pool where I swim. When she said, "I hate you, Eugene Miles," her voice was loud like she wanted all of Washington to know. Instead of blaming her blood, her unlucky life was my daddy's fault, because he cleaned up after "piss-poor, ignorant niggers living off food stamps!"

And then I was mentioned.

"Have mercy! Eyes, teeth, those rubber tires for lips, that child is your mirror image, only yours. He even walks like you, swinging his bony arms back and forth like he's happy. But he don't know the first thing about it. Just like his daddy. But let me tell you something: Left to me, I *swear* his life will not be a carbon copy of yours, you *nigger*. No, *Jeee*sus!"

This is when my daddy hauled off and hit my mother, and she fell down. I heard her shriek then, and the bed I sat on shook beneath me. I went to the door of the bedroom and cracked it open. She was trying to get out of the apartment but Daddy held her from behind. She kicked at him and swung her arms and finally a wild hand smacked him in the eye and he, stunned, let her go. My mother ran into the hall shouting: "Jackeee! Lois Aaaann!" I walked calmly into the room and stared down at my father. One of his eyes was closed and he lay twitching on his back, the breath knocked out of him. He reached out to me, but I did not recognize that man. He was a stranger in my happy father's body. I could hear Momma jiggling the lock out in the hall, trying to get to the street. But the catch on the entrance door was jammed and she could not release it. The stranger on his back heard the jiggling, too. He raised himself up and went after my momma and grabbed her by the hair. He looked at her, and then back at me, standing at the bottom of the stairwell. The whites of his eyes were cloudy and filled with blood and tears. He shook my mother's head from side to side. "You wanna get out?" he asked her. "You wanna get out?" He grunted, and then, all in one swift, clean, expert motion, he shoved the crown of her head into the door and the clear glass shattered.

"Get on out then, you yella bitch!" he said. "Get the fuck out!"

Not long after that my momma and I moved to the suburbs, and I started coming to the pool. To tell the truth, I don't enjoy swimming. I hate that the chlorine stings my eyes. But I keep them open to spy which boy I want to follow into the showers afterwards. This one I'm looking at is new to the suburbs, too. I see him at school and with his parents at the white Baptist church we belong to now. But check this out: I'm not even being slick about staring at him, even though he might get pissed off and shove me into the tile wall like some of the other boys have done. He might call me one of those names. But I'm used to all of that now. None of it bothers me.

Sssh! He's soaping his feet: lifting up first one and then the other foot like he's checking for turds under them. It's funny — somebody dropping a turd in the shower! I have to laugh at this. Hearing me, he turns around startled, and he looks and looks and doesn't stop looking. It's like he had not expected anyone to be there watching him; but it's okay because he recognizes a trait in me, maybe, that doesn't belong to anyone else, but is ours only — mine and his. I have never been stared at like this. Never. Yellows and purples shoot off inside his eyes like tiny bursts of soft light. His eyes have become the ocean on "The Undersea World of Jacques Cousteau," so calm, but all the while hinting at the mysterious nature of evolutionary life. And lo and behold: His hair is crinkly and dark like Jesus' hair, only it's more tangled, as if, perhaps, a seabird had tried to lift his earthbound body into the air with its feet and, with great reluctance, had to let go.

Out of habit, I tense my legs as he stares, preparing to take the punches from his fist if that is going to happen. But this is the deal: He just flashes those eyes, his back to the shower nozzle. The clear water jets out and rinses the soap from his reflecting shoulders and the foam collects 'round his feet. I've never seen feet and ankles so white. It's like he is standing on top of a thick, new cloud and his toes, like cupid-fingers, are reaching out to me through the bubbly spume, their voices whispering:

Steal away, steal away
Steal away to Jesus!

I notice, then, the tiny hairs that trail to his navel. There is lots of hair 'round his thing, down below, and it bounces a little as the water hits it. His is a nice, fat one, much bigger and hairier than mine. I like the color of it — like the inside of a cooked hot dog. I know he is not going to strike me when he smiles. I know this even though I am not looking at his face, if you know what I mean. And all of a sudden I think this is what would make my momma happy: Jesus smiling at her unlucky son. Maybe then she'll think I have religion and will let me visit my daddy for his birthday. I have not seen him since we left the old neighborhood. I miss him teasing me about tongue-kissing a girl. I miss the stormy smell of cigarettes and Wint-O-Green Lifesavers on his breath. I miss the jokes about my momma's crooked toes, though they don't look bad when she wears stockings over them. He only said they did to get her to laugh with us. She doesn't laugh anymore. She's a full-time prayer woman now. The walls are thin here, and every night I hear Momma ask God for the one thing she never had — a big house with a yard and a sturdy tree in it.

She and I live on the ground floor of a five-story apartment building here in the suburbs. Crab apple trees have blossomed along the sidewalk and in the small courtyard. But none of the tart fruit to fall this season, she tells me, will have either her name stamped on the ripe skin or my daddy's. And of course, I can just forget about my own name. "It's not what the Lord has in store for us, baby," she says. "We're meant for something much better than that. Amen."

I watch Momma faithfully lay a dollar bill in the collection plate every Sunday, the corners of her mouth tense, her eyes aimed on Heaven, waiting for the great mission to show itself. I sit beside her small body in that church and feel it quiver and rock with each hymn and sermon. What is it that she expects from a God who would let His only son be nailed through the palms and feet to two beams of wood? If anyone was born unlucky it was Jesus Christ. Nevertheless, He was able to proclaim before His death: *Blessed are ye, when men shall hate you, and when they shall separate you from their company, and shall reproach you, and cast your name as evil!*

It is this passage I re-read every afternoon after I come home from the pool. When Momma sees the Bible in my hands she figures I'm gearing up to be saved any day now. But I am stuck in the Book of Luke for other reasons. I figure Jesus is directing those words not only to His twelve disciples, and to the devoted citizens of Tyre and Sidon, but I figure the Son of God is also schooling my old man and me, because of our own bruises, on the subject of forgiving those who hate us. You see, it's like this: I can't believe my daddy is as cruel and unfeeling as Jesus' father, even though Momma wears a wig these days on account of the numerous stitches required to sew her scalp back together; but Daddy had been drinking the Devil's water on that occasion of violence, and he was anything but himself. I am convinced of this.

My father has to be a blessed man, like Jesus says, and since I am flesh of his flesh I, too, am blessed, in spite of what my mother preaches. In 6:27 of this same Gospel, the Lord goes so far as to say that we should do good to those who hate us. And though that is a hard one, I don't fight those boys back. I will admit that it sometimes makes me crazy as a bedbug for vengeance, but I am not bitter.

In fact, I'm happy this kid is smiling and not spitting on me, or flipping his goodies in my face like I'm dirty. Maybe his momma doesn't like his father either and that is why he comes here. I don't know or care. I just like the lazy way he stares at me like he's not afraid of dying on a cross because he's a believer in the resurrection, too, and all it means, just like Momma. For no reason I smile big at him then, bigger than I have ever smiled at any other white boy. My smile is so big my jaw muscles snap and my teeth stretch to my ears. I can't hear the neighborhood bullies shouting in the pool anymore. I don't even hear the shower running, but it keeps splashing my back like a baptism or a wave from an ocean of voices.

And then this boy is standing right in front of me. He is bolder than I am. He touches his hand to my wet shoulder. A jolt runs through my body like chased fire. His yellow-and-purple eyes are dancing all over my naked ears, throat, eyelids, under the arms, chest, stomach, and down below. Before I can stop it from happening the bones in my face suddenly shatter and my smile grows so big it covers my whole twelve-year-old body. He says something to me and I say something about his crinkly hair reminding me of the sun rising. But I cannot hear the words. All I can be sure of is my heart racing along beneath my warm painlessly expanding skin. I am now a great, big, floating, twisting, turning smile. I am almost as big as my daddy's smile when he's watching Redd Foxx on "Sanford and Son." This kid is smiling, too, and then our two smiles glide forward and press ever so gently against one another like twin brothers in the womb.

It is here that I figure the Jesus in my momma's painting is missing. Can it be possible that I've pulled Him down from the wall of one religion, stolen His unclad body into the room of another ... and bolted the door? I cannot tell where I am, or if the date of my daddy's birth has passed and it's another day, a brand new year, or whether I am older than my age now, or younger. All I know is that the Son of God is smiling upon me and I am jacking Him off with my huge smile of a body. This has to make my mother happy, too, I think: this sudden conversion to a worshipping faith. And if it doesn't, so what. I'm happy enough for the both of us. I am so happy I might let myself explode into a zillion particles of blinding white light...

Oh, *Jeee*sus!

—for Isidro Sesmero

ALAN MILLER

Letter to Gregory

You have never seen the sea-
washed rocks lining the road
to Tiburon, the path winding
to Jack & Annie's home,
now mine. You've never seen
ferry passengers armed with a
smile & a dollar's expensive
innocence. I think of you now
Gregory because nothing I own
stores your memory. Such souvenirs
are easily bought here in Tiburon,
by these bleached rocks,
their picture-perfect reflections.

But I don't own a magical trinket
that re-names, restores you: your ring,
your baseball, or even a letter.
(This last is easily explained.
You never learned to write
very well, wouldn't show me
your difficult, indecipherable messages.)

Jan, an old friend from Massachusetts,
has a stuffed head or a photograph
of his "catch," his triumph, his love.
You can see his finger in the fish's mouth
or his gun mounted on a shelf—

which really doesn't need nails, only
Jan's pride to keep it aloft.
My parents took photos of you & me,
Gregory — us squinting into the camera,
or us again exposed, ashamed, looking hard
for each other, for our secrets.
Dad saw us differently: through the lens
two small detached magnets of equal
& opposite attraction, fearfully clinging
to each other, for a photo.

The cruel boyhood of these photos
accuses me — the shadows falling backward
& forward into the grass or blown large
& ghostly onto bare walls. Now yours
is the unblinking vision of the dead,
the unyielding appetite of the harshest
light. Your limbs are forever full,
your hair a young solid color, &, for me,
you still have, peculiar among Black people,
freckles.

Is it ten years since two boys
barely older than us locked you
in your boyhood body and left me empty-
handed to age & mourn in mine?
Would we perform as they did another day?
Our small black hands squeezing bullets?
I doubt it; but I know someone larger
than either of us pulled the trigger.
Someone: not god and not godly.

No one heard the music the bullet made
against your spine. You were pretending
to swim in the shallow water of a public
pool. (Why does that word "public"
so often mean danger, vulnerability, excess?)
Your last real breath, wet & full
with pleasure & pain, your face kissing
the water for the very first time.

The rest of the telling doesn't matter:
though some are convinced that two years
of electric air pumped into your body
made you whole again — it was enough

only to breathe. But not me:
I'd known your body like my own—
when it had all sensation. We clung together,
you & I, without knowing it, to protect
each other against a lifetime of stray bullets:
the silence spreading in us & around us,
joblessness, against idle hands & stillborn
dreams, against barbers & beards & beads.

I read the newspapers still, read words
like "tragedy," "exploit," & "guilt," read
about boys robbed of their manhood
like Arthur Miller in New York City,
about men robbed of their boyhoods
and their futures, buying & selling
life insurance, like Arthur McDuffie
in Miami, & like you, hoarding the little life
you'd known, cupping your palms
around it, a candle you shielded
from water or wind, even from me, the cameras,
even yourself—

Even now, my own body ringing
with pain, visited in a thousand tourist towns.

JOHN KEENE, JR.

Adelphus King

I

One Saturday, during the summer that I graduated from high school and got a job unloading delivery trucks for Mr. Krone, the Hardware King of St. Louis, I drove down to the Willow Park train depot to meet my cousin, Alma Jean. She was to arrive from Memphis on the 5:25 p.m. train from Jackson, Mississippi. For as far back as I could remember, Alma Jean, the only child of my mother's only sister, would come up to Willow Park by train to spend a good part of the summer with my family. Right after Easter my mother would start preparing for Alma Jean's arrival—she always got here in early June—and by the Fourth of July we were all ready to mail her home. Usually my father or one of my sisters would pick up Alma Jean, but since it so happened that on this particular Saturday they had all gone shopping over in Illinois, I was left to fetch her. My best friend, Roby, who had always had a crush on Alma Jean, let me borrow his convertible Oldsmobile 98, figuring that such a favor would impress Alma Jean. I got to the depot early, so I bought a newspaper and sat down across from the doorway leading to the tracks. Estimating that I had about a half-hour till Alma Jean's train pulled in, I bought a soda and started reading the baseball scores.

"Five twenty-five Jackson train arriving on schedule?" I had been to Jackson many times, always to visit my mother's older brother, Richard, my favorite uncle. My memory, however, always returned to one particular visit. The summer after I turned seven, my mother and I traveled down by train to attend the funeral of Uncle Richard's wife, Charlene. My father could not take off from his job, and both of my older sisters were already at camp, so one week before Alma Jean was to arrive, my mother and I made the journey by ourselves. The ride seemed interminable, and every night I would awaken in a fit from the same dream: I would be standing in an open space, waiting for someone, when all of a sudden a total, seeping blackness would snatch me up: a blackness shinier than lacquer, grainier than charcoal, thicker than tar. I could feel the blackness slowly enveloping me. I would panic, flailing my arms madly about, screaming breathlessly, kicking my feet in every direction. Then I would surrender, my arms above my head, my legs stretched out beneath me, my eyes closed. Smothering in that seeping thickness, blinded by its sheen, crushed by its sheer weight, I would wake up, heaving, gasping, sobbing. I tried to tell my mother about the dreams, but she was convinced that my nightly ordeals were the result of the early summer heat, and that the long trip was aggravating my asthma, so she did her best to comfort me. I did not complain, because I enjoyed her concern and it only took a few minutes after I woke up for my breathing to return to normal. Moreover, I enjoyed the strange, tingling feeling that seized me below my stomach once I had calmed down. Finally we reached Jackson: Our arrival alone took my mind away from the dream.

Jackson: the blistering noonday heat and the heavy smell of freshly laid tar; my ten-year-old half-wit cousin Raymond and his baby sister Denise running figure eights in my uncle's backyard, oblivious to our arrival or the grieving around them; my mother's red and puffy eyes, my Uncle Sonny's tear-streaked cheeks, my Uncle Rome's litany from Revelations, and my Aunt Virginia's fainting spell before the casket at the funeral; above all, my Uncle Richard, silent for the first time that I could recall, somber, his eyes trained on me, while everyone else wept and kept vigil in the house, cleaning, preparing food, and eulogizing Aunt Charlene. Uncle Richard would not cry but just transferred himself from one piece of furniture to another, and seemed too large for the kitchen chairs or the living room sofa or even the swing hanging out on the gallery. He just shifted from seat to seat, silently, watching me, his eyes trying to tell me something that I could not understand, and that no one else around us seemed able to notice.

The night after the funeral, I awakened, coughing and crying from that recurring dream. This time above me stood my Uncle Richard, saying nothing, motionless, in his pajamas, his eyes fixed on me. For as long as I could remember he had reminded me of a bear. His burly build, his huge, pawlike hands, and his bearded, disarming face had always made my sisters tremble, but he had never frightened me: I would fantasize that when I grew up I would look just like him. Now in the dark, his giant, looming shape terrified me. Before I knew it, he was reaching out his arms, then lifting me up onto his chest. With his two square elbows clenching my waist he held me more firmly than anyone — my mother, my father, my sisters, anyone — had ever held me. Then he began to cry: It started out high and soft, but became a man's bellow, heavy and sonorous, from somewhere deep inside him. He trembled as he cried, but held me tightly, and I, no longer afraid, held him as tightly as I could. Slowly he began to rock me and pat my back, and my tears and wheezing stopped completely. When he finished crying, he kissed me on the forehead, then lowered me back into my bed. I closed my eyes and fell asleep. I was sure that I would have that dream again and I was ready for it, but it returned only in daydreams, never with the same force. The next morning, my Uncle Richard drove my mother and me to the train station in Jackson: He was almost back to his old self, laughing and joking some with my mother, talking about the family and about how much he missed Charlene. As we stood on the boarding platform, he kneeled down to me, gave me a thorough looking over and a firm hug. I asked him, "Are you gonna be all right, Uncle Richard?"

"In time, little man," he whispered to me, "in time."

"Five twenty-five train coming in!" Realizing that I had been day-dreaming I looked around for Alma Jean, then surmised that she would probably be the last person off the train, so I sat back down. After a good ten minutes folks started trickling into the lobby, but I saw no Alma Jean. Women and men emerged from the boarding area in every style of sum-mer attire: men in seersucker suits and madras shirts, women in linen skirts and cotton dresses, children in sailor suits and dungarees. As the travelers streamed in, I began to worry about Alma Jean. What was taking her so long? Had she caught the train? Still more people, and still no Alma Jean. More, then a few, then no one. A white conductor entered, wiping his brow: A few more passengers followed him. Where was Alma Jean?

And then, there she was: Miss Alma Jean Reaves, in a natty, hardly wrinkled white linen suit, white pumps, white gloves, white clutch purse, pearl-colored cat-eye glasses and a small-brimmed white trilby. With her hair elegantly bobbed and her face gingerly colored, she was as I had last seen her: young, glamorous, chic. She sternly marched toward me, but she was carrying no luggage.

"Wherehaveyoubeenmarcuswaynealexander?" she hollered out. "I been waiting a good HALF-AN-HOUR for you. Boy, wait till I tell your MOMMA!" As we both burst into laughter, I gave her a hug. I began to ask her, "What took you so long?" and "Where are your bags?" when *he* came through the door.

"Marcus, I want you to meet Mr. A-DEL-PHUS KING! Del, I want you to meet my first and favorite cousin, Marcus!" I heard only "Del" as he stood there before me. Nearly six-four I reckoned, and built just like my Uncle Richard: He was wearing a white pima cotton sports shirt cut from far too small a piece of cloth, a porkpie hat, khaki pants, and foreign-looking black laceup shoes. Behind him, in a tidy pile, sat all seven of Alma Jean's pieces of luggage, as well as a dingy black duffel bag and what looked like a clarinet case.

"Marcus, let me tell you! I had just gotten on the train at Memphis, and what with all of these damn IGNORANT old Pullman porters just rolling they eyes and not giving me even one FINGER of help, I was a MESS!" His shoulders were nearly as broad as he was tall; for such a big man he was slender, with long, sinewy arms and longer, bowed legs. He wore a smile on his face, and as I tried to break my stare, he extended his hand for a shake.

"Marcus, who — WHO — WHO!! came to my rescue but Mr. Adelphus King! Let me tell you, I did not know WHAT I WAS GOING TO DO, when out of nowhere ... maybe heaven, chile ... comes this MAN and then he kind of whispers, 'You look like you need a little help' and then he just TOOK OVER, do you hear me, putting my bags away — that Pullman porter just rolling his old bloodshot, yellow eyes — and sitting me right down — I couldn't take my eyes off this here man — he says, 'Why don't you rest a little bit, ma'am' — 'MA'AM' — so you know I just sat myself down and rested a little bit!" I looked down, and his hand was still extended. I fumbled with my own hands, then awkwardly thrust my left hand into his. Mr. Adelphus King just smiled.

"Del is a JAZZ musician — a JAZZ musician — from New Orleans!" Alma Jean broke in. "He plays the ALTO sax, that's right isn't it, the ALTO sax, and another kind of sax, and he has people up here in St. Louis — in Willow Park, can you believe it — so he's gonna be staying right out here near ME — ain't that right, Del?"

"That's right," he answered softly. He was still wearing that broad smile. A jazz musician, I thought: How did Alma Jean manage this one?

"His jazz musician friends have gigs going, which is why he's visiting, so we will just HAVE to go and hear him play." Reaching into her purse, she pulled out an embroidered handkerchief, then daintily ran it under her chin, all the while watching Mr. Adelphus King watch her. "It's warm in here ... would you please get your DEAR cousin Alma Jean an orange pop?"

I reached in my pocket for some change, but then remembered I had used my last bits for my soda. In the process of digging for coins, out flew my car keys. In one motion Mr. Adelphus King swept them up. Grinning, he dropped them in my left hand, and with them fell soda change.

"Thanks, Mr. King..."

"Del, man..."

"Del..." I went to get the soda. Del and Alma Jean followed me. I was amazed that Del was able to bear, with little obvious effort, all of Alma Jean's traveling implements, as well as his duffel bag and his saxophone case.

As I handed Alma Jean her soda, I offered to take some of the bags from Del.

"Just grab my duffel bag, man..." He hoisted it onto my left shoulder, and I immediately noticed, in addition to its incredible heaviness, the intoxicating scent of freshly washed clothes and sweat.

When we reached the car, Alma Jean looked as though she were ready to faint. "Marcus Wayne Alexander WHOSE CAR IS THIS!?"

"It's Roby's car, he let me borrow it..." Del was watching my response, so I built myself up a bit. "He *owed* me. You know, Alma Jean, I'm the one taught him how to drive this thing..."

Alma Jean smirked at me. "YOU taught HIM? You been around Roby so long you startin' to sound like a FOOL yourself." Then turning to Del: "He's just got this car 'cause Roby's sweet on me." With this, she jumped into the passenger's side up front and started touching up her makeup. Del and I began loading the baggage into the trunk. I had yet to ask him if he needed a ride.

"Can I give you a ride to your folks' house?"

"Sure. Now, what they call you: Marcus?" I didn't know what to say.

"Some people ... Marcus Wayne ... Mark ... Little Man..."

"Little Man?" he grinned. "Big and tall's you are? Can I call you that?"

"Sssure," I stuttered. I normally allowed no one, save my mother and Uncle Richard, to call me by that name. As Del finished putting away the bags, I studied him. He was so at ease, as if he had composed this whole scene beforehand.

"I like your cousin Alma Jean..." he began.

"Yeah, she's a mess..."

"I knew from the minute I saw her standing there in the train that she was good folks," and with this he closed the trunk. "I was trying to figure out a way to meet her, but she took care of that for me."

"I heard y'all back there talking about me," Alma Jean protested, as we both got in the car. "Turn on the RADIO or else I'll get mad," she said, pulling off her hat so that the wind would not send it flying. "I want to hear all the new tunes. You KNOW that down in Memphis we don't get ANYTHING till at least three months after they get it in St. Louis, which is three months behind Chicago, which is at least a YEAR behind New York!" I glanced in the rearview mirror to see Del, who was looking intently at Alma Jean. "Of course, you ONLY hear the COOLEST music in those little JOINTS. I used to go to this one down on the riverfront in Memphis, and they would give you JAZZ and RHYTHM and BLUES!" Although I was trying to concentrate on Alma Jean, it was only when Del threw me a coy wink in the mirror that I realized I had been staring.

"Well, uh, Del ... how long you gonna be here for?" This was not the question I wanted to ask.

"For the summer at least..." Alma Jean arched her hand over the seat, and Del clasped it. "Maybe for good."

"Where'd you learn to play the sax?"

"Well, first off, my daddy taught me ... he was a musician too, a pianist. Later on, I studied music ... at Southern."

"Marcus Wayne is a Morehouse man ... or should I say, will soon BE a Morehouse man, like his daddy." Lighting up a cigarette, Alma Jean grinned at me.

"I used to play the piano..." I began, but before I could finish Alma Jean started in: "Well, I could never even play CHOPSTICKS, so you will HAVE to teach me, Del..." We were at his folks' house. I leapt out of the car to help Del fetch his duffel bag from the trunk. As he pulled it over his shoulder, he said, "You know, Little Man, you really favor a teacher I used to have back in high school, a math teacher ... your face, your mannerisms, your build, just like him."

"That's kind of funny ... I never thought I'd end up looking like a New Orleans math teacher..."

"Naw, Little Man, I grew up in Jackson ... Jackson, Mississippi... This teacher, he was a really good man, he got my act together. Math didn't come any easier, but he knew how to make it all make sense..."

"What was his name?" I asked, as if I were going to recognize the name of some obscure math teacher in Jackson, Mississippi.

"His name was Mr. Peters. Mr. Richard M. Peters."

It took me a few seconds to realize why I was out of breath: I recognized the name. Of the math teacher. My uncle. Richard.

On the way home, Alma Jean prattled on and on about how wonderful and handsome and cool Del was. She apprised me of how she was going to date him and marry him and mother a remarkable tribe of jazz musician-warrior-scholar "Kings" who would eventually rule the earth and allow her to hold court with all the world's most famous, fashionable people at her bidding. I forgot to tell her everyone had gone to Illinois for the day, but I knew that as long as I seemed willing to listen to her, she would be happy. I also knew it would take me a while to regain my senses: I barely heard anything more she said.

II

By the time August rolled around, I had been so busy working and preparing for school that I had not seen much of Del. When I did, he was either coming or going: coming by to pick up Alma Jean — a hot little romance had developed between them that made my sister Peetie extremely jealous — or the two of them going off somewhere: to the drive-in, to the museum, to his gigs. Roby and I were hanging tight, especially after he had let his deranged cousin wreck his car one night during a drinking spree over in East St. Louis: His father had banned him from *looking* at cars till he turned forty. My father was letting me use the family car more often, which was convenient, since both Roby and I were dating the Buckner twins.

But Del was always on my mind. I wanted to tell someone, especially him, how I felt, but who? I knew I could not tell my parents: My father would just freak out before shipping me off to the Marines, and my poor mother, after recovering from the shock, would press me to take up the cloth. I could not tell my sisters: Neither Angela nor Peetie liked Del (because he was Alma Jean's), and Theresa and Charlene were too small to make good confidantes. I thought about telling Roby, because he had once told me something kind of similar, but then I remembered that later he had said he would kill himself before he ever associated with a "punk," so I told him nothing. I thought about calling my Uncle Richard, but I was sure he would not understand. And then there was Alma Jean: Of all the people I considered, she was completely out of the question. Del was her boyfriend, her "man of life," she said, and she went crazy anytime anyone even mentioned his name. Recently, she had begun saying something about some men making good friends and other men making good lovers or something like that, but I had paid her no attention, because I was busy just trying to remain calm whenever she mentioned his name. As a last resort, I even considered speaking with Reverend Wiley, my pastor, but I remembered that he treated all confidences as sermon material, so I kept it to myself.

Since I could not get Del out of my mind, I avoided him. Whenever I knew he would be coming by I made a point to be away: at my girlfriend Marlene's, at Roby's, anywhere but home. But then he would come by unannounced. I would hear his voice — that smooth, melodic, burdenless voice — through my bedroom door, and as soon as he had greeted Alma Jean he would ask, "So where's Little Man?" and my chest would start burning up, and I would ask myself, God, what is wrong with me? Why do I feel this way? Why *me*? I had never felt this way before about anybody or anything that I could remember, and now I had barely any feelings *but* these. I was dating one of the best-looking girls in my entire high school class, I had a scholarship to Morehouse, I had a good-paying summer job, I was a decent-looking, six-foot-tall, popular, *normal* guy — and yet every time this smooth-voiced, jazz-playing Mississippi giant came around I came completely undone! Then that daydream would start, leaving me tongue-tied and dazed! It was so bad I could no longer look him in the eyes or shake his hand or even talk about him without falling apart. I kept wondering, can Alma Jean tell? Can Alma Jean see through me? I was afraid I would give myself away, and then what? Oh, but the horrors that might follow.

But Alma Jean was always begging me to come hear him play. "Marcus Wayne, you should hear him BLOW! Lord TO-DAY, I swear every time he puts his lips to that reed I'm gonna MEET MY MAKER!" Then she would dramatize his playing, hopping and swaying across the living room, wiping her brow, raising her empty arms into the air with a flourish. "And Marcus Wayne, you have just GOT to see this little band that plays with him! The MENS! You can bet your bottom DOLLAR that if Del starts walking you would SURE see Miss Alma Jean Reaves on the arm of that bass player or that drummer!" This she assured me of with a quick nod. "And Del can play EVERY single TUNE that everybody EVER WROTE. Little Miss Bettye Mae Rollins — who can't NOBODY stand — THINKS she is just THE next DINAH Washington — but Marcus, she sings like GEORGE without his DENTURES! — and she'll hoist herself up onto the stage, begging for tunes, so then everybody comes up with stuff we know she CAN'T sing a bar of — and the band will just sit there, until Del comes to her rescue by picking up a bar of something — 'Perdido,' the one little tune she can sing — and when he starts, Marcus Wayne — THERE GOES MY HEART!" At this point, she would fall back upon the sofa humming the bars of "Perdido." "And what he DOES with those songs! Real spare, you know, the new thing, real cool so you can hardly hear it — it keeps coming and going, but it's always THERE!" Trying my best to imagine Del's handling of "Perdido," I almost failed to recognize that Alma Jean had become something of an aficionada. "So you ARE going to come with me to hear Del SOON, OKAY?"

I could see him craning forward and backward, the notes leaping out of that saxophone, the audience swooning in an orgy of excitement and appreciation...

"OKAY?"

"Uh ... okay—"

"PROMISE?"

"Promise."

"Promise to cross your heart, hope you die, stick a needle in your eye PROMISE?"

"Come on, Alma Jean ... okay, I promise with sugar on top won't never stop promise ... next time Del's playing."

"GOOD!"

"Marlene and Roby..."

"Who said ANYTHING about THEM coming along? Marcus Wayne, just wait, you'll see, once you're there you won't be needing no Marlene or Roby..." Her wry smile unsettled me, but I figured that she was up to something that I should simply not probe.

III

Alma Jean, who normally told even the tiniest details of her every experience, had become increasingly terse in recent weeks. Del was visiting us less and less, and Alma Jean rarely mentioned his name. Initially I thought that they had broken up, but then one night I saw them sitting on our porch, hands in hands, talking very softly and giggling. Everyone attributed Alma Jean's lack of conversation to the fact that she was announcing, Alma Jean–style, her immediate return to Memphis; I, however, was sure that something else was going on. One thing that she definitely was keeping secret was that I would be accompanying her to the infamous T Lounge to hear Del play. Although my mother was a Sarah Vaughan fan and although my father had listened to jazz from his boyhood days in Chicago, neither of them would tolerate their seventeen-year-old son hanging out in any kind of bar or lounge, particularly the T, which owed its continued existence to its long-standing reputation as a hangout for bootleggers, pimps, bookies, and junkies. Fortunately for all involved, my parents decided to spend two weeks' vacation in Minneapolis visiting one of my father's fraternity brothers, so Alma Jean chose the first weekend of their absence for our outing.

I was worried about seeing Del. The increasing infrequency of his visits was working inverse magic on my senses: The less I saw his face or heard his voice, the more my mind dwelled on those same attributes. From time to time I would encounter him in the store or on the street, and each time I fell apart worse than before, mumbling, finding nothing to say, staring. I was sure that Roby had figured me out: One day he joked around that I was eventually going to have to choose between Marlene and my "Jazz-man," yet in the next breath, he too was urging me to go, by myself, to see Del play. I could not figure out whether Del knew something too, because although he stopped calling me "Little Man," he always seemed delighted to see me. He was now leaving different jazz records with Alma Jean for me: Dexter Gordon, Jackie McLean, Cannonball Adderley, Miles Davis. In each he would leave a short note, writing something like "MW: I hope you enjoy it. Wait till you see what I can do. Del." I had seven of these notes, and kept each of them at the bottom of a shoebox full of baseball cards in the back of my closet: Whenever I felt I could bear it, I would pull one out and read it over repeatedly. Since Alma Jean had almost caught me once, I looked at them only when I knew she was out.

I called up Roby to invite him along, but his father had caught him in his endless web of lies involving his nightly whereabouts with his girlfriend, so he was effectively homebound until he left for Xavier. He ended up giving me advice on how I should dress for the evening: I should first consider the T's reputation, then opt for a suit of armor. Trying my best to fit the atmosphere Alma Jean had described, I decided to wear my father's midnight-blue worsted jacket, which was almost too small, a white oxford shirt, a red ascot, and olive gabardine slacks. I combed my mustache to thicken it up and brushed my hair back to age my look. As an extra measure of insurance I grabbed the packet of Camels that Jessie Leland had left in my room the time she came by to study algebra. Alma Jean told me that I should wear my brown suede shoes, which I thought looked extremely ratty, but which, she assured me, were *the* vogue. As I stood there looking at myself in my full-length mirror, she sashayed into the room. She was wearing an ivory sharkskin suit with matching silk blouse, gloves, pumps, glasses, purse, and jewelry, all of which were standard for Alma Jean. But she had topped it all off with an ivory pillbox hat, and for added drama she had draped an intricately designed Mexican scarf, with ivory as its background, deftly around her shoulders. She spun around several times to show herself off. I had to clap. "Audrey Hepburn ain't got a THING on ME!" she said, then she told me to wait as she scurried out of my room and returned with something hidden behind her back.

"Okay, Alma Jean, what are you up to now?"

"Close your eyes."

"Why?"

"Close your eyes." Before I knew it, I felt her slipping something onto my head: not a cap, a beret. "Look at yourself." I checked myself in the mirror: I could not believe how much older and sophisticated I looked. Posing in the doorway, Alma Jean continued, "Marcus Wayne, if you weren't my cousin, I'd HAVE you tonight!" We both had a laugh. First she told me that I looked like Del, then she told me that I looked better than Del, both of which were enough to leave me speechless until we reached the club.

Alma Jean's newfound friend, Geneva Todd, was driving us to the T Lounge. Geneva had originally been two years ahead of my sister Peetie — or five years ahead of me — in school, but despite years of disciplinary problems and a general inability to complete even the most basic assigned work, she had finally graduated with my class. Everybody knew that she associated with, as my Aunt Helen called them, the "riffraffs and rudipoots," but according to Alma Jean, Geneva had cleaned up her act and she was now *the* St. Louis jazz maven. Still, I was apprehensive, particularly about her driving, since I knew how she had *earned* her passing grade in driver's education, but again Alma Jean assured me that Geneva knew how to handle herself, as well as her car. When she picked us up, I spoke, got into the back seat, and tried to keep up my reputation as, in Marlene's words, "Sidney Poitier's lost twin."

Jammed deep into the narrow alleyway behind the waste dumps of the Harris-Feld Shoe Company warehouse sat the T Lounge. Everywhere wafted the smell of rotting garbage and cheap perfume: The alleyway itself was a river of debris. My first thoughts, however, were whether Alma Jean had been here outside Del's company and if so, how many times? A throng of wild-eyed young men and women, none of whom looked like St. Louis folks, were congregating beneath a glaring marquee which read, "THE T O GE." As we pulled up, a chorus of "Geneva! Geneva!" surrounded the car. Alma Jean noticed the expression on my face.

"Now DON'T look so crazed ... you did NOT come to rummage through the GARBAGE CANS, so don't WORRY about how it looks on the outside!"

"But Alma Jean..."

As I looked more closely at these people, I knew the inside could not be much worse. Alma Jean, scowling in the direction of the rowdy gathering, would have none of my trepidation, so she tugged me behind her through the crowd, snapping, "Come on, come on, act like a MAN!"

"Alma Jean, baby! Come on innnnn," crooned a sweating, over-weight older man wearing gold chains, gold rings, gold teeth, and a gold earring. After beaming at Alma Jean, he cast a sharp glance at me.

"Tee, I want you to meet my cousin, MARCUS WAYNE, the one I told you about. Marcus Wayne, this is my friend TEE, he owns the club, isn't it outtasight?" Alma Jean wrenched my hand toward this man who looked older than both my grandfathers put together. We shook hands, then Alma Jean allowed him to kiss her — on the lips! In the meantime, Geneva Todd had vanished: I did not want to imagine where we might find her ... and this Tee ... as we walked in I held my breath.

A grey-blue haze of smoke, silk-clad bodies, and lilting chatter filled the long, red, narrow room. To the left of the entrance was a bar which ran nearly the length of the room: Men and women lined it thickly. Before us and to the right stretched the floor, which was a maze of decorated little tables, each with settings for two: About half were occupied. Up front, at the end of the expanse of seating rose the stage: It looked barely as high as the chairs or as deep as the bar. There stood upon the stage a piano and three chairs, but only the bass player was out. I was amazed at how thoroughly this interior contrasted with the façade: Again, Alma Jean knew what she was talking about. With me in tow, she sliced through the bodies and chatter, to a front-center table, then told me she was going in back to see Del.

"Do you want to come or are you going to wait?" she whispered, scanning the room while smoothing her dress.

I nodded no, pointed to the table, and smiled. Alma Jean gave me a surprised smile, then headed through a tiny door to the right of the stage. Trying to settle down I rifled through my pockets for that pack of Camels. There were at least ten matchbooks on our table, so I, as suavely as possible, extracted and lit up one of the cigarettes. I was too nervous to notice whether or not anyone was watching me, but as soon as I started gagging and choking, I heard a high-pitched laugh, then standing above me was a robust, honey-colored redhead in a tight, low-cut red dress.

"Baby, you okay?" I was still hacking when I answered.

"Fine ... fine, I'm fine..."

"I was standin' ova theh when all of a sudden I seen this good-lookin' man go up in a cloud a smoke ... I ain't never seen y'heah befoh ... my name's Bettye Mae ... Bettye Mae Rollins ... I sings heah sometime..." It took a few seconds for me to connect the name with Alma Jean's frequent depictions.

"Marcus, Marcus Alexander. I'm here with my cousin Alma Jean..."

"Miss *Memphus*?" Bettye Mae rolled her eyes.

"That's right," I paused. "That's right ... I'm here to see my friend Del King play." Bettye Mae eased herself onto my table.

"Del King? ... he showww can play ... y'look like a musician yo'self ... what you play?" Before I could answer, she leaned down toward me and cooed, "Evah heard a tune called Bettye Mae Rollins?"

"YES, MISS GUTTERSNIPE," Alma Jean burst in, "and it's ALL in the WRONG KEY!" As soon as Bettye Mae saw Alma Jean, she shot up from the table, blew me a kiss, then disappeared into the crowd at the bar.

"I can't leave you alone for ONE MINUTE," Alma Jean admonished, adding, "Del says tell you HELLO and he better see you after the set." Then she spotted my cigarettes. "MARCUS WAYNE, don't TELL ME you've started SMOKING!"

"Where's Geneva?" I interposed. Alma Jean threw me a cutting look.

"That Bettye Mae's just like you said, Miss Memphis..." Before I could go on, Tee, holding a microphone, was standing at the front of the stage, nearly right above us. I quickly looked around the room. It was filled to capacity: People were bantering back and forth, emptying glasses, giving eyes. A little trollop in a waitress uniform swerved by our table, but Alma Jean waved her away. "You won't need anything to drink tonight," she said to me. Some white people, two ladies and a man who looked like they were from Paris or Berlin, sat two tables to my left. They did not seem pressed in the least by the surroundings. When I looked beyond the floor, I saw Bettye Mae Rollins wedged between the bar and a man who looked like Tee's double. I turned back to the stage, and the entire quartet had come out.

"Ladies and Gentlemennn, welllllcome to another Friday night Jazzzz set at the Teeeee Lounge..." After thanking the audience for coming — he singled out one of the white ladies sitting two tables to my left, the "avant-garde Miss Elsie de la Forge" of the St. Louis candy-fortune de la Forges, as a particularly "stalwart" patron — he introduced the combo as the "James Fortune Quartet," then thanked the patrons — this time winking at Miss de la Forge, who licked her lips back. "I promisssse a reallly hotttt grooove tonight, so get setttt, ladies and gentlemennn, the James Forrrtune Quartettt..." Del, in a black cotton suit, a white shirt, a red ascot, and those foreign-looking black laceups, leaned against a piano on the stage to our left. Looking out into the crowd, he calmly held the alto sax in his left hand and stroked his mustache with his right. "That's the cue," Alma Jean whispered, barely containing her glee. "Mustache means 'Hot House.'"

All of a sudden, Del started in alone with Charlie Parker's familiar intro line, more leanly and less forcefully. The rest of the quartet picked him up. Within seconds Del was at center stage. He just took over, seizing bars of the melody and then driving them over the harmony laid down by the piano and the bass. He was constantly changing direction, juking, pausing, grabbing notes from beyond his range, but the playing was not the quick, frenzied overlaying of bebop. It was something tighter, sparer, cooler. Watching him and listening to him blow, his eyes closed and his forehead bathed in sweat, all the emotions that I had been containing because of nervousness and fear came forth and I felt myself rising in a delirium of awe and respect. People in the audience started testifying.

"Play that shit, man!" Del was laying it down.

"Goddamn, he blowing that groove!" In and out.

"Dig it, brother, dig it!" A snatch, then improvisation, then a snatch. Del stepped back to let the other musicians mine the tune. His eyes were closed, his body rocking to the sweet art around him. Finally, he lifted his sax back to his lips. One final, lean line, then the groove was over. James Fortune, the pianist, stood up and introduced the members of the quartet. When he got to Del, I felt tears welling in my eyes.

"And on alto saxophone, Adelphus King!!" Applause went up. I looked over at Alma Jean. She was gazing intently at Kenno Harper, the bassist, who seemed to be mouthing something to her. The quartet began a new tune, "Fortune's Blues," which was melancholic and slow: Del again took the role of virtuoso, though this was Fortune's feature. Del slowly wrapped the lines of the blues around me; I could feel that total, enveloping blackness: the shininess, the graininess, the thickness. I could feel it slowly drawing me inside, but there was no panic now, no flailing my arms in the air, no screaming breathlessly, no kicking my feet in every direction. I had not only surrendered but was now becoming a part of it all. On the notes rose and on the combo went, through "Market Street" and "Arabesques" and "St. Louis Blues." Then I recognized Del's voice.

"This one is called 'Marcus's Mood'..." He began with the opening bars of "Solitude," low and mournful, his notes alone among the sounds in the lounge. Slowly he began to build the tune, the rest of the quartet following him. Soon he began stretching out notes, laying them down, pulling them out, refining them. Del would call and Fortune would respond, then Harper, then the drummer, Shadrach Phelps. I closed my eyes and I could see the call and response, I could taste the layering and receiving, I felt the notes now, the only reality and nothing else around us; I smelled the smoke and the vapors of the gin and the scotch and the vodka rising, rising, gone, and my ears full of the richness of this lean, low, smooth, sweet song...

Applause? The applause! Everyone was standing, clapping and whistling madly. I looked at Alma Jean. Testifying, she was waving her right hand in the air, while her left hand lay on her heart. Wiping the tears off my cheeks, I stood and applauded. Alma Jean smiled toward me, then rose, heading for the dressing rooms. I slumped down in my seat. As I lifted my head I caught sight of Del, sax in his hands, moving toward the wings. I felt so exhausted, I slouched back in my chair, and took a few deep breaths. I rolled my head over the chair's back, shutting off my senses to the din around me. I needed a little time to recover.

IV

"Marcus Wayne, Del is waiting on you..." When I opened my eyes, Alma Jean was hovering above me, peering down, her eyes focused not on my face, but further along my body. I quickly stood up.

"Where..." I looked around the lounge. It had mostly emptied out, but there were several couples leaning against the bar talking. A lanky, dapper man with thick eyebrows and a gap between his two front teeth was standing at the bar, watching Alma Jean. It was Kenno Harper, the bass player. He looked as if he were waiting for her. Neither Geneva Todd nor Bettye Maè Rollins were anywhere to be seen.

"Come on ... I'll show you..." I was expecting her to snap out these words, but they left her tongue like purrs. I looked closely at her face: she looked as if she knew everything, as if everything were going according to one of her designs. I turned back toward the bar: Kenno Harper was still intently watching Alma Jean. Through the side door she led me, down a narrow, barely lit hallway, then into a dark, low corridor, until we reached a door on the left.

"Go on in ... I'll be at the bar ... take your time." There was no emphasis in her voice; the words just glided out. I felt delirious.

As Alma Jean headed down the hall, I entered the room. A single, naked bulb lit the tiny red space, which had only a wooden chair against one wall and a smaller table on the other. Bent over the table, Del was examining his saxophone. I just stood there. The room seemed too small for either of us. Del turned around, his face forming a smile. I felt my feet giving way, my head jerking forward, my body going slack, I felt dizzy ... started to fall ... Del reached his arms out ... lifted me up ... into the chair ... his left palm on the back of my neck, his right hand holding up my head by the throat ... I was inhaling slowly ... he crouched down so that his face was level with mine.

"Hey, Marcus, don't feel so hot, hunh..." Del was speaking much more softly and slowly than usual. I could not get any words out. "Feeling dizzy?" Under the bald light I saw that his face was still bathed in sweat.

"Bettye Mae Rollins come after you, huhn?" I just sat there, mouth open, head shaking, my eyes fixed on Del's face. "Not your type, I know..." I just kept staring into his eyes, but instead of drifting off, my mind began to focus. "Just like me and Alma Jean ... she Kenno's type, a lady, a fine woman, you know, just not what I'm looking for right now..." It was as if I could see more sharply than ever before: Del's face, his flaring nostrils, his heavy eyelashes, the full, punchy lips, the skin blacker than tar, all more focused, more intense, more startling than I had ever realized before. "Kenno say, 'What's the deal with Miss Alma Jean?' and I say, 'She a fine woman, man, check her out,' 'cause I know it's gonna work for him..." The tiny blemishes, the few ingrown hairs, the quarter-moon scar on his chin. "In my short time I've come to learn that unless things play a certain way, won't nobody be happy..." The thick, bristly hair on the top of his head, the nearly perfect white teeth, the arching eyebrows. "...and this way, Marcus, everybody'll be happy..." He was still down in a crouch, the bows of his arms resting on his knees, his eyes now fixed on the floor.

In the seconds before I said anything I scanned his hunched, squatting form. The huge, expressive hands, the heavy trunklike legs, bent and bowing out, the broad yoke of his shoulders arcing inward now, the thick, bristly expanse of hair. Looking at him I began to see the whole entity, the entire person, the man: He was no longer just the image that had been gripping me since I was seven, no longer just the figure that I saw on that Saturday in the Willow Park Station. He was no longer just the dazzling saxophonist or the handsome boyfriend of my cousin Alma Jean: no longer just hands or shoulders or lips or knees. He was before me on the floor a fellow man, a man I respected above all, a man I admired, a man whose total person left me in awe. A man that I now realized I loved. So many thousands of thoughts, so many pictures flooded my mind in the seconds before I could say anything, that I blurted out, "Why don't you call me Little Man anymore?"

"'Cause, Marcus Wayne Alexander, you ain't no Little Man anymore ... The day your Uncle Richard stopped calling *me* Little Man was the day I realized how grown I really was ... if it hadn't been for him, I might not be here playing anything ... I was headed in the wrong direction, and he helped me straighten myself out ... naw, Marcus, you ain't no little man ... the Marcus I'm looking at is a man, like me."

He reached out his arms, grabbing mine. He pulled me up, slowly it seemed, forever it seemed, pulling me, closer, closer, closer until I was flat against his heavy, soaked chest.

"See, I understand what you been going through ... you asking yourself why you feel this way ... I remember the first time I asked myself the same question ... but like your Uncle Richard say, 'It's when you start to ask yourself that question, and when you realize what the answer is, then you know you a man' ... you ain't got nothing to worry about, you'll see..." His arms clasped against my shoulder blades ... I felt the knot of his entwined hands resting in the small of my back ... I was having no trouble breathing ... I felt his neck press against mine ... he was not too much taller than I was ... I felt myself holding him tighter ... tighter ... crying ... and our legs pressed together and his heart just beating solemnly, mine following ... and we stood there for what seemed like forever ... an eternity ... embracing ... right here, he in my arms ... I in his ... and there was no music, no blues, no applause, but our own ... I lifted my head and kissed him squarely on the lips.

At this Del gently pulled away, his hands sliding from my back across my hips to my hands which he now held. His eyes were half-closed, his nostrils flaring slightly, his body nearly touching mine, his hands gripping me tightly. Then he pulled me back into an embrace, and this time he kissed me on the lips, heavily, fully, thickly. When he had finished, I stepped back. Keeping his eyes on me all the time he smoothly gathered his jacket and his saxophone case, and he ushered me toward the door. As I reached for the handle I felt his warm breath on the back of my neck, his full lips flush against my ear. I asked, "When, Del?"

He whispered, "In time, Marcus." Del placed his left hand on my left shoulder. "In time..." Opening the door, he started grinning and I started grinning. We were still grinning when we reached the floor full of empty tables. Alma Jean was standing there, alone, a smile on her face, looking at both Del and me. She walked up to us, gave Del a long, gentle kiss on the cheek, then said to me, "See, I told you, you wouldn't need Marlene or Roby..." Del looked at me. I looked back at him. In time, I said softly to myself. Alma Jean was already headed out the door.

CALVIN GLENN

In my own space

It was with extreme precaution that I came to know myself. I had concluded, as a young boy, that there was a part of me that I did not want to be; but there was nothing I could do. Almost all of my life I had felt like a drone, following some set path toward my future, not living, but operating according to some preprogrammed specifications. I am older now, and understand who I am. I am thankful I didn't listen to all those people who told me I could only be what the rest of the world would let me be.

Going away to school was a shock for me. I had attended a small college prep school that was very conservative. I wasn't quite liberal, but I surely wasn't conservative. During my life at the prep school, I had several run-ins with people who thought I was outrageous. I wore the same types of clothes they wore. I spoke the same language that they spoke, and I certainly used the same type of money they used. I was "outrageous" simply because I didn't think their thoughts. When I graduated I moved to the Northeast, to a small private college in the country.

When I arrived on campus, I was sure I had not done a great job of selecting a college. The college was just as conservative as the school back home. I had looked for a small campus where I hoped to explore my identity without inhibition. The day I graduated from high school, I made a pact with myself to "come out" on campus before returning home for winter break. I had no fears. I had come this far and didn't care what anyone else might think of me. My parents knew I was gay, which I considered a plus, but being typical black parents, they first berated me, then alienated me, then sent me to a psychologist to be cured. The local Baptist minister was called in to scare the sickness out of me. (If there had been any sickness there, believe me, he would have scared it out.) My parents have simmered down since then, but I am not sure they accept my sexuality; we simply don't discuss it.

I got off the bus in early September, feeling very good about being at college, away from the stifling silence that engulfed my home. I looked around a bit, and finally mustered the courage to ask someone for directions to my dorm.

"It's straight down the road," a fellow student instructed me. "You'll know it when you get there," he continued. "It's the only building that doesn't look old." I thanked him and proceeded on my way.

When I found the new-looking dorm, I walked in and went up to the second floor to search for room 204. I found it and entered. I was assigned to a triple — three rooms, to be occupied by three very different roommates. One was Jim, a quiet fellow from the Midwest. My other roommate, Sam, was a pseudo-jock from the South. And, of course, there was me. When I moved into my room, I had no idea Jim and Sam would never become my friends.

A couple of weeks into the school year, I decided my room was just a little too drab. Everyone else had vivid posters and cut-outs from magazines plastered all over their walls. I thought I should do that, too. It took two weeks to complete the job. I started out, innocently enough, with a poster of a lion that I hung directly over my bed (with that image, anyone would think twice about upsetting me). And I progressed from there; being a typical teenager, I put up posters of my favorite rock bands. And then, it dawned on me; there was something I really wanted but didn't have on my walls: a picture of a perfect man. I looked through my various catalogs and ordered the most innocently seductive poster I could find. When it arrived, I closed the door to my room and tacked up the poster. "There," I said with satisfaction, "now the walls all have a spirit that is purely me."

Later that week, Jim came in to talk with me. "Great posters you've got," he said, walking in. "Kinda picks the place up." We sat on my bed talking about our classes and complaining about our social lives. And then it happened. He turned and spotted the poster on my door. He asked hesitantly, "What — who is that?"

"Some model. It's just a poster I ordered. But he is gorgeous." When those words came from my mouth, Jim gasped and jumped up from the bed. I became wide-eyed, and somewhat offended. I asked, "What's wrong?"

The fear in his eyes was apparent. What was he afraid of? I'm sure I hadn't touched him at all since he waltzed in commenting on the new scenery.

"Are you," he started, then hesitated. He sighed and continued slowly, "Are you gay?"

Equally slowly, I replied, "Yes, I am gay." Jim looked as though his heart had stopped. I had prepared, somewhat, for this confrontation, but I didn't know how to handle his fear. "Calm down," I said, but he just stared at me, his eyes bulging out of his head and his mouth agape. He turned quickly and left. I sat looking at myself in the mirror. What could he have seen to make him so afraid?

It was not long before Sam knocked on my door and entered. I was still sitting on my bed facing the mirror when he walked in.

"Jim told me about the poster you have up on your wall. Where is it?"

"Turn around; it's behind you," I said wearily.

He looked at the picture and gave it a few nervous taps. Pointing at the poster, he said, "You *can't* have this picture up." His plea was in vain. He looked at me with desperate eyes as though I had physically abused him.

"Why can't I have it up?"

Sam paused to search his fears for coherent reasons. "Look, Chris, when people see this up here they'll think you're a homosexual."

"But I am gay."

Sam's nose began to twitch. "Why the fuck didn't you tell us?"

"What the fuck does it matter?"

"I can't believe this," he screamed, putting his hands on his head. "I'm living with a black faggot." He slammed the door behind him as he left. That was the end of our short friendship.

The next day my roommates confronted me. They said they had been conferring and had come to a conclusion. They put it simply: I had to move out.

"No."

"Come on, Chris," Jim urged. "Wouldn't you be happier in a single?"

"I'm comfortable where I am," I replied.

"But you'd be more comfortable in a single," Sam added.

"You guys are out of your minds. I'm not moving out." I got up and went into my room. "Fucking idiots!" I yelled, as I slammed the door. What the hell was their problem? I hadn't made any advances at them; I didn't even think either was attractive. I hadn't even had any over-night visitors. "How the hell am I bothering them?" I asked myself.

I woke up the next morning feeling lousy, and when I left my room I became angry. Someone had written the letters *F* and *G* around the *A* sticker on my door. I had never been so angry. I went back to my room and pulled out a sheet of paper and began to write. But I stopped. "I'm not going to let myself stoop to their level." I crumpled the paper and went on with my life.

There was a small gay and lesbian organization on campus, and I attended the weekly meetings. I told some of the members about the situation with my roommates. They couldn't believe it. Nothing like it had ever happened before. But then, they told me, none of them had ever had the courage to "come out" to their roommates. "Why?" I asked. "Am I the only one who isn't afraid? Am I the only one who is tired of hiding?"

The next week I received a letter from the director of student life. I was told that my roommates had brought complaints against me to her attention. I had to report to her office the next morning for a conference.

The director called us in separately to get an overview of the circumstances. Then we all sat down: Jim and Sam on one side of the table, me on the other, and the director at the head.

"Now what seems to be the problem?"

"Well, a couple of weeks ago we found out that Chris ... he's a homosexual," Jim began.

"He put up this big poster of a guy on his door," Sam added. "Everybody can see it."

"We think he would feel more comfortable in a single," Jim concluded.

The director looked at me. "Is this so?"

"Yes, I am gay," I replied, "but I'm comfortable where I am. There's no reason for me to move out."

"But think about us, Chris," said Jim.

"I'm not hurting you," I paused, and then added, "You mean to tell me I can't put up a poster of a man in my own space?" There was silence. "I don't even bother you. Unlike Sam, I don't even have people staying overnight," I sneered.

Sam yelled, "If the guys find out I'm living with a fag—"

"That's enough!" the director interrupted. "It seems to me that this is a very simple case. Chris is gay, and according to this school's policies, there is nothing wrong with that. He's done nothing wrong, as opposed to you two. You will both share the expenses to have his door repainted, and you both may possibly appear for disciplinary action if Chris plans to pursue harassment charges. Finally, I cannot, and will not, force Chris to move out of his room."

"But what can we do? He makes us feel uncomfortable."

"Gentlemen, you will have to learn to handle your own insecurities. But, if you feel so uncomfortable, I suggest that *you* move out."

LAMONT B. STEPTOE

Maybelle's boy

I get from other men
what my daddy never gave
He just left me a house
full of lonesome rooms
and slipped on in his grave

Now
when muscled arms enfold me
A peace descends from above
Someone is holdin' Maybelle's boy
and whisperin' words of love

CHARLES HARPE

At 36

You can trace my history back to July 23, 1953, in Philadelphia, Pennsylvania. My father sorted mail for the post office. My mother, at that time, was an on-again, off-again domestic worker. I was their first son. I was named after my father and his father.

In 1956, my parents bought a three-bedroom row house in West Philly. I entered school at William Cullen Bryant Elementary. Every day at recess I played hopscotch with the girls. Even during those early years as I was becoming aware that I was somehow different from the other boys my age — they played with the girls, too, but instead of hopscotch they chased them around the schoolyard trying to feel up their dresses — I did not believe that there was anything wrong with me. It was not until I was in the sixth grade that I began to understand what the boys were really saying when they called me a "sissy."

That same year I also learned the meaning of the word *faggot*, when my mother became the first person ever to call me that name. She was angry, demanding that I give up hopscotch and start participating in more masculine activities like other boys. She called me "faggot" only once and that was enough. It did more than echo. It kept me silent and ashamed for years.

Skipping ahead, through high school and college to July 3, 1974, you can find me at a friend's house talking and drinking wine. He is preparing to go out. While he is ironing his shirt, he turns to me and asks, "Are you gay?" For the first time I answer, "Yes."

That night I went with him to the Olympia Ballroom at 52nd and Baltimore Avenue. This was my first visit to a black gay club. It was hot, hazy, and humid, and the men that filled this place wore short-shorts, cut-offs, tank tops, or no tops at all. No one could tell me I was not fierce in my platform sandals and Harry Belafonte–tied shirt standing there, as in fact I did, all night, thinking about fucking, making love, and how the music makes you want to dance. I studied chests, arms, and thighs glistening with sweat, and the tricks light can play when reflected off a mirrored ball. That was the beginning. The beginning of feeling that the word *faggot* did not accurately name the man I was or the man I was aspiring to become. The beginning of thinking thoughts that started off with "I have nothing to be ashamed of..." and "I have a right to..." The beginning of discarding the silence and the shame. The beginning of seeing the truth through all of the lies.

On July 3, 1989, after fifteen years of living as a black gay man, I sat down at my desk and decided it was time to write something about all of this. On July 23, 1989, I turned 36.

I guess age does have a lot to do with my need to put things into their proper perspective. Jokingly, I have told my friends that I am now the age of the men I have always found most attractive. To me, men in their mid-thirties seem to be at a point where they can begin to apply the lessons life has taught them to reconciling themselves with their pasts, dealing constructively with their present situations, and planning their futures. They are clear about where they are coming from and where they are going, what they want and what they don't want. I believe that now, after twelve years of therapy, of confronting my pain and just plain struggling, I, too, am at a point of clarity. I know who I am.

At 36, my homosexuality is no longer an issue in my life. It no longer defines me or confines me. It is simply a part of me, a relatively small part, in relation to the talents, ambitions, skills, dreams, hopes, desires, and needs that make me the man I am today, and the man I will become. In accepting this, I liberate myself from the silence, the shame, hate, pain, anger, frustration, and bitterness I have experienced from accepting so many lies as truths. I am a black gay man. There is nothing wrong with me! This belief is now my armor and my weapon to be used in reconciling my past, dealing with the realities of my present, and shaping my future.

❂

My father died in 1981. He was an alcoholic and my mother complemented his disease with her equally serious addictions to pain and anger. Together they created a household full of tension, chaos, and violence, but empty of love and nurturing. I hated my father for being a drunk. I hated my mother for not leaving him. I hated myself for not being able to make things better. It was in this context that my mother called me a faggot and I began to confront my sexuality.

At 36, I am learning to stop hating, to forgive my parents and, most of all, myself. I have memories of my father carrying me on his back, helping me with my homework, picking me up in his arms after I was hit by a car. He was an intelligent man who loved to read. He encouraged me to excel in school and to go on to college. These things, even when weighed against all the horrors of his drinking, were enough for me to have loved him.

I am talking more to my mother now and understanding her better. I believe that she always did the best that she could. Her own father was an alcoholic and I have allowed that this was, in part, the reason she loved and stayed with her husband until the day he died. While she still holds a great deal of anger and bitterness inside, I know she is a woman of great strength and determination who has passed on to me her sense of humor and her appreciation of the finer things in life. She accepts the reality of my homosexuality and works to be loving and supportive of me.

Forgiving myself has proven to be the far more challenging task. It has meant confronting the truth that I grew up and entered adulthood with practically no self-esteem, a desperate need to love and be loved, and an ingrained sense that I was unlovable. In confronting this truth, I have been able to see how much self-hatred has been manifested in all areas of my life, particularly in my relationships with black gay men.

I have had three significant long-term relationships in my life so far. My first lover called an agency that had just hired me for an important management position and told the executive director I was a "practicing homosexual." I forgave him. My second love was cruelly unavailable to me emotionally. I clung to him. My third lover would literally abandon me for months at a time. I would sit and wait for him to come back. No one could tell me that I did not genuinely love each of these men at the time I was involved with them. But at 36, reflecting back, I know that any kind of genuine love between us was impossible because we did not love ourselves.

❂

The community of black gay men is very diverse. We are short, tall, average height. We are light-skinned, brown-skinned, dark-skinned, and every shade in between. We are tops, bottoms, versatile, fats, fems, teachers, lawyers, poets, doctors, filmmakers, computer analysts, marines, and sailors. What we have in common is the fact that we do not always treat ourselves and each other very well. If we loved ourselves more, we would be less likely to place each other in one of three categories: the object of calculated desire, the competition, or the irrelevant. If we loved ourselves more, we would be less likely to measure our self-worth in terms of chests, arms, stomachs, legs, asses, dicks, quantity and quality of sexual partners, fashion-sense, popularity at a particular club, or attainment of diva status.

At 36, I am learning how to love myself, how to take pride in my accomplishments, how to accept that my needs and wants are important enough for me to work to fulfill them, and how to accept my own value and worth. Through loving myself I have managed to attract into my life some truly dynamic men that I am honored to call friends. With them I have come to know a safe place where there is caring and support; where I can find escape from the pain of racism and homophobia that so fills the world; where I can receive validation of my experiences and perspectives; where I can truly just be me and be loved for it.

Through loving myself I have been able to deal constructively with the present reality of AIDS. My grandmother, who is 89, has seen the death of her parents, all of her brothers and sisters, her husband, four of her nine children, one grandchild, and most of her friends. At 36, I have also seen the death of so many and felt the grief and the fear.

I have known what to do to protect myself and anyone I have sex with for at least five years now, and I find it hard to believe that there is a sexually active person alive today, especially a black gay male, who has not received the same safe-sex information. And yet I find it equally hard to let go of a scene described to me by a friend who does AIDS outreach work in our community: A young black man is on his back, on the floor of a public bathroom in a commuter rail station with his ass thrust under the partition between the toilets being brazenly fucked by another black man. My friend threw condoms into the stall but to no avail. I can only pray for myself.

There was a time when I did not use condoms and it is that time that terrifies me now. For many months I have struggled with the decision whether to be tested. A part of me feels I would not be strong enough to keep on dreaming, and loving, and working if I came to know that there is something inside of me killing off my T-cells and, inevitably, me, much sooner than I had expected. Yet a part of me, recently discovered, also feels my life is worth living and that I should do whatever is necessary to prolong it. Having myself tested then becomes an act of self-love and something I can and will handle very soon.

❂

At 36, I am planning my future. I want to write a play that has been creating itself in my soul for the last two years. I want to get my body in shape, stop smoking cigarettes, and start eating right. I want to form my own production company, buy a house and a car, adopt a child, and travel. And I want a loving, healthy, long-term relationship with another black man.

For most of the past fifteen years of my life, two mental images have stayed with me: One is of an older man, late forties or early fifties, with a sizable paunch and balding, sitting in a bar somewhere smoking cigarettes and drinking gallons, trying to persuade a well-built, smooth-skinned, 20-year-old to spend time with him. The other is of a naked man. He is in his late thirties, six feet tall, possessing full lips, wonderful teeth, a thick mustache, a football player's physique, a beautiful ass, and a perfect nine-inch dick. I was fearful of becoming the first image, and I felt I could only have been saved by the second.

At 36, I really don't know what my salvation is going to look like or who it will be. I only know that he will talk to me about himself, his feelings, his impressions of the world. He will love himself and me. He will be prepared to fight for what he wants. He will not be afraid to look back over his life to see his successes and his failures. He will know how to dream. He will not be afraid to learn something new, nor afraid to be the best he can be. I am trying to be just such a man.

At 36, who am I? I am a self-empowered black gay man.

ESSEX HEMPHILL

Commitments

I will always be there.
When the silence is exhumed.
When the photographs are examined
I will be pictured smiling
among siblings, parents,
nieces and nephews.

In the background of the photographs
the hazy smoke of barbecue,
a checkered red-and-white tablecloth
laden with blackened chicken,
glistening ribs, paper plates,
bottles of beer, and pop.

In the photos
the smallest children
are held by their parents.
My arms are empty, or around
the shoulders of unsuspecting aunts
expecting to throw rice at me someday.

Or picture tinsel, candles,
ornamented, imitation trees,
or another table, this one
set for Thanksgiving,
a turkey steaming the lens.

My arms are empty
in those photos, too,
so empty they would break
around a lover.

I am always there
for critical emergencies,
graduations,
the middle of the night.

I am the invisible son.
In the family photos
nothing appears out of character.
I smile as I serve my duty.

II. Baby, I'm for real

DON CHARLES

Comfort

When you looked and
    saw my Brown skin
Didn't it make you
    feel comfortable?

Didn't you remember that
    old blanket
You used to wrap up in
    when the nights got cold?

Didn't you think about that
    maplewood table
Where you used to sit and
    write letters to your daddy?

Didn't you almost taste that
    sweet gingerbread
Your granny used to make?
    (And you *know* it was good.)

When you looked and
    saw my Brown eyes
Didn't they look just like
    home?

DAVID FRECHETTE

Safe harbour

Though Destiny did not decree
That we become lovers
It's in your arms I find
Safe harbour from
A tidal wave of woes
Threatening to engulf me.

Your smiling eyes are my lighthouse,
Your lips seal out chaos.
The smoothness and warmth of your body
Keeps the coarse chill of
The everyday world at bay.
And I'm not afraid to christen you
My temporary shelter from the storm.

D. RUBIN GREEN

Names and sorrows

I have walked the distance of the earth
since first I saw you
In your carpet of milk,
perpetually shining. Thinking,
revolving beneath streetlamps,
among laundromats and sundials
I have wandered,
troubling myself with questions:

Shall I disfigure chandeliers?
Or shall I with teeth and liver and spine
swallow whole shores of stone and twilight?
Shall I tell you?
Burn down cathedrals?
Shatter the membrane not to enter,
but to exit?
Abandon myself in your wilderness?
Give my mind to the text of flowers?
How simple-minded life is.
How tiresome that we are still
the outlaws of the grain, Luis:
we who are as unbodied snow — fragile,
open and mild.
How strange that we must be so careful,
you and I.

For night cares nothing for we humans;
as neither do pine, nor wave,
nor the lunatic stars
contemplate our names or sorrows.
But here doubt invades us,
and everywhere the cities
drown the dove
in waves of mud and hatred.

But even so — even though
I have wandered in the boulevards,
and the red lakes may grow
tired of our weeping,
even though we are alone,
and the public microphones cry
with the venom of old charlatans—

let me speak openly and say:

I could take up residence in your hair.
I could weep and turn to dust,
or light, or poppies in your arms,
for I have been a ghost,
a shroud of smoke.

I could sing for the bright muscle
of your voice,
your smile of linen,
your oceanic eyes.

I could take up residence in you.

You, who came to me as a garment of flame,
of coal ore,
and luminous rain.

DONALD WOODS

Couch poem

wake in yesterday's clothing
roll the T
to a damp ball
your fingers tweezers
separate cotton briefs
from sleeping member

futon rolled and
neatly sheathed
lonely by choice

poor bed
no stories to tell
no dreams to soak up
shame

sigh for the new day
fall into the morning on
the rattle of your own breathing
alarm clock tweets like
birds above a tent on a lake in Burkina Faso

stretch
unfix the benevolent smile
of Good Morning America
plod on tiptoes to privacy

your reflection
of questions symbols signs
poses reminiscent of poses
when someone else is backdrop
their eyes cameras
recording you
climbing into the shower
all manly and such

wash yourself quickly
soap your privates
rinse them   towel them dry   powder them   blame them
even as you swallow vitamins
too numerous to mention and shit
all the time pleased at the effortless disposal
the regularity of your movement

iron a shirt to wear
dress them
your limbs
are softer now
fashionable in your mind

leave the crib
walk the row of brownstones
speak to the single man and Tiffany his poodle
smile at children
their lucky mothers
busy fathers and
walk this way to work

like a dog
work like a fiend
work like this is your first day
work like this is your last day
and folks will remember you

so respectable
so responsible
he worked like a dog or cat or a kite
in a balmy breeze

blowing the way fortune blew
and sitting up nights on the
couch watching people make their millions

unlock the cubicle happy
at the something to do
day-long escapade
a transparent fascination with decay

(at night when the others make love
laugh at dinner in Soho
sit and write down your writing
you can memorize your fingers at a keyboard
you can leave micro bytes of your living
to be deciphered by
people who loved to love you
who hated to hate you and
loved to hate you and hated to love you all
out of fear and no damn choice)

when nothing else will come you may
search for significance in the farewell
of the security guard who never inquires your life
beyond the walls you share

the waitresses all by name
who love the lord and hate crack
and call you baby
they don't question
they bring the plate
liver and onions or chicken smothered
call you darling and ask if you tired
call you baby and listen
for your answer at the Apollo restaurant

where you eat
with conviction
the meals of mighty men and women
as if you belonged to them
eat quickly solemnly chew
swallow in all seriousness
your nourishment and you

tip her tonight the usual tip
move into the street a new man
walking in an instant like a freed slave
and wait on the subway like a warrior
stand on the subway and leap the stairs
and glow with your own strength

walk past the brownstones
humming a spiritual
and up the stairs
and up the stairs again and
with three more flights to go
it has left you

and you reach the door
defeated in your head and retreat to the couch
that has waited all day
expectant

RORY BUCHANAN

Summer chills

I was lonely that day. More lonely than I had been since the beginning of the summer. I hadn't been involved in a relationship with anyone in years. Not because I didn't want to be. I just couldn't find anyone that excited me the way I needed to be excited. I needed a man I could hunger for and dream about when he wasn't with me, but so far, I hadn't met that kind of man.

It was hot that particular day. When I looked out the window it seemed like everyone was coming out of their clothes. I decided to go for a walk in the park. I had to get away from the heat in my stuffy apartment. I had to get away from myself.

I put on the briefest outfit I could find. I snatched up some old white gym shorts made of cotton jersey that draped and clung to my body. They were soft and comfortable and made me feel sexy. I always felt like I was wearing nothing when I put them on. I threw on a worn red undershirt that was more holes than fabric. The undershirt and shorts grabbed at my body in the moist fire of that summer day. I slipped into a pair of rundown banji sneakers and intentionally left the laces untied. I looked in the mirror and was pleased with the image I created. The outfit was hot. I was glad I had spent the summer cycling, swimming, and lying in the sun until I was a golden, coppery shade of brown. Even I was impressed with the way my body had responded to the exercise program I started a few months earlier. My body was toned and healthy, every muscle visible and proportioned just the way I wanted it to be. It made me wonder why I was always so alone.

I left the apartment and headed toward Prospect Park. I only lived three blocks from the park, but because of my anticipation, the walk seemed to take forever. When I got there, I found the park filled with men in the same horny, hungry state of mind I was in. They were as undressed as I was. Everyone looked and smelled like they had just finished a hard game of basketball. They were hot, sweaty, musky, tanned, well proportioned and well endowed. I can't remember ever seeing so many gorgeous black men in any one place. The sun glistened on taut ebony flesh. I was in a candy store of melting chocolate, and my sweet tooth demanded more attention with each passing moment.

There was a slow but noticeable procession of men into a special area of the park. I decided to follow the crowd and see what was causing the attraction. One by one we disappeared between two trees into the thickest part of this urban jungle.

Passing through the trees and bushes transported me through time. I found myself in a lush tropical jungle. I could feel the humidity wrap itself around my body. I could smell the vegetation smoldering and seething with a life all its own. I looked at the other brothers near me and felt I was in an uninhibited village in Africa. I looked at gym shorts with wonder as they blurred and changed into rough animal skins covering hard sable thighs and loins.

A short distance away there was a clearing. In the middle stood one tall, regal figure that everyone began to circle. The man was coal black and the sun reflecting off his skin gave him an iridescent sheen. His dreads fell onto wide shoulders and gave the appearance of an unadorned yet elegant crown. Around his neck rested a necklace made from the teeth of some vanquished predator. He was a commanding dark tower. Waves of strength flowed from him sending chills up and down my spine in spite of the 97-degree heat.

I moved closer and joined the men already slowly circling him. It wasn't planned. There were no directions given. Instinctively we knew we were supposed to move around him. As we swayed from side to side the movements became rhythmic and intoxicating. Gradually a collective moaning and chanting began. I don't remember what we chanted. It was tremulous, primordial, raw.

I don't know how long we moved around and around him, but suddenly, we stopped. He turned and looked directly at me. His eyes flashed like diamonds in chiseled black velvet. I felt compelled to go to him. As I walked toward him, his eyes locked onto mine. I had no control over what was happening. When I was close enough, he reached out and grabbed me; gently, slowly, but with a grip that spoke of ancient powers. I could feel hard, rippling sinew in his forearms and felt comfortable surrendering to his strength. His will.

He pulled me closer to him until all I could smell was the musky sweetness of his body and all I could taste was the salty essence covering him. Without warning, he reached down and ripped the skins from my body. I couldn't move. I was paralyzed by the intensity of the moment. He grabbed the back of my neck and pulled me toward moist, full, inviting lips. My own emptiness seemed to pull him inside of me. I could taste the inferno that was him as I lost myself in the arms of this ancient warrior.

A lifetime later he escaped my mouth and I felt him move down to my neck. He chewed and sucked until all I was conscious of were his lips, tongue, and teeth on my body. Just when I thought I couldn't stand any more he slid off my neck and slipped further down my body. He took one hard nipple between his teeth while he firmly massaged the other with a massive hand. He licked my chest for what seemed like hours, then stopped and slowly turned me around licking, biting and sucking every part of my trembling body. His tongue was rough like a cat's. I lost myself in the ecstasy of the moment. He rubbed and licked my back. When he pulled me against him I felt his hard stiffness.

He reached around my body and gently held my own stiff throbbing erection in his hand. He slid his hand slowly up and down as I felt his other arm encircle my chest and continue the erotic massage. My body was relaxed and there was only the barest twinge of delicious pain as he penetrated me slowly, a fraction of an inch at a time. A deep groan escaped my throat as our spirits blended together.

Our bodies moved as one as we sinuously pulsed against each other. Our rhythm quickened as the intensity of our movements increased to match the ferocity of our rising passions. Our synchronous motions seemed to last forever. I lost all sense of time. I was only aware of each exquisite moment as a separate and complete entity.

I don't know how long we slipped and slid against one another. Gradually, and with increasing strength, I started to feel our bodies vibrate and throb. The men circling us swayed and moaned in time with our ecstasy. A growing heat surged from the center of my being and spread rapidly throughout my body. The anticipation of what was to come was more than I could bear, and then suddenly, my whole being exploded. I was simultaneously consumed by fire and cooled by ice. My mouth filled with indescribable tastes. I was aware of everything and nothing but the fire burning in my head and groin. The moment was infinite but over long before I wanted it to end. I felt part of this African god who had totally possessed me.

Then he let go and I slid off of him onto the ground, collapsing like a broken puppet at his feet. I was totally spent and sensed the rapid approach of the kind of sleep that comes after a delicious and complete exhaustion. As my eyes started to close he reached down and pressed his animal-tooth necklace into my hand. My last memory was of this African king bent over me and the sensation of his necklace biting into my hand as I clutched it tightly.

When I awakened, I was back in my apartment in my own bed. I realized I had fallen asleep in the muggy heat and dreamt the whole thing. I decided to get up and take a shower. For some reason I was soaked with sweat and covered with a sandy grit. I couldn't figure out why. I felt something pressing into my back. I reached behind me. It was a necklace, a crude necklace made of the teeth of some animal.

ALAN E. MILLER

At the club
(Excerpts)

like their cigarettes
　　alive only at the tips
　　　　these lovely fireflies

　　　　　　　in this strange eden
　　　　　　　　delicious wax apples
　　　　　　　　　fragrant plastic roses

his eyes howl at me
　　coyote separated
　　　from the roving pack

　　　　　　under the table
　　　　　　　where everyone can see, we touch:
　　　　　　　hand to burning hand

is it relief
    I see when the condoms fall
        from my bulging wallet?

                    The wedding band clanging
                        against glass causes a thousand
                            tiny explosions

after the music ends
    we will hold each other
        till the lights come up

ADRIAN STANFORD

In the darkness, fuck me now

for Donald Thomas Williams

In the darkness, fuck me now.
speak not, for the rustling of white linen
will make music,
and the occasional zooming of cars
below, will add to the rhapsody
and as silence, deep and pregnant, settles
in our ears (taking us beyond lust's ocean roar),
we will drift on our minds' eternal sea.
falling stars will be our witness. the wetness
of my loins proclaims the rite.
i am pinioned in your arms. silent, and hard breathing.
each breathing creating galaxies; where unnamed
children call me god—
and shout in their private gloom, as i do:
fuck me now.

ESSEX HEMPHILL

The tomb of sorrow

for Mahomet

> *I cannot say*
> *that I have gone to hell*
> *for your love*
> *but often*
> *found myself there*
> *in your pursuit.*
>
> —William Carlos Williams
> "Asphodel, That Greeny Flower"

I

Gunshots ring out above our heads
as we sit beneath your favorite tree,
in this park called Meridian Hill,
called Malcolm X, that you call
the "Tomb of Sorrow"
(and claim to be its gatekeeper);
in the cool air lingering after the rain,
the men return to the Wailing Wall
to throw laughter and sad glances
into the fountains below,
or they scream out
for a stud by any name,
their beautiful asses
rimmed by the moon.

Gunshots ring out above our heads
as we cock dance
beneath your favorite tree.
There are no invectives
to use against us.
We are exhausted
from dreaming wet dreams,
afraid of the passion
that briefly consoles us.

I ask no more of you
than I ask of myself:
no more guilt, no more pity.
Occult risks await us
at the edge of restraint.

These are meaningless kisses
(aren't they?)
that we pass back and forth
like poppers and crack pipes,
and for a fleeting moment,
in a flash of heat and consent,
we release our souls
to hover above our bodies;
we believe our shuddering orgasms
are transcendental;
our loneliness manifests itself
as seed we cannot take
or give.

Gunshots ring out above our heads,
a few of us are seeking romance,
others a piece of ass,
some — a stroke of dick.
The rest of us are killing.
The rest of us get killed.

II

When I die,
honey chil',
my angels
will be tall
Black drag queens.
I will eat their stockings
as they fling them
into the blue
shadows of dawn.
I will suck
their purple lips
to anoint my mouth
for the utterance of prayers.

My witnesses
will have to answer

to go-go music.
Dancing and sweat
will be required
at my funeral.

Someone will have to answer
the mail I leave,
the messages
on my phone service;
someone else
will have to tend
to the aching
that drove me
to seek soul.

Everything different
tests my faith.
I have stood in places
where the absence of light
allowed me to live longer,
while at the same time
it rendered me blind.

I struggle against
plagues, plots,
pressure, paranoia.
Everyone wants a price
for my living.

When I die,
my angels,
immaculate
Black diva
drag queens,
all of them
sequined
and seductive,
some of them
will come back
to haunt you,
I promise,
honey chil'.

III

You stood beneath a tree
guarding moonlight,
clothed in military fatigues,
black boots, shadows,
winter rain, midnight,
jerking your dick slowly,
deliberately calling attention
to its proud length
and swollen head,
a warrior dick,
a dick of consequences
nodded knowingly at me.

You were stirring it
when I approached,
making it swell more,
allowing raindrops
escaping through
leaves and branches
to bounce off of it
and shatter like doubt.

Among the strangest gifts
I received from you
(and I returned them all)—
a chest of dark, ancient wood,
inside: red velvet cushions,
coins, paper money
from around the world.
A red book of hand-drawn runes,
a kufi, prayer beads,
a broken timepiece—
the stench of dry manure.

And there were other things
never to be forgotten—
a silver horse head
to hold my chain of keys,
a Christian sword,
black candles,
black dolls
with big dicks
and blue dreads
that you nailed

above my bed
to ensure fidelity.
A beer bottle filled
with hand-drawn soap,
a specificity—
a description of your life,
beliefs, present work,
weight and height;
declarations of love
which I accepted,
overlooking how I disguised
my real motivations—
a desire to keep
some dick at home
and love it as best I can.

I was on duty to your madness
like a night nurse
in a cancer ward.
Not one alarm went off
as I lay with you, Succubus.
I've dreamed of you
standing outside my soul
beneath a freakish tree,
stroking your dick
which is longer
in the dream, but I,
unable to be moved
and enchanted
rebuke you.
I vomit up your snake
and hack it to pieces,
laughing as I strike.

No, I was not
your pussy,
she would be
your dead wife.
I believe you
dispatched her soul
or turned her into a cat.
I was your man lover,
gambling dangerously
with my soul.
I was determined to love you

but you were haunted
by Vietnam,
taunted by demons.
In my arms you dreamed
of tropical jungles,
of young village girls
with razors embedded
in their pussies,
lethal chopsticks
hidden in their hair,
their nipples clenched
like grenade pins
between your grinding teeth.

You rocked and kicked
in your troubled sleep
as though you were fucking
one of those dangerous cunts,
and I was by your side
unable to hex it away,
or accept that peace
means nothing to you,
and the dreams you suffer
may be my only revenge.

IV

It was an end to masturbation.
That's what I was seeking.
I couldn't say it then, no,
I couldn't say it then.

When you told me
your first lover,
a white man,
wanted you to spit,
shit, piss on,
fist-fuck and
throw him down stairs,
alarms should have
blared forth
like hordes
of screaming queens.

When you said
in the beginning
you beat up Black men
after you fucked them,
when you said
in the last year
you were buying crack
for Black men
who let you fuck 'em,
alarms should have
deafened me for life.

When you told me
you once tied a naked man
between two trees
in an isolated,
wooded area,
debased him,
leaving him there
for several days,
then sent others
to rape him and feed him,
my head should have exploded
into shrapnel
and killed us both.

When you swore you loved me
and claimed to be sent here
to protect me,
I should have put bullets
in my temple
or flaming swords
up my ass.

Feeling my usual
sexual vexations,
I came here then,
seeking only pleasure,
dressed for the easy seduction.
I never considered
carrying a cross.
I had no intention
of being another queen
looking out

at the morning rain
from the Wailing Wall,
hoping to spy a brutish man
with a nearby home.

Slouching through Homo Heights,
I came to the Tomb of Sorrow
seeking penetration and Black seed.
My self-inflicted injuries occurred
when I began loving you
and trusting you.

V

Through some other
set of eyes
I have to see you
homeboy,
fantasy charmer,
object of my desire,
my scorn,
abuser of my affections,
curse, beauty,
tough/soft young men,
masked men,
cussing men,
sweet swaggering
buffalo soldiers.

Through some other
set of eyes
I must recognize
our positions
are often equal.
We are worth more
to each other
than twenty dollars,
bags of crack,
bullets piercing our skulls.
I can't hope to help
save us from destruction
by using my bed
as a pagan temple,
a false safe house.
There are other ways

to cross the nights,
to form lasting bonds;
there are other desires
as consuming as flesh.
There are ways
to respect our beauty.

Through some other set
of common eyes
I have to behold you
again, homeboy.
I rummage through
ancestral memories
in search of the
original tribes
that fathered us.
I want to remember
the exact practices
of civility
we agreed upon.
I want us to remember
the nobility of decency.

At the end of the day,
through some other vision,
perhaps the consequence
of growing firm and older,
I see the thorns of the rose
are not my enemy.
I strive to see this
in each of us—
O ancient petals,
O recent blooms.

ADRIAN STANFORD

Remembrance of Rittenhouse Square

black sarah ruled
and we of lesser divinity paid homage to her
with our pansy smiles.
we breathed magnolia air, dreaming other visions
through the velvet of our mascara lashes;
and blessed ourselves with water from the shallow pond,
and kissed each handsome boy as he passed by.
the low-hung moon brought expectation to our hearts.
we chattered endlessly: mingling within, without,
seeking happiness, finding nothing
but the sad green beauty of the trees.
our priestess has another temple now,
and we the keepers of this sacred ground
have been raped, our harpstrings broken,
we sing no more—
ah, good queen sarah, why did you never speak of reality?

CARY ALAN JOHNSON

Hey, brother, what's hap'nin'?

You know, it has occurred to me as of late that gay men are still hung up on roles. Only now, instead of the question being who's on top and who's on bottom, the question has become "Who's more of a top?" Everybody is so *Yeah-I'm-Down, What's Hap'nin'?* Of course there are still queens, and plenty of 'em, but even they throw on their Reeboks and step out cruising Flatbush Avenue. Out looking for *fellas*. If you a *fella* then you cool. If you a queen, well honey, you are not "in" this season.

Everybody's at the gym pumping iron, 'cause it's all about appearances. We've rejected the leather and the boots (too white!) and the limp wrists and snapping fingers (too effeminate!), and where are we now? Everybody wants to be the boy next door — and *have* the boy next door. And I'm no exception.

Last winter I wore my Reeboks and my alligator shirt buttoned all the way up to the top. It was a costume, the "in" one. You'd spy someone who looked like you, or what you hoped you looked like, all ghetto-ish with not a trace of that fag-juice. You'd approach.

"Hey troop! What's hap'nin'?"

And within thirty seconds, your hopes of finding the last real man were dashed, and maybe his were too. But it was cool, 'cause the night was young and there were plenty of chunky possibilities running around. Plenty of would-be homeboys in *fella* outfits. All you had to do was find the right one.

Last Saturday night, at the Garage, I was so desperate, I got on the loudspeaker and made an announcement:

WOULD THE LAST REAL MAN PLEASE STAND UP!
WOULD THE LAST REAL MAN PLEASE STAND UP!

I was amazed at the response.

But you see, I'm looking for the real thing, the A-Team, not a bunch of What's-My-Line impostors. This ain't Halloween, and I am no longer fooled by his urban drag, Jersey haircut, or his name in six-inch letters around his neck. I've got the same ones. I'm looking for a real brother who knows the streets, don't take no shit, kicks ass when he has to, kills white boys for fun, eats bullets for breakfast, drives a mustang, done been to jail. Someone like ... like...

"Hey cuz, what's hap'nin'?"

DON CHARLES

Jailbait

You better quit coming around here like that
with no shirt on
and them gold chains on your neck

In them tight shorts
halfway pushed down the back
and your jockstrap showing

Ass jerking from side to side
and your legs all sweaty and shining

Trying to talk dirty
with that Kangol hat cocked to one side

Some dude's gonna grab you
yank them shorts right down
throw you 'cross the hood of his car
and ram his dick up your little ass so hard
it'll make you walk more funny than you do.

Couldn't nobody blame him neither
the way you walk around
acting like you want something

Hell!
I may be the one who jams you

You just better quit coming around here.

DONALD WOODS

What do I do about you?

holy ghost of my heart
grinding my memory
humping my need

throw your head like the dinka
shake your arms like the masai
a french whore flirting
lickin lips at strangers

been waitin for your lightbulb
to glow for me

waiting
to exchange hard ass love
calloused affection

slapping high fives
capable and competent
listless and lonely

turn the blaze up slow
so I can breathe your
mourning breath
wet my pillow
part your eyelids

I'm a typewriter
randy and selfish and wise
a sonnet
a beat box

serve the next line
in your salty metaphors
and smoked salmon humor

wet me with
the next line

the resounding refrain
of grown men in love

CARY ALAN JOHNSON

Obi's story

At seven a.m. he looked upon her, a fantastic bas-relief against a sea of smarting blue. Brown, open, a thrush of mountains plying down her spine, into a crack, a gully of darker. He had risen from a wet July night in New York, solid black and white with the genies of rising steam on JFK's tarmac, and broken through to a clear African morning. Through the porthole he watched the coast of Mauritania transform itself into the groundnut sand of Mali, only to be replaced by the lush Nigerian bush. The plane fell east and south.

The only black passenger in the first-class section, Stu had expected at least an African diplomat or two, or a businessman flying Air Afrique back home to Doula or Libreville after parlaying gold, diamonds, or oil into VCRs and expensive cars. He was alone with the Burkinabé flight attendant and felt a strange guilt each time one of the coach passengers, overwhelmingly Black Africans, would wander into the first-class cabin by mistake or curiosity.

As the Belgian woman in the aisle seat slept, a haughty nasal buzz came from her mouth. Back in New York, he had thought her French as they attempted the ad hoc friendship eight hours of flight necessitated. During the night she had spoken in her sleep, an ugly Flemish Afrikaans sound, he had thought, and remembered how frightened she was when the plane took off, crossing herself repeatedly, gripping her crucifix, the divider between their seats, and finally his arm as they lifted high above Long Island.

"*Pardon, Monsieur*. Flying makes me so nervous."

"*De rien, Madame*," he responded with the magnanimity he always felt at the beginning of a long trip.

"Oh, you speak French? I thought you were *noir américain*."

"Yes, I'm an American."

She shrugged. "But you speak so well. You've lived in Europe?" she stated her question.

"No, in Africa ... and Haiti," he added the last for emphasis, though he'd never been to the Caribbean. It was just the next deepest, darkest, blackest place he could think of.

She clucked to herself and smiled. "But you speak so well," she repeated. "You are a diplomat, perhaps ... no, no, no. A journalist." She had decided.

He debated momentarily about which answer would most likely shut her up. Both opened a can of worms particularly savory to expatriates in Africa when they have a captive audience. He had already determined that this woman had lived in Africa for many years and was probably more at home on the verandas of private clubs in Kinshasa than in a Paris boutique. He knew her type, hated them, therefore hated her.

"Yes, journalist."

She smiled comfortably. He signaled the handsome Burkinabé to bring him more champagne. Journalist was as good as anything. What was he after all? A tourist, an invader? What had he ever been here?

Now, several hours and bottles of Moët later, he turned back to the unfolding map below. It had been too long since his eyes had feasted on this sight and he'd grown weary and red-eyed from a night of expectation and twisting in anticipation of this particular arrival. Five years since he last set foot on the Continent, since that wonderful and vicious summer with Kate and Obi on the coast and all that had happened since.

He wondered if anyone would be at the airport to meet him. He imagined Kate, drinking tea, her tanned face and red hair amidst the crowd of fiercely turbaned heads and crisp robes on the observation deck. He imagined Obi, a black mountain of a man, calm and imposing in the sea of activity that always reigned at Ntala Airport, its red and black flags flapping in the harmattan. The images disquieted him, and two valiums and the alcohol could not dispel them. Now as the earth approached the plane, miles at a time, his anxiety turned to fear.

God, she must hate him. The years of no words had methodically grown into a wall of dispassion built to shield him from the pain of that summer, of losing Obi, then Kate's friendship, and finally himself. But in New York, and then later in Washington, the losses, the liquor, and finally the drugs had come crashing down on him, leaving him with no choice but to return to the scene of this crime, to Ntala, to the coast, and to what was left of that summer's memory.

Five years ago it had been so different. It was he on the observation deck sipping not tea but *Mbusa*, the national beer, the "water of champions," as its advertising proclaimed. The sun was a cruel slash in the sky that day, its rays releasing the copper in his skin. Ruddy, it had turned him, tanned just like a white boy he remarked when passing reflective shop windows in the capital. He wore a safari suit: Khaki and large, it hung comfortably on his thick shoulders, a gold chain lying casually among the hairs of his chest. His short, well-oiled afro picked up flecks of intense light and shot them back. He was twenty-nine at the time and unremarkably handsome. It was his eyes that set him apart. They had an intensely sad quality to them, as if they'd witnessed too many bitter scenes already at that young age, as if they belonged to a small child who'd been left out of too many games. It was this pain in his eyes that lit his face when he smiled, making his joy all the more important for its viewer.

At the table with him, Obi sat drinking a bottle of the same. Among the handsomely dressed and well-bred Africans in the terrace café, Obi was a commanding figure, tall for an Ntalan, with skin so dark it approached true black in its reflection of light. He did not appreciate the sun in the same way Stu did and sported a blue cap with a visor to shield his eyes. He wore a pair of plaid walking shorts, very fashionable at the time among the *"jeunes premiers,"* the West-looking youth of the capitol. Hairless, muscled legs ended in clean white Nikes. A small brown tanned leather pouch hanging from around his neck seemed to be the only vestige of the traditional in his image. He quietly hummed along with the crackling radio tuned to Gabon and Africa Numero 1 until a fast track came on.

"Papa Wilo," his eyes brightened. "He's in town tonight."

"I know, I know. Best high life on the continent. We'll be there if Kate wants to go. She may be tired after the flight. Damn, must this thing always be late?"

Obi looked at his watch, a black face with tiny silver chips where the numbers might have been, a gift from Stu only last week. Stu wagered it was the nicest watch Obi had ever owned. Obi downed half the bottle of beer and leaned back in the white wire mesh chair. The sight of his body unfurling flipped a switch in Stu; he summoned the waiter. The man came, dressed in a clean white coat and beach sandals. Stu ordered more beers in Kindoma, the words falling easy and light off his tongue.

Obi smiled. "You still speak Kindoma with an American accent."

"How many Americans do you know can speak Kindoma?"

"Just you and the Great White Fathers." Obi laughed loud and killed what was left of his beer. "They're Americans, aren't they?"

"Of a sort."

"But you know more curses."

"You're damn right. That's 'cause I hang around you and Zamakil too much. Too many high-life concerts."

Obi straightened in his seat. "Does Kate speak Kindoma?"

"No, she's never been here, but her French is fantastic. She's great. I can't wait to see her."

Obi reached across the table and pulled the pack of Okapi from the pocket of Stu's shirt. "I think you like her."

"Of course I do. We've been friends for a long time."

"That's not what I mean." He lit two cigarettes, handed one across the table and returned the pack to Stu's pocket.

Stu smiled at the boldness of his lover's actions, amazed at how comfortable Obi had grown over the past six months. "Now Obi," he lowered his voice, "if I didn't know you better, I'd think you were jealous. You know I'm not thinking about anyone else, okay homeboy? Kate is an excellent engineer. We work well together. I need her on this project if I'm gonna get that water pumped in before the river goes down. We want to be in the States by Christmas, right?"

"Right."

"So we'll work together. We're a team, okay? Okay, chief?"

"Yeah, okay, Stu." He answered this last in English. Stu slapped him lightly on the face, letting his hand linger imperceptibly while the noisy chatter on the terrace was broken by the sound of the DC-10 approaching the city.

○

Dear Kate,

Hey sweetheart! Trust this letter finds you well. I sure hope, however, that you've had a lousy winter and want to totally change your lifestyle, 'cause I've got a proposition. The engineer on the water project just quit and we need a replacement fast. I've been doing such a damn good job on these quickies, that I've got the Minister of Works eating out my back pocket, so to speak.

So the other day, we're sitting around talking about how to get a top-notch, crackerjack engineer with small irrigation experience to spend the summer on the beautiful coast of Ntala. Well hon, we thought and thought and couldn't come up with anyone. So I decided to ask you (ha ha).

No, but seriously, you've got to come out. We'll be in the middle of the short rainy season, and Katie, you've never seen anything like this coastline. It'll blow you away. I've really fallen in love with this country. So different than the years we spent in the Peace Corps. Do you remember how frustrated I was? Loving my work, but hating the rest. My God, I couldn't wait to get out of our village, but do you remember how I cried like a baby on the truck? But I seem to have worked things out. Or they've worked out for me.

Most of the reason is probably this gorgeous mothafucka lying in bed next to me. I swear, Katie, I'd given up all prospects of falling in love over here and had resigned myself to taking some desk job with AID in

Washington. But meeting Obi has changed everything. He's just so honest and genuine. He really cares about me as a person. You'll see. If you come out we'll be working together. He's the liaison man. Most of the projects I've worked on that means glorified interpreter and chauffeur, but I swear Katie, the guy is so bright. I'd never get these folks working so fast if it weren't for him. And now everything else seems to be falling into place, too. I'm going to bring him back to the States for a few months, spend Christmas in Detroit. My parents will love him. And then we'll see. See how he adjusts to life in the States. Or maybe back out here. Or, there's a job with Catholic Relief in Harare.

Anyway, I'm going on as usual, letting my imagination run away with me. Let me stop. I really hope you'll consider the job. You need to be out by first July. Cable me as soon as you get this. My love to your dad.

Best love,
Stu

✪

"Katie, you look great. How's Washington?"

"Same old bullshit. Summer was hot as hell. Thanks for the rescue." Kate was a modest and attractive woman in her early thirties, with angular features and a full frame. She had a playful quality that at times made her seem much younger than she was, and at other times her up-front brashness made her seem years older. Her no-nonsense, down-to-business attitude sometimes alienated people, particularly the staff under her, but she was easy to respect, a hard worker, and committed. The last ten years of her life had been divided between graduate school in engineering and work in India and Bangladesh. "Something about the faces of the children," she had confided in her letters, "I just can't stay away."

On the drive from the airport, Obi removed the top off the Jeep. Kate's hair caught the wind and rose. "It's dry as a bone out here." She pulled from her bag a pair of punk black sunglasses, hanging on an old-fashioned silver link chain, and surveyed the dusty maize fields sprawled along the road. Single huts and larger compounds, all washed a sandy brown, dotted the landscape.

"Two years. No rain." They were the first words Obi had spoken since the initial introductions on the terrace. He seemed to be brooding.

"The U.S. and France are doing some famine relief in the North. Soviets mostly in the South," Stu filled in. "Most of the grain's been going to the cities, but what else is new?"

"That's stop-gap shit. What's the solution?"

"That's what we're here for. The government decided a few years ago to dam this great big monster of a river, change the whole ecosystem, and then tell folks to dig irrigation canals. You've seen the plan."

"Yeah, I read through the stuff you sent. It's not hopeless. Water table's high enough. How many teams have we got?"

"Ten. Locally trained engineers on every one."

"Who's your anthropologist?"

Stu shook his head. "Ain't got none."

"Sociologist?"

"Couldn't get anyone on such short notice."

"So you're gonna go in and tell people to stop eating millet, start growing rice, and sell half of it to the government, all by your lonesome." She looked at him over the top of the glasses. "You're cute, dear, but not that persuasive."

Stu smiled, put his hand on Obi's shoulder and squeezed it. "No, I've got a little help." Obi stirred uncomfortably under Stu's grip, raising his eyes slightly to catch Kate's reaction to the small gesture in the rearview mirror.

"So, Obi, you're the man with the plan," Kate quipped. "Care to share it?"

He returned his eyes to the road. "No plan. The land is dry. People have no food. You will come with pipes and canals and pumps and help grow food. People will welcome you. You want them to grow rice. They'll grow rice."

"That simple?" Kate looked doubtful.

Obi sighed almost imperceptibly and continued, "Years ago, the French told us to grow peanuts. We grew peanuts. Everywhere peanuts. You took them. The land died. Peanuts killed the land. Now you want us to grow rice. We'll grow rice. What do you want us to do?"

The crush of the gravel underneath the wheels of the Land Rover and the turn of the motor Obi had tuned to mechanical perfection underscored the silence. An ancient Mercedes truck, loaded to twice its height with bags of imported grain, lumbered by. Perhaps this was food on its way to government soldiers squelching the bush warring guerrillas in the interior. The truck, leaning dangerously to its side, kicked up a great cloud of smoky stinging dust as it headed to the airport.

"Here Obi, you need these more than I do." She removed the Greenwich Village specials from around her neck. Obi hesitated, then looked hard at her reflection in the rearview mirror. Finally he turned to Stu for a reaction. Stu provided his most encouraging smile, lighting his face with eyes that had found their way into Obi's heart at other times, trying now to break that wall that Obi was carefully constructing. With a slight release of breath, Obi put on the shades, his dark face opening into a wide gulf of white teeth as he laughed appreciatively at what he saw.

"You look great," Kate smiled with him through the mirror.

Cameroon John Little was a large, affable, blue-eyed man. He lived in an opulent villa on the peninsula where the river turned its mighty attention to entering the city. Stu had grown to tolerate Cami, probably because he had come to understand him. It was not easy to be a man who liked men on this continent, he reasoned, though being white made it easier. Cami had learned early in his life as a businessman in Africa that he could have almost anything he wanted for the right price. He participated gleefully in the free market economy of the capital, filling his home, its manicured gardens, poolside, and numerous bedrooms with the most attractive young men Ntala had to offer.

There Stu had met several law students from the university, Mohammed, a friendly military parachutist visiting from the north, and Zamakil, the goalkeeper for the national football team. The men Cami kept in rotating residence were always obliging, most quite openly. A few begrudgingly relented, but these were never invited to return. All were in need. The university and high school students were mostly poor fellows struggling through an academic and social system hard-pressed and unwilling to meet their most basic needs. The soldiers were living mean lives with large families on meager government salaries that were always late and occasionally never came. Some, like Zamakil, came out of no particular financial need, savoring only the pleasures that Cami's house offered.

Many found that they could live their sexual lives openly within the walls of Cami's compound. For some, the sex, with each other or with the various expatriates who also passed through, was an amusing addition to the life of decadence and excess lived there. For others, it was what they were forced to give in payment for the relief from difficult lives, or for the few dollars Cami would slip into their pockets when they left.

Cami's had originally been a refuge for Stu, who had lived in enough countries to know that such people were necessary, that to be befriended by the Cami's of Africa meant entrée into a world it might take a man months or even years to discover on his own.

Stu's life as a gay man in Africa swung violently between the poles of the erotic and the neurotic. It swung between the attraction he felt for most of the intensely sure men he saw on the streets and in villages and his mistrust and hatred of the power they had over him. He was quite clear that the men of Ntala had the ability to validate him, to make him feel totally at home and accepted in this foreign land. But he knew all too well their willingness to reject him, to cripple him as a man, and even worse to betray him to a society that tolerated only silent difference. He knew that any unwise act, the wrong man approached, a pass unsuccessfully completed, could be his downfall, could mean in fact the end of his career abroad. When he first arrived in a new post, he would live a life of abstinence, carefully surveying the sexual landscape until he felt safe enough to venture out. Nevertheless, his future often hinged on the whims of his dick, not a healthy prospect for a man of his sexual appetite.

But he knew that Cami could, if he so desired, change the entire nature of his time in Ntala. So just as he'd done in Botswana, Togo, and then Zaire, he subjected himself to the scantily cloaked racisms, the thin jokes, the greedy stingy generous use of men as objects in this city that Cami and his expatriate friends called temporary home, one they hated with a passion and could not wait to leave when their fat contracts came to an end. In the meantime, they ate, drank, and fucked heartily at the villa on the peninsula.

Cami's place was known for its orgies. Stu would sometimes arrive after several weeks in the bush, stopping only to drop his bags off at the InterCon. He would find parties in full swing: Ntalans ranging in age from sixteen to thirty, in various states of undress, would be lounging by the pool, entertaining Cami's friends in tangled liaisons of two, three, or more.

Mostly people seemed to be having fun. These were the times when Stu could enjoy himself the most. Other times the commerce was too visceral. Cami would call a new invitee over.

"Isn't he a beautiful boy? Look at him." Cami would run his hand over the boy's head, under his shirt and finally, always end by stroking his crotch. The boy would invariably smile, knowing what was expected. Stu's skin would crawl, he would struggle to maintain composure as he vicariously felt Cami's hand on his own body, as he felt a chain tug at his neck. But Cami knew better than to try it. Stu was, after all, his equal in every way. An honorary white by these twisted standards.

Yes, the boy was beautiful. Cami entertained nothing but the best. "What's his name?" Stu would ask and then regret. He did not wait for a reply from the white man. "What's your name?"

The boy had a name. He was from a place. Had a history which Stu tried to discover in between bouts of lovemaking, at dinner, or while frolicking in the pool at his hotel where he sometimes took them after leaving Cami's house. The boy was most often not a boy at all, but a man with children, or a wife, or both. With dreams. And at the end of the day or the week in the capital the boy/man always wanted money from Stu, cab fare to go back to his place, to pay his kids' school fees, once even to buy a taxi. Stu gave what he could, took a furtive kiss (he had after all paid for it), and crawled back to the project site, back to whatever distant village he was working in, feeling alone and betrayed, but never knowing exactly by whom.

It was Zamakil who brought Obi to the house. Zamakil was the only African who seemed to approach Cami as an equal. And Zamakil and

Obi were friends. They had gone to primary and secondary school together and separated only when the athlete's fate turned him into a national hero. Obi, too poor to continue on to the university, had taken up carpentry and then finally had become a mechanic for a large transport company in the capital. He'd always been good with his hands. Now, both nearing thirty, their memories of childhood games on beaches, of shadowy touches as boys, brought them together as men with hardened bodies and adult needs. They were fast friends once again, two men who shared an intimate past.

On the day Stu met Obi, he was in a difficult mood. The trip into the city had been particularly annoying. He'd been stopped seven times by knuckleheaded soldiers demanding bribes to tide them over through the first of the month. It had been hot, a day that had desperately needed a strong rain which never came to break the sun's anger. He was exhausted when he rang Cami's doorbell.

"You look a mess, man." Cami ushered him in. "Rough trip?"

"Exceedingly."

"Well, put on some trunks and come for a swim, old man. I've got something out back I think will perk you up a bit." He smiled lasciviously and slid out the back into the yard.

Stu found Cami and Zamakil downing Scotch and soda by the pool. They were enjoying a good laugh about Zamakil's recent trip to Kenya for the Africa Cup finals. Zamakil stood up when he saw Stu. They had always liked each other very much, had even had an affair which ended when Stu realized that the athlete liked fresh trade as much as Cami did and could never be tied down to one man.

"Stuart, where have you been so long? Out working in the field from the looks of it." They embraced and kissed one, two, three times on the cheek. "We've missed you."

"Zamakil was just telling me about the coach of the Kenyan football team," Cami said.

"Not the coach, the manager."

"Coach, manager, whatever. You probably had them both, knowing you, whore."

"I tried." They both laughed. "But the coach was sleeping with the goalkeeper and that bitch wouldn't let me near him. Stuart, what are you drinking?"

Stu headed to the poolhouse. "Whatever's wet, and mix it with something cold."

"Don't hurt yourself," Cami called from his lounge chair and chuckled.

"Huh?" The door to the poolhouse opened and a black man walked out wearing only a bright white bikini and a smile that matched in color and brilliance and left Stu speechless. The seconds before either of them spoke seemed both few and long.

"Excuse me," Stu said finally, "I just wanted to change."

The fine young man, tall, muscular, twenty-five or twenty-six at the most, moved away from the door to let Stu pass. "Yes, sure. How are you?" The voice was earnest and warm.

"Fine," Stu responded, feigning nonchalance, but his voice clearly matched the warmth. He entered the poolhouse and shut the door slowly behind him. Carefully sliding on his trunks, he counted backwards from one hundred in threes, thought about tombstones, asparagus, and car wrecks, waiting for the bulging nylon to recede.

He found Zamakil and Cami smiling conspiratorily. The tall perfect one with the hair a bit too long for his round face was doing laps in the pool. Stu decided to say nothing in response to the obvious plot.

"What's new?" he asked Cami.

"Your reticence, for one," Cami, always master of the sharp tongue, answered.

"Okay, okay. I'm impressed. Who is he?"

Zamakil laughed and pulled off his shirt. "Who is who? Oh, you mean him there swimming. Just someone. Just a boy." He slipped out of his shorts and dove naked into the deep end of the pool. Cami followed suit, playfully wrestling with Zamakil in the warm chlorinated water. Zamakil fought off his opponent and swam to the shallow end, where he hiked himself up and sat on the edge.

The tall one got out of the pool and sat on the grass under a shaded palm, near Stu who watched him watch Zamakil as Cami's head bobbed methodically between the goalkeeper's legs. The stranger's face, a nearly impassive mask, broke only at the corners, which twitched uncomfortably. Was he excited? Should Stu move on him? He was here, he knew the game, the unwritten rules of the house. Stu made what seemed like an interminable trip over to where Obi sat in the shade. He reached his hand out to touch the water beading on the taut chest. A black hand darted out and encircled his wrist. The man looked at him confused, betrayed. The warm look of invitation was gone. A shield had gone up. He let go Stu's hand and pulled on his pants over the wet suit. He stood and shook the water from his thick hair, then walked around the side of the house onto the path which led to the street.

Stu rubbed his wrist. It did not hurt nearly as much as his ego, newly bruised. He felt small and ashamed. He cut through the house to the front yard, racing to catch the man at the wrought-iron gate.

"Wait a minute. I'm sorry, okay?" The other was silent. "I didn't know."

"Didn't know what, nzuma?" He used the Kindoma word which had come to signify foreigner, stranger, but translated literally as white man.

Stu felt as if he'd been slapped. "Is that what you think of me?"

"Is that how you behave?" He threw open the gate.

"Wait, I'll give you a ride."

"I'll walk."

"It's a long way to town. Lots of hungry soldiers. Let me give you a ride. I'm sorry, okay. Okay? What's your name?"

Perhaps it was the earnestness of Stu's voice. Or the memory of the first few moments of their meeting. Or perhaps merely the fear of soldiers on the long road to town, but Obi relented. Stu drove.

❂

That night at the hotel, when Obi took him, he felt warm and full, safe in a forest of circling lions. As the momentum mounted, Obi built a fire of black logs for protection. In the morning, so much later, when he took Obi, the fire was replaced by clear white light as he gasped at the shock of entrance, an entrance so tight and fitting, so perfectly unforetold that he came before he could pump or slide or ride. These would come later, of that he was sure, from Obi's sighs, from the relax in his body, from the wet he felt running down now over Obi's hard black belly.

❂

"Are you married?" The room was lit only by dawn creeping through Venetian blinds, under doors, and across pillows.

"No, are you?" Obi propped himself up on his elbow, slid his other hand slowly down the long of Stu's body.

"I'm gay."

Obi laughed. "I, too, am sometimes very happy."

Stu scanned his face in the scattered light for a trace of sarcasm and found none. "I'm trying to understand your country. How to be happy here. I would like to find a friend. A special friend."

"*I* will be your friend. Zamakil says you will go to work on the coast. It is very beautiful. My oldest nephew will be baptised there during the short rainy season. I will take you to meet my family. They have never met a *noir américain*. Would you like to go?"

"Of course, I would love to meet your family. You aren't afraid they will suspect?"

"They could never suspect such a thing. And your family ... will I meet them?"

"They're in America. Do you want to go to the States?"

"What do you tell us? It's the biggest, the best. What fool would not want to go?"

"I mean what's in this for you, Obi, before I let myself go? What *do* you want from me?"

Obi seemed to consider, lay down on the bed, raised himself up again, took Stu in his arms, and held him. His hand was hot and moist on Stu's thigh. "Your ass, right now, would make me very happy."

Outside the hotel grounds, at the port, market women waited impatiently for the arrival of the barge from up-country. They tied and retied silk wraps over rotund bellies and generous hips, dreaming of dried fish, french perfume, and moonlit nights unalone. They stared intently north, shielding their eyes from the sun's riverdancing glare.

❁

All day the sun had burned white-hot in an unbroken sky. The evening had fallen slow without cloud cover. Stu had spent the afternoon working budget figures in the small hut they used as an office. The last canals had been dug, the pipes were laid, and two business-class tickets to Detroit via Frankfurt lay in the safe. The visa had been simple. Marc, a friend at the embassy, had made all the arrangements and now Obi's new passport lay on top of Stu's old one. All that was left was to close out the accounts and Kate could do that in a pinch.

Obi's absence that afternoon weighed on him. Late in the day, Cissé, the night guard just coming on duty, had informed him that Obi and Kate had taken the Jeep and gone to the baptism on the hillside.

"Great, just when I need him, she's got him traipsing all over the goddamn bush." Cissé smiled uncomfortably. Stu slammed the door and immediately regretted revealing so much of himself to the man, an elder from Obi's tribe. He returned to his desk and looked at the papers in disarray: figures, elevations, men and their salaries, debits ran together in black lines, red dots. His head swam.

Shutting and locking the bamboo door behind him, he took the back roads that led to the beach, down behind the small *pailotte* Obi had had the crew build for himself. Pretenses had, after all, to be maintained. The path, like the hut, was mainly unused. Milky thornbushes cut shallow grooves in his bare legs. He didn't care. The beach was empty except for a group of a dozen or so fishermen returning with the day's catch.

In this part of Ntala, the coastline was a study in natural drama. Within a half-hour's walk, the fine yellow sand lifted to tenuous cliffs and then hilly bluffs at the mouth of the river where the interior of the country drank its thirsty fill and opened itself up to weary passage.

He sat on the sand, wet with the approach of evening, and watched the fishermen. Night fell in patches around him; bits of sky turned themselves in, gave themselves over to higher powers. He could hear the drums from the baptism, urging but not urgent. What was ever pressing in this land of uncountable yesterdays and impossible tomorrows? The wind itself seemed to scoop percussion from the hillside where Kate and Obi surely danced and deposited it on the beach where Stu watched the sea alone now, the fishermen gone.

Tonight, he was waiting for a sign, a word telling him to go on. He got this way sometimes, lethargic, no motives. Earlier in the season,

Obi's presence had kept him moving, prodded him to work the teams at twice their normal speed. Kate had set up evening training sessions for the Ntalan engineers, sharing techniques she'd learned from local crews in Asia. Obi was a native of this region; he was related somehow to everyone. He used his contacts to speed up the delivery of supplies for the canals and spare parts for the Jeep and pumps. The three of them worked like a well-oiled machine, turning to each other at the end of each day, falling steadily into the arms of a growing friendship. Most evenings they sat out by a fire, dodging mosquitoes and sharing stories, smoking and feeling the vastness of the night consuming them.

On a mid-season trip to the capital, they had danced all night to a band at an outdoor club. Kate was arhythmic and knew it, swallowed it with a laugh and a beer. Obi had guided her across the floor through a sea of black faces with one sure hand on her waist and the other supporting the lifted curve of her spine. In his arms she appeared capable and weightless. To Stu, at a table in the corner, methodically getting sloshed on dark rum, the song seemed interminable.

Slowly, through the course of the season, something had been changing. Stu felt this instinctively before he ever admitted it. There was a resistance developing between him and Obi. Despite Stu's admonitions, curses, cajoling, Obi would not allow him to caress, hold, or even touch him when Kate was around. Kate's presence brought out a shame in Obi which Stu could not penetrate, as hard as he tried. When Stu demanded more time alone with him, Obi resisted. "What will the workers think? Some suspect now. We are too much together alone. They want to know why you have no children at your age. No wife."

Stu became angry. "But you're only five years younger than me."

"They begin to ask me the same questions."

"You never cared before!"

But Obi seemed to care now. "Perhaps in the city I am more free. But here, in my place ... and around Kate..."

"Kate is my friend. She wants us to be happy."

Obi smiled slightly and looked him square in the eyes. "Be patient with me, Stu."

Leaving the beach, he headed back up the path. Things would be better once they were in Detroit. Once they left the country of dying soil for the city of dying steel. Obi would be overwhelmed by the strangeness, Stu would be there to comfort him, to be relied upon, to translate their new lives into English, into American. Stu would be there.

Coming up behind Obi's unused hut, his eye caught on a flicker of light from inside, and then a sound of something hard hitting something soft. Robbers, he thought, as he stopped in his tracks. Where were the guards? The sound again, only this time it was more human, a groan, perhaps a moan of pleasure or pain. He crept up to the windowless cabin and with a push of its door exposed its two occupants to the night air.

What he saw seemed cloaked in a smoky gauze. His life was in fact smoldering around him. Obi and Kate lay tangled in each other's arms, legs, and twisted white sheets. Heat gushed from the room, it overwhelmed him. Obi stood up, the words coming quickly from his mouth were incomprehensible, his sex was still hard and wet.

"Shut up," Stu cried. Kate tried to cover herself with the sheet which was caught up in her legs. Obi continued talking, explaining what could not be explained. "Shut up," Stu roared and felt his fist make contact with the soft squish of the man's eye. He was suffocating and the room became a blur. He had to get out, but to go where and to do what, he did not know. He left the door agape, swinging on broken hinges.

"Stuart." Kate came into his room after several minutes, wrapped in a flowered green pagne covered with jungle beasts. "Stu." He started packing, savagely throwing his belongings into a suitcase. Carvings from the region, carefully chosen, a woman's head in bronze, fell at his feet.

"Stu, look at me. I know you're upset."

He stopped and looked at her, slowly focused on her blue eyes, her tanned, healthy complexion, skin still gleaming with sweat.

"You bitch." He hated her completely, there was no question, no holds barred. He wanted to hit her, the way he had hit Obi, to pummel her to the ground, permanently to mar the beauty — female, Caucasian — that he knew had drawn Obi to her.

"I don't know how it happened. It just did."

"Save it, okay. I don't understand you, Kate. You've got your choice of whomever you want. These men would do somersaults for white pussy." He glared at her.

"Stop it."

"Even back in Botswana, you got whatever you wanted. Why do you have to take the only piece of this damned country that ever loved me, the only thing that's ever mattered to me?"

"Obi is not a thing, damn you. He's a man with feelings just like you or me. He has a right to make choices. You don't own him."

"Oh, don't make yourself sound so innocent." Her seminudity seemed to weigh on her now. The pagne looked light, as if it were nothing. "Look at you."

"Oh, so you can sleep with half of Africa and you call it getting in touch with your roots."

"Just what the hell do you know about it?" He slammed the suitcase shut and hoisted it toward the door.

She glared at him, looked into his eyes, and then softened as the years of their friendship came back to his. "Enough to know that you're better than this. Stu, you're not going to find yourself this way, running from one country to another paying for affection."

"Obi loves me," he stopped. "He loved me. It's not about money." He sat down on the bed, confused, his hand still smarting from the blow he'd struck to his lover's face. Kate sat down next to him and tried to take his hand. He recoiled from her touch. "I'm going. I can't stay here. This hurts too much."

She took his hand and held it. He didn't draw back. "Do you want me to leave, Stu? I'll leave. Our friendship means more to me than—"

"Than Obi's love? I don't think so. It doesn't to me. I love you, Kate. But I needed him."

The numbers of the combination lock fell silently into place and the safe clicked open. He immediately erased the numbers from his head. He would need them no longer. He retrieved the two airline tickets and shoved them into the side pocket of his overnight bag. He picked up both passports. He fingered the brilliant red and black of the Ntalan flag embossed on the cover of Obi's. He wondered how the thick raised paper would look burning in a fire, how neatly the seal of the country would tear into two, ten, twenty pieces and then scatter onto the floor of the hut. He wondered of the possibilities. He placed it on the table.

Outside, the fresh of night evaporated the sweat on the back of his neck, dried the wet streaks on his face. Obi stood in front of the Jeep, his eye swollen. He'd been crying but Stu knew that it was not from the physical blow he'd struck. As Stu approached the Jeep, Obi reached out and gripped the handle of the suitcase. Stu resisted, holding on, their hands touched; Obi won, taking the suitcase and tossing it deftly into the back seat.

"Where are you going so late? You know the road is dangerous this time." Obi got into the driver's seat.

"The city. What are you doing?"

"I'm driving you. I'm the chauffeur, remember?"

"The project is finished. Your services are no longer required."

"I'm driving. I'm your friend."

"You're fired." He replaced Obi in the driver's seat and shut the car door. "Give me the key." He turned it in the ignition and the motor began coughing, spitting, and then finally hummed its familiar tune.

"Be careful, Stu." Obi touched the back of his neck and rubbed it lightly.

"Be careful, homeboy." Stu shifted the car into first and rolled out the compound toward the main road. At the gate the ever-dozing guard woke up. He opened the gate and waved bewildered as Stu passed. He did not wave back.

On the road, the Ntalan sky opened before him. It struck him as serenely beautiful, untouched. Perhaps he'd never thought of Africa as anything more than a life-sized postcard, a moving breathing tourist brochure. And even the years he'd spent living and working in the villages, towns, and major cities, crossroads of black life, were nothing more than stepping into (and then out of) still life. There was never a sense of belonging, only of tolerance, mutual, guarded, and temporary.

He was glad it was night. He knew that in each of the tightly knit villages scattered along this main artery lived young black men with big chests and open shirts. In the light of day, they tantalized him with smiles and the aroma of dust and work and hidden, dark places on the body, their physical closeness deceptive in its inaccessibility.

If he made good time he'd be in the capital by morning. It was Tuesday. He could catch a flight to New York on Thursday. And then? And then. The wind whistled past his ears. His hair caught it. It did not rise. It did not move.

○

The plane touched down heavily and after a series of runs and turns came to a definitive stop in Ntalan soil. The Belgian dowager sighed, relieved, and crossed herself again. Stu reached into his travel bag for a mirror. He brushed his hair forward, the slight thinning in the front hardly noticeable. He looked out the window to the terrace.

He spotted them amidst the crowd. They had come. Kate and the beautiful little redheaded boy he recognized from the photos she'd sent year after year (despite his lack of response), a walking replica of his father in everything except color. The scene on the terrace was familiar. Waiters in white coats darted between tables to catch the fleeing customers running to meet their cousins, brothers, lovers coming from America, from the land of plenty. Only one person was missing.

It was the Fever that had taken Obi, the four-letter thing that had come to mean death and destruction in the States, that had ravaged Stu's circle of friends and left his address book bleeding with gaping white sores, victim of white-out, numbers remembered but disconnected, no longer needed. It was the thinning disease that had taken Obi. That had left Kate an uncertain widow and had left this beautiful caramel-colored boy fatherless. And now Stu had come back to turn a new page in his life, to help his best friend, a white woman, raise a black boy to manhood, to perhaps rediscover his own manhood, lost somewhere between the coast of Africa and his youth.

The Burinkabé stood at the door of the first-class cabin, saying goodbye to the passengers. "Welcome home," he said to Stu and smiled, engaging, promising with teeth and a decidedly warm handshake.

"Thank you," Stu returned the warm press of flesh. But this was not the time. On the tarmac, Ntala buzzed with languages he'd not heard for years. He listened to the world as he walked to meet those who awaited him.

Brothers loving brothers

Respect yourself, my brother,
for we are so many wondrous things.

Like a black rose,
you are a rarity to be found.
Our leaves intertwine as I reach out to you
after the release of a gentle rain.

You precious gem,
black pearl that warms the heart,
symbol of ageless wisdom,
I derive strength
from the touch of your hand.

Our lives blend together
like rays of light;
we are men of color,
adorned in shades of tan, red,
beige, black, and brown.

Brothers born from the same earth womb.
Brothers reaching for the same star.

Love me as your equal.
Love me, brother to brother.

III. Hold tight, gently

WRATH

An infected planet

My body is disintegrating
in the fires that created it
I am becoming a planet
Lumps rise on my skin like tiny hills
where shepherds bring their sheep to graze
Rashes like the lake of fire
into which Lucifer was cast
crisscross my flesh
Dry white areas appear
in my mouth and throat
like the sun-bleached sands
of some desert
where a sultan relaxes
with his harem
My bowels are a river
constantly flowing like the Nile
or more appropriately
the Delaware
I am too tired to move
so nothing disturbs the tranquility
of the planet I am becoming
except the occasional tremor
when I shiver with fever
or the all-too-frequent earthquakes
when I convulse in agony
I am a planet
in the agonies of being born

This is not AIDS I suffer
It's not a result
of not practicing safe sex
These are not blisters but land masses
being formed on my nose and eyelids
in my anus
it is not sweat that dampens my sheets
but rather I am becoming
a tropical rain forest
and no
these are not tears
that you see on my face
just a trickle of fresh water
from an underground spring.

ESSEX HEMPHILL

When my brother fell

for Joseph Beam

When my brother fell
I picked up his weapons
and never once questioned
whether I could carry
the weight and grief,
the responsibility
he shouldered.
I never questioned
whether I could aim
or be as precise as he.
I only knew he had fallen
and the passing ceremonies
marking his death
did not stop the war.

Standing at the front lines
flanked by able brothers
who miss his eloquent courage,
his insistent voice
urging us to rebel,
urging us not to fear embracing
for more than sex,
for more than kisses
and notches in our belts.

Our loss is greater
than all the space

we fill with prayers
and praise.
He burned out
his pure life force
to bring us dignity,
to bring us a chance
to love ourselves
with commitment.
He knew the simple
spilling of seed
would not be enough
to bind us.

It is difficult
to stop marching, Joseph,
impossible to stop our assault.
The tributes and testimonies
in your honor
flare up like torches.
Every night
a light blazes for you
in one of our hearts.

There was no one lonelier
than you, Joseph.
Perhaps you wanted love
so desperately and pleaded
with God for the only mercy
that could be spared.
Perhaps God knew
you couldn't be given
more than public love
in this lifetime.

When I stand
on the front lines now,
cussing the lack of truth,
the absence of willful change
and strategic coalitions,
I realize sewing quilts
will not bring you back
nor save us.

It's too soon
to make monuments

for all we are losing,
for the lack of truth
as to why we are dying,
who wants us dead,
what purpose does it serve?

When my brother fell
I picked up his weapons.
I didn't question
whether I could aim
or be as precise as he.
A needle and thread
were not among
his things
I found.

ROGER V. PAMPLIN, JR.

It happened to me

Here I sit at County/USC Hospital in Los Angeles, hating the existence of a very small creature. An organism so small it takes a microscope to see it. So deadly, it has claimed thousands of people's lives, many of my friends included. A little fiend that has changed my life in so many ways that I can't keep count. This tiny killer is AIDS and I'm a person with AIDS (PWA). I hate it with all my heart. I sit here crying and thinking why didn't I listen to the news when word of the disease first surfaced? I'm an intelligent, young, black man with a good education. All I had to do was open my eyes and read the information that was there. Or just open my ears and listen.

But I didn't.

Oh, I'm intelligent all right, too smart for my own damn good. You see, I thought like a whole lot of people think, it will never happen to me, or that AIDS only happens to white, limp-wristed gays, or (this is the *big* excuse) I'm always a top, never a bottom man. So I continued my ways, having sex with people I didn't know, working the clubs and adult bookstores, having three-way and four-way sex, smoking dope and drinking until I was so high that all I cared about was who I could have that night. And I figured, why use condoms? I'm safe (I'm a top, remember?). Besides, condoms are a pain, and I like the feel of flesh against flesh.

I wish I had listened and believed. Here I sit at Los Angeles County/USC Hospital with my third bout of PCP and a host of other medical problems, to bear witness that anyone can catch AIDS.

❂

I was diagnosed with AIDS in June of 1987. My lover (at that time) and I had been sick with flu-like symptoms for about two months. I went to a neighborhood clinic, while my lover tried home remedies. Because I didn't fit the stereotype of a gay man or an IV drug user, my doctor didn't suggest that I take an HIV test. He said that all I had was a bad case of bronchitis and prescribed an antibiotic. The medicine helped some and I got a little better, but I was still weak and still couldn't breathe well. I was relieved it wasn't the Big A, and went back to work.

My friend continued to deteriorate before my eyes, but refused to seek medical attention, until the night I had to drag him physically to the emergency room. While he was in the hospital, for the first time, I sat and thought rationally. Colds, flu, and bronchitis don't last for three and four months, and because of my past behaviors, if anyone was a candidate for AIDS, it was me.

So I went and had the HIV test and it came back positive. At about the same time, my friend was diagnosed with ARC (AIDS Related Complications). I received counseling at the Gay and Lesbian Community Services Center and was told not to be discouraged because being HIV-positive didn't mean I would come down with AIDS.

So once again I held on to my denial of having AIDS. My friend eventually got better and was released from the hospital. In the interim I had embarked on my acting career. I landed a small part in a movie and had just gotten the lead role in an off-Hollywood play. I was on top of the world and felt everything was going to be all right.

During rehearsals for the play, I began getting sick again, so I went back to the same doctor. This time, I was honest and told him about my positive test results. He looked me square in the eye and said that he could no longer help me and that I should go to the hospital. The first words out of my mouth were, "Can't that wait? The play opens within the week." The doc said, "No. Go immediately."

Off I went to County General Emergency Room, where I was admitted within an hour (a hospital record). A few days later, I got the news from my new doctor: "Mr. Pamplin, you have PCP pneumonia, which is one of the two major diseases that accompany AIDS."

Two weeks and a holiday later (I spent the Fourth of July in the hospital), I was released and sent home. As I lay in my bed still sick from PCP and the medicines, it hit me: I have AIDS. I am going to die. Not just die, but waste away, die a horrible, painful death. I thought I'd never see my kids grow up, or love someone again, or play in the park with my dogs again. I was scared and angry at the whole world, especially God.

❂

It has been almost two years since then, and I'm still here. My friend, Robbie, wasn't so lucky. He died from PCP two months after his release from the hospital. I'm still here only through the grace of God. I have the best support system a person could have.

First and foremost, I have God in my life. Before I didn't. Then there is my family in Chicago. And my spouse, Deryl, who sticks by me through thick and thin. Then there is my best buddy, Greg Hill, and a host of other friends too numerous to name. Besides all these loved ones, I have my will to fight, to survive.

Oh, believe me, I get tired of being sick and sometimes I wish God would call me on home. I've even considered suicide (even to this day). The only reason I haven't done it is because of my strong belief that God isn't done with me yet — that He (or She) still has work for me to accomplish. Maybe it's to educate someone about the HIV infection to keep them from making the same mistakes that I did, or maybe it's to help another PWA through hard times. I really don't know. It's all God's will. I continue to pray that God will keep using me in whatever ways possible — that He will continue to give me strength and guidance on this journey through life.

I didn't always feel this way. At first I was angry with God. I mean, what kind of God creates such a monster? What kind of God lets so many people die? And then there is the question we've all asked at one time or another: Why me? Why me, God? Have I been that bad? Since then I've thought: Why not me? I had an active choice in the matter. I decided not to listen and modify my behavior, so I can't blame anyone but myself: Roger Pamplin. Besides, maybe God has a purpose behind this whole thing. Maybe God is using me to reach out to others. I hope so. I wouldn't wish this disease on my worst enemy.

I hope you listen carefully to my story and take heed. I hope you realize anyone can catch AIDS. Protect yourself with knowledge and condoms. And please change your sexual behavior. AIDS is real and it's gonna be around a while. Remember that blacks (and others) do catch AIDS. I know. I'm a witness.

DERYL K. DEESE

Letter to Roger

Dear Roger,

It's been three weeks since you passed away, and it still hurts as much as it did when I saw you take your last breath. I promised you two and a half years ago that I would be there with you through the end. I'm glad I could keep my promise to you. Even though I had a long time to prepare for your passing, it didn't make it any easier for me. I remember telling you as you lay there in the hospice the last two days to let go and cross over and that I'd be okay. Well, I lied. I knew that I wouldn't be fine, but it tore me apart to see you like that. I was glad when you finally let go, only because you weren't in any more pain. You no longer had to deal with having needles stuck in you or a bedside full of medicines to take every four hours. No more hospital beds, no more crying. I have to admit, even though I was glad, I was also a little angry because I couldn't go with you, because I felt as though you left me, and also because no matter what I did or how many times I told you I loved you there was nothing I could do to keep the pain away or keep you here.

Over the course of your illness I felt so helpless, particularly this last year. Even though I rubbed your feet and hands, they continued to hurt. Each day I watched you get a bit more weak. As your appetite grew smaller, and you struggled to eat what little you did, I got angry and yelled at you, but it was only because I was frustrated. All I could do was watch you waste away. It killed me inside to watch you get weaker. There were days when I wanted to cry, but I had to be strong for you and your son, little Roger.

Remember when you asked me a few months ago if I would end your life for you if you began to suffer? I remember how angry you were when I said that I couldn't do it. But baby, as you lay there during your last two days I thought about taking the pillow and putting it over your face many times. I just couldn't bring myself to do that. I couldn't play God.

I miss you so much, honey. My life isn't the same without you anymore. Sometimes I get so lonely and hurt so much that all I do is curl up and hold myself until it passes. What should be home doesn't feel like home, not without you. It's only a place for me to lay my head at night. I avoid going "home" because if I do, I have to face the fact that you won't be there.

I'm not motivated to do anything but get out of bed and go to the gym. It's funny though, sometimes I can hear your voice pushing me like when we trained together. I miss the way we used to hold and kiss each other. I miss the love we made and the way we made each other feel so very special. Every time you looked at me I could see the love in your eyes; I could feel it every time we touched. I miss walking hand in hand with you, or kissing you in public. Roger, you were everything and more than I ever wanted in a mate. I'll never forget the day we stood in front of our family and friends and were married by Reverend Carl Bean. That was the happiest day of my life, being a gay man and marrying the man I loved.

I can't help but feel cheated that all we had was three years together, but then I look at other people and realize they never find the kind of love we shared. God truly blessed us by allowing us to find each other and to have the kind of love we had, even through AIDS.

I feel so empty without you. When you left, you took so much of me with you. I wish I could have gone with you, but unfortunately it isn't my time yet. I'm sure that with time I'll be able to go on, but right now it's still very hard for me. All the memories, both good and bad, still hurt. Sometimes I cry and don't even realize that I'm crying. The love we shared was so powerful, baby.

Thank you for your love and your courage to stand with me as my spouse and friend. Thank you for working out all of our problems with me and making our love stronger in the process. Thank you for fighting this virus the way you did, because each time I looked in your eyes I found the strength to hang in there. You are the best thing that ever happened in my life. There is no one who could ever take your place and move me like you did. Because of you my life is so much better, but at the same time, the emptiness and loneliness I feel hurt so much.

I know that you are happy now with the Lord and I am happy for you. When you hear me crying at night, please come to me and hold me like you used to. You will always be a part of me and I guess now nothing can separate us. When it's my time to cross over, you'll be there to help me across. Until that time, my life goes on and I'll live it and love you as I always did. I love you, Roger.

Your baby always,
Deryl

DAVID FRECHETTE

"Non, Je Ne Regrette Rien"

for Keith Barrow and Larry McKeithan

> *I had big fun if I don't get well no more.*
> —"Going Down Slow"
> as sung by Bobby "Blue" Bland

Sister Chitlin', Brother Neck Bone and
Several of their oxymoron minions
Circle round my sick room,
Swathed in paper surgical gowns.

Brandishing crosses, clutching bibles,
(God, *please* don't let them sing hymns!)
Pestering me to recant the
Wicked ways that brought me here.

"Renounce your sins and return to Jesus!"
Shouts one of the zealous flock.
"The truth is I never left Him,"
I reply with a fingersnap.
"Don't you wish you'd chosen a *normal* lifestyle?"
"Sister, for *me*, I'm *sure* I did."

Let the congregation work overtime
For my eleventh-hour conversion.
Their futile efforts fortify
My unrepentant resolve.

Though my body be racked by
Capricious pains and fevers,
I'm not even *about* to yield to
Fashionable gay Black temptation.

Mother Piaf's second greatest hit title
Is taped to the inside of my brain
And silently repeated like a mantra:
"Non, Je Ne Regrette Rien."

I don't regret the hot Latino boxer
I made love to on Riverside Drive
Prior to a Washington march.
I don't regret wild Jersey nights
Spent in the arms of conflicted satyrs;
I don't regret late night and early a.m.
Encounters with world-class insatiables.

My only regrets are being ill,
Bed-ridden and having no boyfriend
To pray over me.
And that now I'll never see Europe
Or my African homeland except
In photos in a book or magazine.

Engrave on my tombstone:
"Here sleeps a *happy* Black faggot
Who lived to love and died
With no guilt."

No, I regret nothing
Of the gay life I've led and
There's no way in Heaven or Hell
I'll let anyone make me.

WALTER RICO BURRELL

The Scarlet Letter, revisited
A very different AIDS diary

November 3, 1988 — My birthday is tomorrow (the 4th), but since that's a Saturday, the women at the office (I'm the only man) threw a party for me today. I had a very difficult time maintaining a smiling, enthusiastic façade. Everyone was so nice and I didn't want to disappoint them. Couldn't they see how skinny and weak I look? I'm sure they did. They probably didn't want to embarrass me by mentioning it. At least not in front of my face.

It's this damn flu I've had for the past few weeks. The worst I've ever had in my entire life. Chills, fever, sweating so profusely at night that I'd wake up in the morning to drenched sheets. No appetite. The mere thought of food brings me very near regurgitation, even though there's nothing to throw up. And the smell of food is even worse. Extreme nausea forces me to nearly collapse.

Thinking back on this flu, though, I can say that I didn't miss even one day of work. Not one! Even though I lost nearly 25 pounds and had to drag my body out of the bed and into the office with the greatest effort. Sometimes I actually felt as though I was going to lose consciousness. God! I hope it isn't the Big "A" — AIDS. Naw. You don't get over the Big "A." Once that hits you, you die. And I'm getting better. The fever has left. The delirium has ceased. Now, if I can just get my appetite to return, gain some weight, and get on with my life.

Man. This has been the worst flu I've ever experienced.

❂

November 8, 1988 — I saw the pictures from the party today and, man, do I look terrible! Like an emaciated scarecrow. There's one shot of me being hugged by a couple of the women. Only it looks more like they're holding me up. I shuddered when I first saw the pictures, trying not to let the people around me see my reaction. I never looked like this with any other flu I ever had. And my appetite is showing no sign of returning. Even though I've gained a little weight, I'm still only 162 pounds. Down from a normal weight of close to 180 or so. Something isn't right here. This is no normal flu.

✸

Christmas, 1988 — I'm still showing very slow signs of recovery. And there's something new: dark purple, raised blotches appearing on my arms and lower legs. And my feet are turning purple, as though the blood is coagulating and my feet are dying. I'm losing feeling in my big toes as they get darker and darker. My face is also getting darker, which is weird, since I've always been a very light brown color. Some darker people have even referred to me as high yella, though that was, at least in my opinion, an exaggeration. My fingers are changing, too. I was always so proud of my fingers. They had pink coloring under the nails and white moons at the tops near the cuticles. I always felt my hands were among my better features. When I looked at them the other day I was shocked. The pink flesh has been replaced by the ugliest of dark, dead tones. My fingers are almost black beneath the nails. My first thought upon seeing this was a mental image I've carried for years of monkey fingers. During the early years of my marriage, my ex-wife worked in research (neuroendocrinology and cardiology) at UCLA, and once when I visited her laboratory I saw these pitiful, frail little monkeys. Aside from their pleading, sorrowful eyes, which stared out from faces capped with plaster of paris globs holding electrodes in their unwilling brains, I remember their cold, tiny hands jutting out of their cages when I approached. They wanted to touch me. Not to harm me, but, I suspected, simply to make contact with another living being in a social, as opposed to merely clinical, manner. My heart sank when I saw them, and I remember those hands because in addition to being tiny replicas of human hands, the flesh under the miniature fingernails was black. Now my own formerly great human fingers resemble larger-scaled versions of those black monkey fingers. I'm so ashamed of the fingers now. Several people have made comments and I quickly responded that it was because I'm a black man. Some darker-skinned black men do have such black flesh beneath the nails of their fingers and toes.

I've noticed something else: a lightheadedness. Sometimes I become dizzy and have to struggle to remain standing. Sometimes I have to concentrate really hard to remain conscious. The other day I felt myself losing consciousness and walked over to the health center at the university where I work as a writer (my actual title is manager) in the Public Affairs Office. When I got to the center, I was standing at the counter describing my symptoms to one of the nurses when I simply fainted. The next thing I remembered was waking up on a bed somewhere in the center. A nurse with warm hands and an equally warm, maternal smile was taking my blood pressure. She put her soft, time-worn hand on my forehead and it felt so good. I closed my eyes and hoped she could leave her hand there forever. I tried to sit up, but the room started tipping over on its edge like one of those rooms in the fun house at a carnival. The nurse reprimanded me and said I'd have to continue to lie down for at least another half-hour. I made up my mind to see a doctor, even though I'm terrified of what I may discover.

✪

January 9, 1989 — I've decided to find out what's going on inside my body. Something is terribly wrong and I've simply got to know what it is. Of course, the biggest fear is that the answer will come back "AIDS," but at least knowing it will end this awful physical and emotional floundering. I've made up my mind to find a black doctor, preferably in the area where I live, Baldwin Hills. I looked on the "list of preferred physicians" supplied by the benefits office here at Cal State L.A. and selected one in The Community, assuming the doctor would be black. Just to make sure, when I called his secretary to make an appointment, I asked if he were black and was assured that he was. He looked just as I thought he would: in his sixties, conservative, fair-skinned, paternal. He examined me, but told me nothing. I could see in his face that he had an idea of what my problem was, but he didn't want to tell me. That was the moment I instinctively knew I had AIDS. An all-consuming hot flash swept over my entire body. The doctor droned on about the symptoms and the possibilities, never once mentioning the dreaded "A" word, and took some blood. When I spoke with him again by phone, he first said the tests had been delayed, then that they were inconclusive. He wanted me to see a colleague of his, a dermatologist also located on Santa Rosalia Drive. My meeting with this second doctor left things equally unresolved. He was a physical and spiritual clone of the first, and his examination was equally as cryptic. He tried hard to appear casual following his cursory examination, but I felt the same embarrassment and reluctance to be candid on his part that I had experienced earlier.

I remember sitting in his examining room and experiencing the most incredible sense of calm. I have AIDS, I thought, and these doctors don't want to tell me, nor do they want to take me on as a patient, but at least I'm not afraid anymore. If anyone had asked me several months ago (even yesterday!) to predict how I would have reacted to such a terrifying situation, I probably would have conjured up reactions of stark terror, panic — the worst possible emotional scenario. But there I was in that exact situation and the dominant feeling I experienced was a soothing, all-embracing peacefulness The real terror, that of uncertainty and fear of the unknown, was gone.

"I've never seen anything quite like what you have," the dermatologist said in drawn-out, baritone, Southern tones.

"What do I do now?" I asked feebly, knowing full well this was going absolutely nowhere.

"I think you should consult a specialist, someone conversant in internal medicine."

I decided not to remind him that I was referred to him by just such an internist.

I left the doctor's office feeling frightened and isolated. I will never forget the disdain and condescension that were so blatant in the faces of those two good doctors. I was surprised at how calm I felt. I knew I had AIDS. I knew it as surely as I knew the sun would rise the following day. And I felt so genuinely sorry for the doctors. AIDS was totally out of the realm of their medical and social realities. They were simply too old, too established in their predictable, comfortable worlds to be introduced to AIDS and its myriad implications. The world will quite simply leave them behind to wither away in their self-imposed ignorance as it fights to understand and deal with this newest, most devastating emotional and medical challenge.

As I climbed into my little Daihatsu and drove away from Santa Rosalia Drive that morning, my purple feet throbbing inside my loafers, I felt a quiet desperation verging on doom.

❂

February 6, 1989 — I gleaned my "list of preferred physicians" and came up this time with a third name, in the 3400 block of Wilshire Boulevard, an area where most of the physicians are white. The hell with trying to find a black doctor. My life is on the line here. At this point I simply want a diagnosis and whatever treatment is possible. I called today to make an appointment and was impressed with the swiftness and professional manner of the people on the phone. The doctor will see me tomorrow.

Tonight as I stepped from the shower I caught a glimpse of myself in the mirror and was horrified. I'm so skinny, and the purple, raised blotches are showing up all over my legs and arms. And they seem to be growing. I feel as though something alien is in control of my body; something intensely evil that is intent not only on taking my very life but taking it in a drawn-out, horrible, long-suffering way, as if to punish me for having committed some dark, unpardonable deed by inflicting my mind and body with excruciating pain and ceaseless humiliation. I try to overrule it, but a small voice in the back of my mind continues to naggingly suggest what I'm being punished for. It's the same thing that was a reason for my divorce. It's at the root of my estrangement from my son. It's the very sexual act through which I contracted this disgusting virus in the first place.

On one rational, intelligent, commonsense level, I know that the puritanical outcries against homosexuality are wrong. I know that my own manhood is not determined by the sex of the person with whom I choose to sleep. I know that AIDS is not, as many religious fundamentalists proclaim so loudly, a punishment heaped on sinning homosexuals. I know all of that, but still, that nagging suggestion haunts me, as it surely must haunt all men who dare to stray across traditional heterosexual lines.

I turned off the bathroom light so I wouldn't have to look at myself. There was comfort and reassurance in the dark. I groped my way through the unlit hallway to my bedroom and sat on the edge of my bed. My friend and constant companion, Shaka, a 120-pound Rhodesian Ridgeback dog, followed me through the darkness into the room, sensing that something wasn't right. As I contemplated what I imagined to be the horror of the coming months and my certain, impending death, I sat naked in the dark, slowly lowered my face into my hands, and sobbed deep, rocking cries of the utmost despair. Shaka whined softly, sympathetically, and licked the salty tears from my face.

My thoughts drifted to a book I'd read way back in grade school, *The Scarlet Letter*, by Nathaniel Hawthorne. I remembered the heroine, who, accused of committing adultery with a married preacher, was forced to wear a scarlet "A," for adulteress, on her clothing so all the townspeople would know of her sin. Like her, I'm forced to wear my own scarlet letter in the form of these abominable purple blotches; a blazing visual condemnation for all the world to see so they can pass judgment on me and become part of my perpetual penance.

I slowly slipped my frail, blotched body under the covers, clinging to the comforting blackness of the room like a shroud, and the tears flowed as they never had before.

❂

February 7, 1989 — My new doctor is a nice, clinical, takin'-care-of-business type. Tall, white, neatly dressed in a suit and tie, busy, no nonsense, no coddling. He questioned me for a full forty-five minutes before he began his physical examination. He asked me questions no doctor had ever asked before. That was a first for me as far as physical exams go. I was impressed. He asked me about my sexual encounters, their frequency, whether or not anal sex was involved. I was as surprised at the apparent ease with which I responded as with his forth-rightness in asking the questions. His interview demeanor was nonjudgmental, warm; clinical and thorough, yet humanistic. I liked him from the start.

I told him about the flu I'd had, how it had dragged on for several weeks, the weight I'd lost. I told him everything I could think of relating to the illness.

"Is it AIDS?"

"The symptoms could indicate several things, AIDS included. I recommend a thorough series of blood tests, then we'll take it from there. If it is AIDS, there are alternatives available today that weren't available as recently as six months ago. I can get rid of the purple lesions. You can feel better."

"Then let's do it."

Did I really say that? He drew several vials of dark blood. I thanked him for taking me on as a patient, then I left. The mere act of meeting with him made me feel better, both physically and emotionally. I left his office feeling I was finally, after virtually years of blind, ignorant fear, on the right track.

❂

February 9, 1989 — The doctor called around 10:00 a.m. A hot flash swept over me so fast that I became dizzy and almost lost control of my voice. I felt suddenly that I had to go to the bathroom. I took a couple of deep breaths.

"Well, your test results are back."

"And?"

"You want me to tell you on the phone?"

"I figure we're both grown men. I'm gonna have to deal with it one way or the other anyway. Go ahead."

"Well, it is AIDS."

A silence followed which seemed to swallow us both. The word *AIDS* echoed in my brain like the Notre Dame bells rung by Quasimodo. Then, slowly, the peaceful feeling I had experienced in the first doctor's office returned. I smiled to myself, the kind of smile that recognizes not something funny but something ironic. I thought to myself that now I was one of those people with AIDS. I recalled a guy I'd known who'd attended a meeting at my house a couple of summers ago. He was suffering miserably from AIDS and had asked for a glass of water. When he finished, I debated with myself as to whether I should wash the glass or throw it away. I considered the dilemma briefly, then threw it into the trash and returned to the meeting, confused and ashamed. A month later, the guy was dead.

"Are we talking years as opposed to months?"

"I certainly think so."

"Where do we go from here?"

"I want to start you on medication immediately. And there's something you might have a problem with."

What could possibly be a problem when the alternative is death, I thought to myself.

"What's that?"

"You're going to have to take this medicine every four hours, which means that you'll have to wake up during the night."

"Are you serious? We're talkin' about the literal difference between my life and death and you think I'll object to waking up at night to take a goddamn pill?"

"Don't speak too quickly. A lot of people simply can't adjust."

"Faced with such a choice, how can they not adjust?"

He decided that I would take 200 milligrams of a derivative of the drug AZT, at 10:00 a.m., 2:00 p.m., 6:00 p.m., 10:00 p.m., 2:00 a.m., and 6:00 a.m.

"There's a lot going on in the area of AIDS research nowadays. There are encouraging new drugs on the horizon, so we'll fight this thing a day at a time. You hang in there. I think you're going to do fine. Your body has fought a good fight by itself. Now, let's give it some help."

I hung up the phone and just stared at it for a few moments. I was emotionally numb. I had confided in a friend and coworker, a woman I'd come to care a great deal for, and told her that I feared I might be HIV-positive and that I was having myself tested. Now I told her the results were positive.

This lady is one of those amazing people who is loved and trusted by virtually everyone. People who can't stand each other still manage to like her. And she has a reputation around campus for keeping a secret. When you tell her something, you can be sure it's not going any further.

My doctor suggested that I not tell anyone at my job about being HIV-positive. I decided that this particular coworker, who was also my closest friend, would be the only exception. Jesus! I had to have someone to share this incredible secret with. And she was wonderful.

"You're going to be fine," she responded without hesitation, and even though I had difficulty believing her at that moment, I needed to hear her say just that.

When I took the prescription to a local drugstore near the doctor's office, the middle-aged, obviously gay pharmacist was very short and rude with me. I handed him my Blue Shield medical card and he tossed it back to me.

"This prescription is going to cost more than two hundred dollars and we aren't allowed to make any third-party transactions on a sum that large."

"But my insurance will pay for this," I pleaded.

"Then I suggest you pay cash and bill them later."

"Thanks a lot," I retorted as sarcastically as possible.

Jesus! I thought. Was I going to have a major problem getting this prescription filled? I could see months of fighting with pharmacies over this medicine that I needed to literally stay alive. It was bad enough I had AIDS. Now I was going to have to fight to get the very medicine I needed to hold the disease at bay. I immediately thought about all the street people, poor people, people who didn't have the resources I had, the job I had, the insurance I had. Christ! What would happen to them? Were they doomed to death simply because they're not middle-class enough to afford to fight AIDS? I left the pharmacy more angry than depressed.

I decided to go to the Thrifty drugstore in my neighborhood. They were wonderful. The sister behind the counter didn't hesitate as she took the card, ran it through her machine, and told me the prescription would be ready in an hour or so. I breathed a sigh of genuine relief.

❂

March 15, 1989 — Wow! The difference in the way I feel since I've been on the AZT medication is phenomenal. Aside from a little drugginess once in a while, I hardly know it's in my body. And waking up at night is a cinch. I simply roll over and go right back to sleep. I put exactly the number of pills I need to take on the nightstand and in the morning, they're all gone. Most of the time, I don't even remember taking them. I've always enjoyed sleeping anyway. At times, I suspect I even use it as a means of escape from unpleasant reality. I remember falling asleep in the waiting room at Daniel Freeman Hospital in Inglewood while my mother was dying. They had to wake me to tell me she had died. So waking up in the night to take the pills is no problem. I could go on like this for years. Certainly, I can go on until a better drug or, hopefully, a cure comes along.

I suppose I've known all along that I was going to face this basically alone, with the exception of my coworker and my doctor. The doctor has suggested that I join a support group of other AIDS patients, but the last thing I want to see is other AIDS patients suffering, dying, wasting away. I'll fight my demons by myself. And while I'm doing it, I'll go on with my life as normally as possible. I will not become a flag-waving, consummate AIDS patient. That sounds depressing.

❂

June 14, 1989 — The change in the drug's effect on me has been drastic. I sometimes think it's worse than the AIDS disease itself. In the beginning, when I first began taking AZT, it was great. I actually felt normal most of the time. Now, however, I'm nearly always consumed by a heavy, drugged feeling. My legs feel heavy and I sleep a lot. Sometimes the muscles in my cheeks and neck twitch and I am almost constantly being attacked by the drug; there are recurring headaches, stomach pains, loss of appetite, dizziness, a terrible taste in my mouth, and a ringing in my ears. But the worst thing is the drugged feeling, which inevitably brings acute depression and melancholy that lasts for hours, sometimes days. It's so very difficult under these physical conditions to put forth a façade of cheerfulness, especially at work. Yet during all of this, I've yet to miss a single day of work. Even during those terrible days before I was diagnosed and thought I had the flu and lost nearly twenty-five pounds, I still managed to drag myself to the office, and if anyone suspected anything, they never said it to me.

❂

September 27, 1989 — I simply can't take this drug anymore. I've been thinking a lot about death lately. I have fantasies about throwing away all my AZT pills and just letting the disease take over and run its course. Surely, death would be a welcomed release after the roller coaster hell AZT has put me through. And to think I go to work every day and attend meetings and write stories and do photography and all sorts of other people-oriented activities.

Ever since my initial visit in February 1989, I've been returning to my doctor's office once every month to have my blood drawn and tested to make sure my white blood cell count is okay. He always asks me if I'm feeling all right and I answer enthusiastically that I'm doing just fine. What else am I to say? That I'm feeling lousy? And what would be the alternative? As far as I know, the only alternative is death, so complaining wouldn't help a damn bit. But this time when he asked me how I was feeling, tears welled up in my aching eyes and I actually told him the truth: that I simply couldn't take even one more day of AZT.

He looked at me with more compassion than I ever saw him express and said, "You've been on AZT for six months now. I think it's time to adjust your medication."

And just like that he came up with a possible solution to the nightmare AZT had become. He kept me on AZT for four of the daily medications, but switched me to another antiviral medicine for the other two medications, which I will now take at 6:00 a.m. and 6:00 p.m. Perhaps there is a God in heaven after all. The new medication doesn't have the harsh side effects common to AZT. I have my fingers crossed, but considering the alternative, what choice do I have?

❂

October 16, 1989 — Knowing that this virus is flowing through my veins has forced me to focus more sharply on how I see myself, what's really important in life, and, perhaps most importantly, what I will leave behind.

Since my very earliest recollections, I've always wanted to be a father. And as sexist as it will perhaps sound, I always thought in terms of having a son. I've talked with many men and boys over the years and nearly all of them have admitted having had similar or identical thoughts throughout their lives. There's a very special bonding between

–129–

fathers and sons, just as there must be between mothers and daughters.

I also decided very early in my life (I can recall thinking about it as early as age ten) that I wanted to be the kind of father I never had. Not that my father wasn't a great provider, because he was. Our family's living standards, especially during the fifties and sixties, were noticeably above the vast majority of black Americans throughout the country. I didn't realize it at the time, but during those years few black families could boast of three generations of graduates from the same black university (Hampton), a head-of-household who was a successful mechanical designing engineer (for Hughes Aircraft Company), and a home in a predominantly white suburb of Los Angeles. So the physical needs for my parents, two brothers, and sister were being met. It was in the area of emotional nurturing that there was a very definite need.

My father and I have a truly warm, loving, mutually supportive relationship these days, but I remember him through the filtered haze of childhood as being an extremely volatile, mean, unfriendly, and emotionally hostile man. I was terrified of him. All of us were, including my mother. He screamed and yelled and slammed things about. Plates of food would go crashing against walls unexpectedly. We kids would hope among ourselves that something would delay him at work so we could have a couple more hours of peace before he came home.

As an adult, I came to understand some of the deeply rooted reasons for his intense anger. In many ways, he was born a couple of generations ahead of his time. He was so bright and articulate: a very talented, creative mechanical-draftsman-turned-engineer. But he was also black, and during the forties and fifties, the two just didn't jell. He contributed greatly to his department at Hughes, but less capable, less productive white males received far more publicity, better salaries, promotions, even credit for work he did. Added to this was the fact that he was far from being one of those handkerchief-head niggers who would grin in the white man's face and scrape and bow and accept whatever was handed down. He stood up for himself, for his manhood; he defended his ability. Naturally, that didn't sit well with the whites.

Even as a child, I viewed him with a mixture of awe and fear. I saw him through my naïve, innocent child's eyes as a powerful, though tyrannical, figure who ruled over and protected us, but only on his conditions. Looking back, it's easy to see that his home was just about the only place where he could exercise such power and control. He certainly had boundaries at his job beyond which he simply could not traverse.

And there were the social constrictions he was forced to contend with, especially those relating to his race. Other black men of his generation were able to adjust, to accept, to make do, but not my father. No one — *no one* — was going to treat him like a nigger. I remember once during the fifties when my father, my younger brother, and I were motoring across country through the South to my grandmother's house in Virginia. We couldn't sleep at night in any of the motels, because nearly all were for whites only, and the ones blacks were allowed to use were so disgusting, Dad wouldn't even consider using them, so we slept in the car.

But we still had to eat and I remember this one particular day when Dad had been driving virtually all day and we were starved. He pulled up to a roadside fast-food joint somewhere in the vast wasteland of redneckville and tried to order some burgers. Without looking into Dad's face, the white proprietor snarled at him that they didn't serve niggers, but that if Dad went around to the back door, they might let him buy a cup of coffee.

I knew something terrible was going to happen when I saw the veins in Daddy's neck begin to bulge and pulsate. My mind flitted from my younger brother to the gun in the glove compartment, then back to the scene being played out in front of the burger joint. My terror mounted when Dad returned to the car, started the engine, and drove slowly around to the back door. His normally brown color was now deep red, and tears of rage welled in his eyes. I prayed he would leave the gun where it was.

He turned off the engine, got out of the car, and approached the dirty, dilapidated screen door hanging defiantly by one rusted hinge to the door frame. The fat, greasy, white man held out a steaming cup of what I supposed was coffee.

"Here you go, boy."

Oh dear god! He didn't call Daddy *boy*!

I slid down in the back seat of the car, trying like hell to become invisible. Dad took the cup, then tossed the scalding contents into the man's face.

"The next time you see a boy, you give 'im that coffee. Meanwhile, you can kiss my black ass!"

My heart pounded fiercely as we sped away down the dirt road and headed back to the highway.

There were many other such incidents where Dad simply refused to be treated in less than a manly way. That was a dangerous attitude for a black man to have during the fifties. It's truly a miracle that he wasn't killed somewhere along the way during those tempestuous times.

Even when his life — or ours — wasn't being threatened by one of these incidents, there was still an incredible amount of tension and embarrassment.

Like the time when I was a senior at Compton (California) High School and my white English teacher failed me on a paper I wrote, accusing me of plagiarism. I'd worked hard on that paper and was proud of it. Since early childhood, I'd always liked — really enjoyed — writing. So I was genuinely hurt when she accused me of cheating.

"You couldn't possibly have written this," she said in a most condescending tone. "Colored children are born with an achievement level beneath that of white children and the sooner you learn to function within your limitations, the happier you'll be."

When I told Dad, I could almost see smoke burst forth from his nostrils. He took his shotgun from the back closet, put two shells into the chambers, motioned me toward the family station wagon, burned rubber peeling out of the driveway, and headed for the high school.

Luckily, he left the shotgun in the car, but he gave my English teacher a tongue-lashing like none other. The principal, another white woman, who boasted of having been the highest-ranking woman in the Navy at one time, was brought in, and my father insisted that I be allowed to sit down in the presence of the assembled gathering, be given a new topic by the teacher, and write another essay. I did, and it was of the same quality as the first.

As I look back on these and similar incidents, I realize the wonderfulness of hindsight. What I originally viewed with fear and embarrassment are now tempered with admiration and unabashed pride.

Still, the one thing dramatically missing from my and my indomitable father's relationship was the kind of closeness that I believe all children need with their parents: a closeness that involves touching and stroking and holding. During all the years I lived under my father's roof, I cannot ever recall even once being held or hugged by him. Neither did I ever see him embrace another man. Even his handshakes were cursory, brief, consummated more out of adherence to polite tradition than out of genuine warmth.

Though I couldn't articulate it as a child, I know now that this physical as well as emotional closeness is one thing I wanted to pass on to my own son one day. And when my children were eventually born, I was indeed very open, warm, and physically demonstrative with them. Contrary to my childhood premonitions, I have emerged far closer to my daughter than to my son, who has refused to speak to me for more than a year now. The last contact I had with him was a terribly depressing letter he wrote to me in September of 1988. He accused me of having disgraced the family and ruined his mother's life. He said he couldn't see how I could possibly hold my head up before the family ever again. Ironically, he said that he had, during his early childhood, been afraid of me (as I had feared my own father!), but that he no longer feared me, and he even went so far as to imply bodily harm to me if we should come face to face.

Needless to say, I was stunned and in no small way confused about the letter, his hostile attitude, and his reluctance to be specific about his grievances toward me. To this day, his chilled attitude and bitter silence have remained the most troubling aspect of my current life, even more than the AIDS virus.

Since those things of any real value that we leave behind after death are usually works of art (writing, music, painting, etc.) or other lifetime accomplishments or children, resolving this thing between my son and myself has taken on a dedication approaching that of the Holy Grail.

I see the black family in danger of extinction, at least from where I sit. Young black girls are having babies and rearing them without the aid of the babies' fathers. I see a lopsided, matriarchal society evolving in the inner cities, and I am brazen enough to contend that it is up to all of us, even gay or bisexual men, to take on the responsibility of piecing it back together before it's too late.

I have felt this way for many years. That was one reason I got married in the first place, but AIDS has made me focus on ideas like this even more acutely.

I want my children, all children, to know and understand that manhood, womanhood, and humanhood are not determined by the sex of the person with whom one chooses to sleep. A man is no less a man because he chooses to sleep with another man instead of (or in addition to) a woman. And neither is one's manhood increased or decreased by what one does in bed, or by who does what to whom.

Manhood, I would tell my wonderful children, is determined by how man lives his life, how he cherishes and guards all forms of life, how he carries himself, how he defends and practices truth, how he applies ethics to everything he does, every decision he makes. Certainly with these standards in mind, a gay man can be just as manly, just as good a husband and father as a so-called straight man, and make just as significant a contribution to society as virtually any other human being, regardless of sexual preference.

Once this is understood, the way is open for gay men and women to either adopt or parent children naturally and in either instance emerge as wonderful, competent, nurturing parents.

It is the lack of belief in this most basic human concept that lies at the heart of the AIDS crisis, and once the long-awaited cure emerges onto the scene, this humanistic aspect of the problem will still cry out to be addressed.

Yes, AIDS certainly does clarify one's thoughts, if only through a sense of urgency. AIDS places restrictions of time on our otherwise timeless, casual attitudes regarding our parting this world. It also forces us, especially those of us who are engaged in this ghastly game of tag with death on an hourly basis, to redefine certain key words which have been used throughout our lives in oddly ambiguous ways. Words like *right, wrong, good, bad, masculine, feminine, normal, natural.*

I've found myself examining such words under the glaring micro-scope of my own individual life and morals and redefining them to fit my standards. Perhaps one of the advantages of knowing of one's impending death is that, if we're wise enough and disciplined enough, we can write a new dictionary for ourselves, digest it, then glory in its singular truth for what time we have left.

❁

October 30, 1989 — Dr. Richard Keeling, the noted AIDS expert who teaches at the University of Virginia, spoke on our campus today. I'd been looking forward with great anticipation to his coming. His medical expertise is augmented with such unbounded compassion. He speaks of the need for all the various strata of society to deal not only with the clinical, medical aspects of this disease, but with homophobia, heterosexism, and racism as well. He manages to combine a medical perspective with that of a social scientist.

While I thoroughly enjoyed listening to him (I sat in the very front row for more than two hours), I left his lecture feeling deeply depressed. He showed horrible slides of people with AIDS who resembled inmates of Nazi concentration camps, and he reminded us that not only is there no cure but a vaccine is at least a decade away, and some researchers say that a vaccine will never be found.

I felt a heavy cloud of doom as I had never experienced before. I can't stop thinking about my own death, when it will come, what I will look like, how long I will linger, whether or not I'll look like those horrible creatures in his slides. All the haunting questions return. Will I have time to resolve the situation with my son? Will I finish the books I'm working on? How many more birthdays will I celebrate? How much longer will I be able to work? Am I fooling myself by becoming excited about the new drugs being tested? How will my family react when they realize that I've died of AIDS? Will they stay away from the funeral? And what will happen to my beloved Shaka?

No one ever said that life would be fair, but this is ridiculous. I am not a bad person. So why do I feel so guilty? I feel guilty about my sexuality, about having AIDS, about having, as my son insists, ruined my wife's life by marrying her, about wanting to be loved at least once before I die in a way that I've never been loved — ever.

I've told myself during the past year that it's perhaps easier for me to deal with the loneliness imposed by AIDS since I've known loneliness and rejection virtually all my life. I've always been on the outside, different, "odd man out," strange, the last kid to be picked to play on the team in P.E. class.

Logic would tell one that such a person's entire life had been spent in preparation for living with (and dying from) AIDS. Well, it just ain't so. The loneliness is even worse, more penetrating, more terrifying. I've memorized every speck on every wall in my house. I've washed every spoon and fork, carefully folded every piece of linen, gone on countless walks and tried my damnedest to go on living a "normal" life. But it's a lie.

The frightening truth is that I have AIDS and there's a bomb ticking away inside me. And I'm alone. It's little wonder that my computer has become my only lover, my ever-present confidant, my father confessor, the recipient of the desperate, passionate regurgitation of my mind and soul in a ceaseless effort to leave something behind; something that will let the world know not only that I was here, but that I was a valid, frightened, compassionate, caring human being who wanted only to be accepted for who and what he was, and who wanted so much to be loved.

There is a terrible temptation here to wallow in extreme self-pity, wailing over the lack of love in my life. Some will undoubtedly interpret these lines in exactly that way. I would say to those readers that I deserve the right to subscribe to my own definition of love, just as I would allow you yours. It is true that I have known the love of friends, family, children. I've even known the very special love of a wife. But all those forms of love have left something lacking, something that defies description with mere words. There is love that extends beyond all these, and it exists between people of different sexes as it does between those of the same sex. I know that it exists, because I have seen it, and it is selfless, uncompromising, and total. It says I accept you just as you are and I would never change you; I know everything about you and I still love you. This love knows no jealousy or insecurity, and communication is achieved as often through exchanging mental energy as it is through words. Some of you who are reading this know what I'm referring to. I want to experience that love at least once before I die. Thus far in my life, I haven't found it. And precious time is running out. To make matters worse, who is going to love someone with AIDS? AIDS patients don't even warrant hugs, much less passionate love. And yet, ironically, it was very often a search for love that exposed many of us to AIDS in the first place.

A wife loves her husband, but, at least in my experience, I suspect that her love is tied very much to what I call the "nesting instinct." How well she is provided for materially plays a big part in the intensity of her love. Children love their parents, but that love is one basically of respect, admiration, and veneration. Friends express love for each other in various ways that encompass respect, trust, mutual interests. And all these various forms of love overlap and intersect.

Still, there's that special, very personal, private, all-encompassing love that goes beyond all of these. The kind that makes the hairs on the back of your neck tingle, that makes you joyous inside, that makes you sit for hours gazing into a fireplace, that makes you think about sharing even an afterlife. And knowing it's possible, attainable, makes me want it even more. AIDS has made me focus on it more intensively, and it's made me realize that I'll more than likely leave this life still longing for it.

ASSOTO SAINT

Hooked for life

There were no tears. There was no time for tears that year. Just a tight knot in the pit of my chest where it hurts more each day. Yet, it had all come to this: a two-pound plastic bag filled with ash, bits of bones, and fragments of teeth that didn't completely burn. It had all come too quickly.

It seems only yesterday that Riis Park bustled with laughter and WBLS blasted everywhere. Beautiful bodies languished on the sand in colorful swimwear. Volleyball players along with joggers ran up and down the beach. Lifeguards whistled to swimmers straying too far. Vendors hawked soft drinks and ice-cream sandwiches. Others hustled cheap cologne and fake gold bracelets. That day of wine and smiles we were all walking on sunshine.

Next to me, on our "I Love New York" beach mat, dreads cascading down his head, Duke eased through his hundred daily push-ups. Every inch of his six-foot taut body glistened deliciously like honey. Many a passing glance sized him up, but the man was all mine and had been for ten years. He was so fine that I paid no attention to a spot on his left foot, right below his big toe; a spot, small ... purple like the stain of a crushed grape.

Soon after, it multiplied like buds on a tree in early spring. It multiplied all over his feet, his legs, up his ass, inside his intestines, all over his face, his neck, down his throat, inside his brains. For nine months of fever and wracking coughs, nine months of sweat and shaking chills, nine months of diarrhea and jerking spasms, it multiplied, and wrenched him skinny like a spider.

"Sky, I don't understand this. I don't want to understand this," Duke said as he awakened from the anesthesia.

"It's all right, baby," I answered, "I'm right here. I know just how you feel."

"No, you don't," he angrily protested. "I'm sick of this hose in my nose. I'm sick of this tube in my dick, all these IV's in my arms. I'm sick of being strapped to this bed," and he coughed out a scream.

"Easy, baby, easy," I whispered, smoothing my gloved hand over the side of his head that they hadn't shaved for the biopsy. I was glad to hear him starting trouble again. I hoped he could see me smiling behind the mask they made me wear.

"I ain't joking," he continued, "I'm really tired and I'd rather be dead."

"Sir Duke, don't you talk like that. You ain't gonna die. You're only thirty-one. You're too young to die. We're gonna beat this shit," I kept repeating, "that's why I want you to come home where you belong. One month is too freaking long to stay cooped up in this room. This hospital food ain't fit for dogs. You'll see, I'm gonna make you strong, baby. We're gonna cheat death, you hear me. Sky and Duke — hooked for life. Come on, say it. Say it like we used to sing all the time. Say it, Duke."

"Sky," he muttered, "I'm gonna die."

"No! No! No!" I kept yelling in the corridor, running to the nurses' station, where three of them stood reviewing charts.

"Here he goes again," one of them whispered.

"Mr. Carter, please calm down," the heavy-set Haitian head nurse told me as she rushed into Duke's room.

"What's the number of the administrator on duty?" I asked this tiny Filipino nurse. "I want to take my lover home."

"Take him home? What do you mean?" she asked.

"I do believe I am speaking English. I said I want to take my lover home."

"But your friend is dying. His brain biopsy shows Kaposi's sarcoma is present."

"*You* are killing him. You and this hospital ain't doing shit for him. You're all idiots," I screamed at her.

"Mr. Carter!" the head nurse summoned me as she walked out of Duke's room.

"What?" I yelled back.

"Stop it! Stop this nonsense right now. You are not going to come into this ward and upset my staff and these patients. No more temper tantrums on this floor. I've told you that many times before. Is that understood?"

I kept quiet, watching the Filipino nurse walk away.

"Mr. Carter!"

"What?"

"I'm still waiting for an answer."

"Understood!" I shouted.

"You can do all the screaming you want as loud as you need, but from now on you do it outside. That's exactly where you should be carrying on in the first place. It's obvious to a duck that if enough of you homosexuals were acting up in the streets the politicians would take you quite seriously and allocate more money for care and research. Now, I don't need to teach you history. You told me you're from the South. From what I used to hear back in Haiti, if most black people in this country hadn't gotten into civil disobedience, marches, sit-ins, and what have you, brother, all of us black people would still be riding at the back of the bus today."

"Really! Fresh off the boat, you should talk, sister," I said sarcastically. She gasped in Creole.

"*Qui sa ou permet ou dim la?*"

"You're probably one of those black folks who *think* that we gays are getting just what we deserve."

"That's way beneath you, Mr. Carter, and I won't bother to dignify your comment with an answer." She started to walk away, but then turned back. "Look around you," she said, "you see all these little cabinets outside these rooms? I don't have to tell you what's in them or why they're standing outside these rooms, do I? Count them. Go ahead, count. That's right, nine! Nine rooms with AIDS patients in a ward of seventeen beds. Nine! Eight young men and one young lady who is so demented the poor thing doesn't even know her name. Do you think I like to see this misery? Do you think it doesn't break my heart to be working in all this hopelessness? I don't like this. I'm telling you I don't like it one bit, but most of us in this hospital are trying to do the very best we can. Unfortunately, that isn't enough. Lord help us all."

I stood facing her in silence.

"Why don't you go get some rest," she said. "You'll be doing your friend and yourself a disservice if you keep up this vigil. Come on, Mr. Carter, sit down. Come — drink some water." She filled a paper cup and put it to my lips. "It's all right," she said, "I understand." And she held me.

❁

From then on I wasted no time. My indefinite leave of absence from work was approved rather quickly. Ever since the day I told my coworkers about Duke's illness and why I've been so stressed, they've been wiping the office phones that I use with alcohol. This year they asked me to bring rum and vodka to the Christmas party instead of my tasty fritters, which they used to love, taking the leftovers home for their kids.

I applied for a bank loan, claiming it would be used for educational purposes. With the money I rented a wheelchair, a walker, and a commode. I bought sheepskin pillows, a portable suction machine, a stand-up bed tray, hot water bottles, all kinds of medical supplies, and bundles of paper towels. I stocked up the refrigerator. I vacuumed, dusted, and waxed the parquet floors. I called on friends and neighbors to volunteer for chores. My sister, Belzora, a retired registered nurse, said she'd come up from Georgia to help care for Duke.

Instead of a hard narrow bed in a sterile room, Duke would die in the dignity and beauty of his own home on our big brass bed.

❂

"Sir Duke, do you remember the first time we met at Peter Rabbit?" I asked him, the night I brought him home, as we sat on the living room sofa, his head resting on my chest.

"How could I forget. You and your bunch of loud friends..."

"Loud!" I protested.

"Yes, very loud. You were all bitching at the bar, singing soul ballads so off-key. Sky, you were stoned-drunk."

"I was not. I was just enjoying a nice Sunday soirée until you walked in wearing tight bell-bottom jeans and yellow platform shoes."

"Oh, Sky! Remember them heels on those awful shoes?" he said as we laughed hysterically.

"Do I ever! Baby, you had my heart pumping and jumping. Duke, you looked so good..."

"I did then, didn't I?" he muttered.

"And when the deejay played 'Hooked for Life,' I had to ask you to dance."

That night we played "Hooked for Life" over and over. We were two disco divas with ten years of memories: the trips, parties, the steps, orgies ... laughter.

"Sky," Duke whispered, as I tucked him in bed and kissed him good night, "Sky, I'm glad I'm home. I love you."

"Love you too, baby," I told him, "thanks for all the good times."

❂

The days went by swiftly. Duke made a will and named me executor of his estate. He couldn't get up or eat by himself. Belzora flew in as she'd promised. She fixed all those deep Southern meals Duke used to like but could hardly eat now. He would stare at the wall with a glazed, faraway look in his eyes. Some nights he gagged, choked, and vomited. I helped him sit up and cough. I changed his diapers, washed him, massaged his back, smoothed the bed sheets, caressed him until he'd fall asleep, then awaken from a nightmare struggling for air. Every four hours Belzora would give him shots of morphine to soothe the pain.

One Monday the doctor visited and said he didn't expect Duke to live through the week. I called his mother, Doris, despite Duke's forbidding me to. She took the bus from Chicago, too scared to fly. She arrived late on Wednesday evening, huffing and puffing, waving her righteous finger in my face.

"What you done now to my baby? What you done to Duke? Duke! Where is he? I want to see my..."

"Woman, I ain't taking you into the bedroom until you calm down. Duke's too sick and much too weak to put up with your jive."

"Who do you think you are, talking to me like that? I'm his mother. I have a right to..."

"You ain't moving from this living room until..."

"Come on, you two," Belzora whispered from the bedroom door. "Quit that cat 'n' dog fight right now."

"Bel, stay out of this," I said, as I pushed my sister back into the bedroom and shut the door, just in time to block Doris from getting in.

"Let me go!"

"Shut up!"

"You're crazy, boy!"

"I ain't crazy, yet, and I am quite sure that you don't want to see me going crazy on you. Do you?" I kept repeating, as I dragged her back to the middle of the living room.

"Lord Jesus, save me!"

"You better pray harder 'cause as long as I, Sky Carter, am here, you ain't moving one inch from this room until you, Doris Taylor, and I discuss some serious business."

"You ain't got nothing to say to me that I want to hear!"

"Oh, yeah!"

"You done perverted my son, you low-down immoral..."

"Don't you ever, ever talk to me about morality. Not ever! You have been blessed with four sons, but as I understand it, each one by a different father, and you have never even been married to any of them."

"Shut your dirty mouth before you say things God can't forgive you for!" she yelled, lifting her hand to strike me.

"Don't you try it," I warned her, holding back her arm and stuffing my hand in her mouth to muffle her screams.

"Go ahead, why don't you bite me!" I urged her, "You'll get blood in your mouth and who knows, I might be infected, too. Go ahead! We'll see if this disease discriminates between gays and straights. Go right ahead! Take a big bite!" I kept taunting her. She froze.

"Now, you are finally going to hear me out," I told her, restraining her as she tried to move away. "I met you once, nine years ago, when Duke and I came to Chicago for Thanksgiving. It was our very first trip together. Duke was so excited and anxious about introducing me to you. Unfortunately, you didn't like me then and from what I see, you still don't. Well, I didn't like you then and you better believe it, I still don't. Damn it, I was willing to give you a chance. I was willing to put up with you simply because you are Duke's mother and I respect, no, I respected that. You were so mean when he told you about our relationship. You ordered him to break up with me and move back to Chicago because New York City was corrupting him. I bet you didn't think I knew about that one, did you. He was all in tears on our flight back to New York. I remember he couldn't wait to get to the dorm that Sunday night to call you. He was shaking from all the nasty things you kept telling him on the phone. How you didn't want to have anything more to do with him if he didn't repent. How you couldn't have such a sinner as a son. My Duke was so broken, and it hurt me that you had hurt him so. I could not believe a mother would actually be that cruel to her own flesh and blood. I remember taking him in my arms and rocking him all night long. Right then and there we promised each other we would stay together forever, hooked for life. We helped each other through college. After graduation, I accepted employment with a record company, and Duke became a damn good accountant with a prestigious firm. We bought this apartment and we've been living here ever since as man and man. Doris 'Sweet Mama' Taylor, I have been good to your son, and your son, Duke Emmett Taylor has been so good to me in ways you can't even begin to imagine. I don't expect you to like it, and I do not give a fuck, a hoot, or a damn that we don't have your blessing. This is our story, just the way it is. Either you deal with it or leave us alone."

It was then and only then that I released her from my grip.

"Can I see my baby, now?" she asked softly...

❂

That Friday, at 3:00 p.m., while his mother sat on the bed, held his left hand, and read the Twenty-third Psalm, I sat on the bed, held his right hand, and relived all our good memories, trusting the instant Duke yielded his soul.

There were no tears. There was no time for tears that year. Just a tight knot in the pit of my chest where it hurts more each day. Yet, it had all come to this: a two-pound plastic bag filled with a promise gone, scattered dreams, and I can't even pick up the pieces...

CRAIG A. REYNOLDS

The worst of it

Death is not the worst of it
    for I have died before—
at the hands of gangs who guzzled their courage
or boy/men who cuddled then cudgeled me to death,
at the hands of healers who electroshocked my brains
    as if they were frying eggs,
    and at my own hands.
So death is not the worst of it
    for I have known death—
gang death on the docks, sudden death in my bedroom,
slow death in the sanitarium, and chosen death on my chaise.

Because I have known death I have thwarted it.
I learned to avoid deserted streets, to stay in on Halloween,
to ask my sisters how tricky a trick was,
to distrust all psychiatrists, and psychologists, and even M.D.s
    who asked too many questions,
    and to be my own best friend.
The worst of it is knowing that neither
street queen brazenness, nor middle-class discretion,
    nor Wildean wit and hauteur,
neither being active nor passive, neither avoiding doctors nor
      visiting them—
nothing I have done before can snatch
    me from the oncoming headlight of death.

The worst of it is to stand naked before death's harsh glare
which stuns like the dread paparazzo's flash
    once he's breached and betrayed my boudoir,
naked before death, the policeman's spotlight
    which has caught me in *flagrante delicto*,
naked to be sun-poisoned, naked without radiation shielding.
    I am reminded of the worst of it each day;
as if at Hiroshima, I see about me freshly blasted *kage*,
the palest apparitions of former lovers, friends, and desires.
The worst of it is that it poisons not through enemies but through
        friends
The worst of it is that there is no catastrophic moment, no zero hour
        flash,
but that it lingers, lies, and insinuates itself
    worse than the subtlest homophobia.
The worst of it is that I may not have seen the worst of it,
that today's horror may be to tomorrow's
as a candle is to the sun, and the sun to a supernova.

    But ... I have survived the worst of it before...
the raids, entrapment, and pissy paddy wagons,
the bashings, prison rapes, and background checks turned exposé.
Each solar flare of hatred and fear
I have survived, then sifted the ashes — a prospector.
No fire has destroyed my best and most malleable stuff;
each time I have risen a purer gold iridescing lavender.
So, if the worst of it is a supernova, I will remember:
when stars burst in death dark new worlds begin.
I have risen before; I will rise again...
After the worst of it ... I will rise again.

KENNETH MCCREARY

Remembrance

I am distressed for thee ... thy love to me was wonderful, passing the love of women."   —I Samuel 1:26

He said he wanted his body burned and thrown where I would not go to that pile of nothing and weep. He also said he wanted all of his possessions given to the poor.

I have pictures of us on our vacation in the Keys. He was a strong 190 pounds; I have no pictures of him at 93 pounds. He had such a soothing and persuasive voice that it was difficult to disagree with him, but I will never forget the hoarseness and rattle of his voice when he had pneumonia. Even in the hospital, I cared for him because the nurses were afraid. AZT was only a false hope. What am I going to tell his parents?

Last Sunday, I rode a ferry to Mayport to release his ashes. Except for the helmsman and two fishermen, I was alone. Only the muffled rattle of the engine and the lapping of water against the sides of the boat intruded into my thoughts. It was a beautiful morning. The gentle breeze caused his ashes to float several seconds before landing in the water. My tears burned as they streamed down my face; I could not see through this liquid veil.

Several weeks later I was cleaning the garage and found one of his old shirts tossed in a corner. It still smelled like him — that light orange odor. I also found our old beach ball, but I could not let the air out — his breath was in it.

MELVIN DIXON

Aunt Ida pieces a quilt

*You are right, but your patch isn't big
enough.* —Jesse Jackson

*When a cure is found and the last panel
is sewn into place, the Quilt will be
displayed in a permanent home as a
national monument to the individual,
irreplaceable people lost to AIDS — and
the people who knew and loved them
most.* —Cleve Jones
founder, The NAMES Project

They brought me some of his clothes. The hospital gown,
those too-tight dungarees, his blue choir robe
with the gold sash. How that boy could sing!
His favorite color in a necktie. A Sunday shirt.
What I'm gonna do with all this stuff?
I can remember Junie without this business.
My niece Francine say they quilting all over the country.
So many good boys like her boy, gone.

At my age I ain't studying no needle and thread.
My eyes ain't so good now and my fingers lock in a fist,
they so eaten up with arthritis. This old back
don't take kindly to bending over a frame no more.
Francine say ain't I a mess carrying on like this.
I could make two quilts the time I spend running my mouth.

Just cut his name out the cloths, stitch something nice
about him. Something to bring him back. You can do it,
Francine say. Best sewing our family ever had.
Quilting ain't that easy, I say. Never was easy.
Y'all got to help me remember him good.

Most of my quilts was made down South. My mama
and my mama's mama taught me. Popped me on the tail

if I missed a stitch or threw the pattern out of line.
I did "Bright Star" and "Lonesome Square" and "Rally Round,"
what many folks don't bother with nowadays. Then Elmo and me
married and came North where the cold in Connecticut
cuts you like a knife. We was warm, though.
We had sackcloth and calico and cotton, 100% pure.
What they got now but polyester rayon. Factory made.

Let me tell you something. In all my quilts there's a secret
nobody knows. Every last one of them got my name Ida
stitched on the back side in red thread.
That's where Junie got his flair. Don't let nobody fool you.
When he got the Youth Choir standing up and singing
the whole church would rock. He'd throw up his hands
from them wide blue sleeves and the church would hush
right down to the funeral parlor fans whisking the air.
He'd toss his head back and holler and we'd all cry holy.

And nevermind his too-tight dungarees.
I caught him switching down the street one Saturday night,
and I seen him more than once. I said, Junie,
you ain't got to let the world know all your business.
Who cared where he went when he wanted to have fun.
He'd be singing his heart out come Sunday morning.

When Francine say she gonna hang this quilt in the church
I like to fall out. A quilt ain't no showpiece,
it's to keep you warm. Francine say it can do both.
Now I ain't so old-fashioned I can't change,
but I made Francine come over and bring her daughter
Belinda. We cut and tacked his name, *JUNIE*.
Just plain and simple. "*JUNIE, our boy.*"
Cut the *J* in blue, the *U* in gold. *N* in dungarees
just as tight as you please. The *I* from the hospital gown
and the white shirt he wore First Sunday. Belinda
put the necktie *E* in the cross stitch I showed her.

Wouldn't you know we got to talking about Junie.
We could smell him in the cloth.
Underarm. Afro Sheen pomade. Gravy stains.
I forgot all about my arthritis.
When Francine left me to finish up, I swear
I heard Junie giggling right along with me
as I stitched Ida on the back side in red thread.

Francine say she gonna send this quilt to Washington
like folks doing from all 'cross the country,
so many good people gone. Babies, mothers, fathers
and boys like our Junie. Francine say
they gonna piece this quilt to another one,
another name and another patch
all in a larger quilt getting larger and larger.

Maybe we all like that, patches waiting to be pieced.
Well, I don't know about Washington.
We need Junie here with us. And Maxine,
she cousin May's husband's sister's people,
she having a baby and here comes winter already.
The cold cutting like knives. Now where did I put that needle?

CRAIG G. HARRIS

Hope against hope

i.

"Marc with a 'c'
Steven with a 'v'
and a hyphen in between,
thank you,"
he'd explain,
and God help you
if you spelled either
incorrectly

couldn't cook to save his soul
except for baked chicken
and steamed broccoli

couldn't match his clothes
and I never found him
particularly handsome
but he was my first true love
and a seminal thinker

he could interpret Kant,
Descartes, and Fanon
over breakfast or half asleep,
pump out a more than respectable
first draft of a one-act
in two hours or less,
and recall every line

Joan Crawford
ever spoke before a camera

besides
he was incredibly sexy when
sweat irrigated his bare rib cage
while he twirled
under danceteria's strobe lights
he swore no virus would beat him
armed with rose quartz
and amethyst, homeopathic remedies,
Louise Hay tapes
and the best doctors
at San Francisco General
he fought it
like a copperhead going
against a mongoose

when he lost
we all wore purple,
tucked him in white satin
with his crystal shields,
and thought of Icarus
soaring toward the sun.

ii.

Jameel was what he preferred to be called
even though his mother still called him Glenn
pronouncing both 'n's
it had something to do with
rites and rituals
and the Baha'i faith
he tried to practice

he was six-six
and built like a linebacker,
the last man in 96 West
the night we met

made me feel like an eager virgin
on the Jerome Avenue express
uptown

home
his full lips peeped out
from bristles of beard
that tickled my cheeks and thighs
before he turned over
on his stomach
demanding service

when I heard
I made the trip
to St. Lukes-Roosevelt
to find his spirit
drained by Bactrim,
isolation and embarrassed relatives

he asked me to write his story
an assignment I declined
suggesting he start a journal
we'd publish once he was well

he did
and during later visits
I proofread each entry

when he stopped writing
his mother discarded the pen,
folded his hands,
donated the journal
to the church
with the condition
it be cloistered
and stored his memory
in Woodlawn Cemetery.

iii.

Calu, he explained,
was a name he
lifted from the side of
a passing milk truck
in the Tenderloin
'cause even as a boy
in Oklahoma
he hated being called
Cecil

he had the prettiest skin,
the axe-sharp features
of the Masai,
the carriage of a Panther King
and big bad feet like an
Alabama lunch counter waitress

I remember the night
he, Don, and I sat drinking wine
and eating salmon souffle
on my bedroom floor
with our guards down
and our egos in check
we teased him
about his stock rap
that always began:
"Black and brown babies are dying..."
but health officials listened
and funders listened
and the community listened
and he did good work

long-distance wires
first told us of his misfortune
we sent messages of support
asking what we could do
and wondered what could be done
for someone with
as much access as ourselves
or more
someone considered an expert
so we prepared ourselves
for the slow mourning of months ahead

It took only eight days
for the streptococcal meningitis
to overcome him,
much longer for his lover
to explain to himself
and their son
how they'd come
to find themselves alone.

iv.

He always went by Eddie
never Edward
which was too formal
too staid
for someone so playful
and full of life

he was the pride of his family
and the hero of Baltimore
having built a reputation
on his ability to make
everyone around him feel
at ease, yet at risk

when he spoke
it was hard to tell
if he was a preacher
or a saint
and amazing to see
the power of such a big voice
blown from his tiny frame

his energy and weight
steadily diminished,
he perfected his avoidance skills,
only partially answered
questions about his health
and if pushed
cited youthful
dalliances with drugs
as the cause

he denied any close
association with men
but offered no substitute
significants

when his energy crossed over
still in denial
the biggest tears
fell from the eyes
of the man
who used to call him
three times a day

at the office
and pick him up
every afternoon
from work.

v.

"You can call me Frederick or Fred
I don't care as long as you call me
and if you misquote me it's okay
just make sure you spell my name correctly,"
he'd joke

he was a ready griot
with stories of his Chicago childhood
and disco days in New York,
a gentle mediator
who always kept us focused,
a proud warrior
who wore a lavender
badge of courage

his diagnosis was the catalyst
for his activism,
his schedule filled
with speaking engagements
and television appearances
and interviews and conferences

he never let poor health
keep him away
even when we had
to carry his bags
to the airport
cautioning him to stay home
he boarded the flight anyway
and moaned discomfort
all the way to the desert

when we landed in Las Vegas
we told him to sit and relax
while we retrieved the luggage
but when we returned
Gil and I had to peel
him away from the

airport slot machines
and the next morning
he was the first
to arrive at our meeting

his luck ran out
at George Washington Hospital
nearly a year later,
his body was shipped
to Chicago for a generic
requiem mass

days later
we gathered
at the Friends Meeting House
in Adams Morgan
for a Quaker memorial
where we held hands,
sang his favorite Joan Armatrading tune
and cried tears
of hope against hope.

BOBBY SMITH

For colored boys who have considered

A s I rounded the corner from Eighth Street, I saw a red-and-white emergency vehicle turn out of sight at the other end of the block. A police car with lights flashing on top was blocking the middle of the street.

He's already dead and I'm too late, was all I could think as I recklessly parked my car. I jumped out and made a mad dash for the top of the stairs. A badge and a uniform stopped me.

"I'm sorry, sir, you can't go any further until my supervisor comes."

"Why?" I blurted back. "What's happening up there? Is Jerry dead or alive? I just saw the red-and-white van turn the corner. Did the paramedics take him away? Can't you even tell me if he's dead or alive?"

"No sir, I'm sorry, I can't tell you anything," he said in his redundant monotone.

"But you don't understand. I'm the one who called for help. I was talking to him on the phone. He told me that he swallowed some pills and that it was all over. Then the phone went dead. Please," I pleaded, "I have to go up. I'm a volunteer at the Minority AIDS Project. Jerry is one of our clients. I have to know if he's okay."

The rookie cop was not moved by anything I said. I stopped trying to reason with him and tried instead to catch my wasted breath. I couldn't believe what was happening and that I was playing a part in this life-and-death scenario. It seemed more like daytime television, like a rehearsal for one of those tear-jerking soaps. But this was real — too real for me.

I was glad, but not much relieved when his leather-faced supervisor arrived a few minutes later. The three of us took the elevator to the third floor. Before we got to the small one-room apartment, we saw nosey gawkers crowded in the hallway trying to see what was going on inside.

We pushed through the crowd. The dumpy landlady, a dishwater blonde, was standing in the center of the room surrounded by three uniformed police officers. Her brother was there, too. He was telling the story of how he had climbed up to the third-floor balcony and broken through the sliding glass door to let the paramedics in, because in the hysterics of the moment, his sister couldn't find the passkey to apartment 307.

Jerry was lying completely motionless on one of the matching twin beds. I couldn't tell if his body still held breath or not. One of the officers handed me a suicide note.

"Is he ... is he dead?" I asked, trying to swallow the lump in my throat at the same time.

"No, his vital signs are stable, but he's going to be out for a long time. He shouldn't be left alone. Do you know him? Are you gonna stay?"

I glanced over at the shell of a man that I hardly knew. He was lying in a fetal position. His slim frame was quivering slightly now, searching for a peace and a permanent calm that still eluded him. I didn't know if I should be the one to stay or not. Surely someone in the gawking crowd knew him better, but no one came forward.

"Are you gonna stay?" the policeman repeated. He was anxious for an answer.

"I just met him last Tuesday ... he has a lover, Roy," I said.

The landlady spoke up, "He's at work and I don't know the number. He won't be home 'til midnight."

"Are you gonna stay?" The policeman's patience was wearing thin. I could tell by the tone and the urgency in his voice that the big man in blue who had once sworn to protect and serve was more than willing to forget that pledge now, and just get the hell out of there.

He was the senior officer present. There was no doubt about that. But it was also clear that he was as fearful as the rest. There was no recognizable difference between him and the others who stood around the room snickering, at safe distances, snickering at the bed that cradled the frail diseased black body. Acquired Immune Deficiency Syndrome was not on the books when they trained at the Police Academy, and God knows that compassion was never a prerequisite for the job.

"Yes, I'll stay." That was what everybody wanted to hear right then. It meant they could safely return to their separate places, untouched and uncontaminated by the scourge of this new leprosy that was loose in the land. They really didn't want to get involved. They just came to watch the drama of somebody else's pain and suffering.

The landlady and her brother hurried back to the first-floor office under the guise of stopped-up toilets and leaking faucets. The curious neighbors scattered to spread the news about what had happened in apartment 307, pointing accusing fingers at a person and a disease, neither of which they knew anything about. And the boys in blue with the lone female officer scattered too, back to writing parking tickets, sipping stale coffee from styrofoam cups, and the safety of harassing the locals.

After everyone left, I sat in the evening's early darkness. Mute black-and-white shadows flickered from the television screen as I listened to the clock tick away the time.

Twice in the night, Jerry rose up dazed and angry. His weak silhouette moaned in the darkness. "I'll be all right, you can go now and leave me alone."

I went to his bedside and tried to calm him. I rubbed his shoulders and told him to try to get some sleep. When he dozed off again, I remembered the note. I read it by the light of the television.

Dear Roy:

I know when you read this it's going to hurt a lot. I'm sorry. I love you so much, and would never want to hurt you in any way. When it's all over, and you find me here, asleep forever, I will still be loving you. You are the one that I have loved more than anything or anyone in the world. Just knowing that you were here with me made me feel so good. Thank you for fourteen beautiful years. But AIDS changes everything. I'm sick, and I'm going to die anyway. I don't think that I can face the suffering. And I don't want you to suffer either, watching me get sicker and sicker. Please tell my mother and Ronnie, and my cousin, Bubba, how much I love them. Tell them I'm sorry. They won't understand but tell them anyway. Most of all, I'm sorry for leaving you Roy, my handsome, beautiful black man. Who is going to take care of you now? God only knows.

P.S. Get a haircut tomorrow.

❂

My silent vigil ended hours later, sometime after midnight, when I heard a key turning in the lock. I rushed to the door and backed the handsome man out into the light of the hallway.

Finally ... it was Roy. He looked just the way Jerry had described him. He was tall and well built, a gorgeous man of Afro–Puerto Rican parentage. He had long lashes and big brown eyes that were well set above his high cheekbones. His hair was wavy and shiny black. A full trimmed beard framed his honey-brown face.

"You must be Roy." He nodded yes. I continued. "My name is Bobby Smith. I'm a rap group leader at the Minority AIDS Project over on Pico Boulevard. I met Jerry there last week. He took some pills today, after you went to work. He tried to commit suicide. No one knew how to reach you, so I stayed with him."

Roy was stunned. He leaned back against the wall. His face went blank. "Suicide? But why?... That doesn't make any sense. Jerry knows how much I love him, and that I'm going to take care of him — no matter what. I need him. We still have so much to..." I could tell that Roy was focusing on what he hoped would be their future together. But now he stopped short and looked directly at me. "How is he ... is he going to be all right?"

"Yes, it looks like he's going to be okay. He's been sleeping pretty good for the last few hours." I reached in my pocket and pulled out Jerry's note. I handed it to Roy. "I think this belongs to you," I said. "I'm going to go home now and get some sleep myself. It's been a very long day."

Roy lowered his head a little and read the first lines of Jerry's good-bye. Then he looked up and took hold of my hand. "Thanks," he said. "I really appreciate it — your staying with him. I'm sure he'll thank you later, too."

"You're welcome, both of you. We've got to take care of each other... I'll call you guys in a couple of days. I left my phone number on top of the television just in case you need anything or want to talk before then. Be sure to call me if you do. Okay?"

"Okay." Roy smiled back. A single tear splashed on his cheek.

I headed for the elevator.

❁

Jerry lived for another year and a half. He became very active in the fight against AIDS, and remained so life-giving until his last hospitalization in October 1986. He became a spokesman for the Los Angeles Minority AIDS Project. He documented his experiences with the disease in a training video for the Veterans Administration Hospital, and received rave reviews for portraying himself in one of the first plays to deal with the subject of AIDS. His lover, Roy, survives him, and continues to live in Los Angeles.

JOSEPH BEAM

Brother, can you spare some time?

*Pride is more than going into a bar or
going on parade.* —Ted Smith

"Ted Smith" is a closeted black gay man. His real name and picture have never appeared in the gay press. He has never attended a gay pride rally or signed a gay rights petition. Although in his mid-forties, he has entered a gay bar exactly three times. Yet Ted is an activist, in the most literal sense, performing vital and essential tasks as a volunteer to the Philadelphia AIDS Task Force.

Ted is a buddy to a person with AIDS. Out of the thirty-five men who have been buddies since the program's inception in mid-1983, Ted is the only black man who has volunteered in this capacity. Ted and I met over coffee. A huge salt-and-pepper Afro frames his face, and his smile is warm. Immediately I sensed his generosity and sincerity. What follows is an excerpt from our meeting.

JOSEPH BEAM: What is the AIDS buddy program?
TED SMITH: It's a group of volunteers who provide different kinds of support for people with AIDS. My particular part is to provide friendship and any kind of services that I can on a nonprofessional level. That might be simply being a friend to that person, taking him shopping, going to the movies — in short, providing whatever care I can, which doesn't involve nursing care. And then if there's a problem, there are people higher up who know all the ins and outs of the AIDS situation: Social Security benefits and all that stuff. Ideally there are two buddies who work with a person with AIDS, so that they back up one another. If one goes on vacation, the person with AIDS still has a support system functioning. Should there be any problems, one takes them to the service manager.

Considering all the ways you can be involved in the gay community, what motivated you to become an AIDS buddy?

Well ... I like to help people; I'm altruistic and I do for people what I would like someone to do for me if I were in that particular situation. It could be AIDS, it could be cancer, it could be anything. People should do for other people because what you put out you get back, and I've gotten a lot back. I've learned an awful lot about myself by being an AIDS buddy.

Will you talk some about what you've learned? You are dealing with a very difficult sickness, which is often fatal. How is that satisfying?

I had two people I was working with, one of whom has died. When I was working with the fellow who died it was fulfilling because I was needed. I was doing something that was important and I learned a great deal. I got from that particular man the sense that life is important. It's not necessarily the length of your life, because certainly that man knew that in all probability he would die in a given period of time. Honestly, there were times when it was difficult. This man lived in Philadelphia and I live in Jersey; as a result, my phone bills were about $50 more a month. We'd have two-hour conversations because this man didn't have any other friends. It felt good to know that I had something that someone else needed. Ironically, after four months of these phone bills, it occurred to me that this man had never once tried to call me. So, I did a bit of a turnaround: I changed. If I had been in that situation ... it's supposed to be a two-way street ... I think I would have responded differently. There were no more two-hour phone calls. The other man in New Jersey is just the exact opposite; I call him, he calls me.

I don't regret having put out the time and the money. I would like to have known that I was somehow appreciated by just a call or something. So perhaps in that respect it was draining. I felt I was being taken advantage of, but that was the way this man was with his other buddy. I don't feel bad now that he's dead. I did for him what I could while he was alive.

Has being a buddy changed your notion of time or life expectancy, in that the next twenty or thirty years are not necessarily guaranteed?

No, that came to me before when I had deaths in my family. It was then that I became aware, hey, nobody promised you sixty years or whatever. So I was prepared, but had I not been, this would have made me realize that I may not have seventy or sixty years. You're guaranteed today. And you do the best you can today because there may not be a tomorrow. It may be true for other members of the buddy group that this is their first time coming face to face with a death they can't deny and that their relationship is a short-term one. They put everything into it and when their person dies they have to take a vacation because they have to come to grips with their own mortality.

Do you think that as men we have trouble reaching out to each other and saying "I need to talk"?

Yes, I think that's very true. As men we sit and suffer.

What do you have to say to other black gay men about the reality of AIDS from the perspective of someone who is dealing with men with AIDS on a weekly, ongoing basis?

What I want to say is that just because you turn off the lights that doesn't mean your room is not cluttered. And just because you close your eyes to a particular situation doesn't make the situation go away. And too, as with a lot of things, people are quick to talk, but very slow to do anything — whether they're black, white, whatever. I don't really understand, with the large numbers of black gay men who are contracting AIDS, why we aren't helping our own. I don't understand that. To me it wouldn't make any difference whether the person was pink, black, purple, or green. Why aren't there more blacks involved? I think it's inexcusable. Even for the whites, considering their numbers, there aren't nearly enough involved. I just think that people don't give a shit until it happens to them. Then they want everything; it's just me, me, me. And you just can't take, you have to give. You get out of life what you put out.

DONALD WOODS

Prescription

no point in crying injustice
shooting off in public places
they are slack-handed and wet-eyed
with sympathy

can confession aid the process
the fellowship of mourners
propping themselves up
on heart-rending commiserations
brave corners bending
blank eyes staring

time waits for no man
it comes for you
alone   you spit
yank your flaccid member
cry envious tears for
young folks caressing
at your side

strike back with amorphous ammunition
refuse the paisley-patterned despair
take the violate in hand
massage with the oils of
your heart valve
wash your battered spirit

in the salty extract
of self-pity

shore up the heart for the
thankless task of living
breathe through your nose
taste fruit with your tongue

loiter at crosswalks
while crowds pass by and laugh at the rush
of euphoria when your mother calls you
from a sweaty sleep

yawn loud
make noise
make love to the body you have
now bathe it in african oils
now dress it in royal cloth
now lay it in a single bed and listen for it
digesting raisins and bananas

full of your self get
ready to battle a raging fool
a venom-dripping motherfucker
lurks behind a green door of shame
and pain and guilt and bullshit

fight back with stuff that lasts
the melody in your head that massages your insides
the name jesus in repetition
toenail polish on sandaled feet

fight back with roughage
personal spinach
spiritual broccoli

call on herbs
ginseng for heartache
and seamoss coats the lining
of an empty stomach
hungry for full mouth kisses

medicate the time
the hours

the moments
with a mantra that
grows in your temples
and radiates your fibers
your busy weekdays
and quiet evenings

your own arms
against a sea of trouble
take them
wrap them
round and round
what belongs to you and
hold tight
hold tight
hold tight gently

IV. The absence of fear

ADRIAN STANFORD

Psalm for the ghetto

let there be planted the seeds for an intellectual, moral, and social revolution out of which a new culture can be formed; out of which a new civilization can be fashioned; out of which a new world can be hewn; wherein the black man can walk confidently and unafraid in that truth and that light which is freedom.

let there be issued no call for violence, unprovoked; but let the black man be admonished and prepared to confront every incident of force with greater force. to do so at his own discretion, in his elected manner, and on his chosen ground.

let there be emblazoned upon the inmost consciousness of the black man a preference for death in the cause of liberty and equality, rather than life in the toils of tyranny and racial servitude.

let black folk everywhere be clothed with a flesh that will not tolerate oppression, an intelligence that will not countenance injustice, and a spirit that will not suffer degradation.

let there be prepared the means by which the black man can convince himself that he must and shall be free.

let this be the black man's offering of love. let it be proffered in the glad conviction that the black man will survive, gloriously.

ISAAC JULIEN AND KOBENA MERCER

True confessions
A discourse on images of black male sexuality

*I went through a lot when I was a boy.
They called me sissy, punk, freak, and
faggot. If I ever went out to friends'
houses on my own, the guys would try
to catch me, about eight or twenty of
them together. They would run me. I
never knew I could run so fast, but I was
scared. They would jump on me, you
know, 'cos they didn't like my action...
Sometimes white men would pick me up
in their car and take me to the woods and
try to get me to suck them. A whole lot of
black people have had to do that. It happened to me and my friend, Hester. I ran
off into the woods. My friend, he didn't
... I was scared.*   —Little Richard

In recent years, issues of sexuality, pleasure, and desire have been
prioritized for political debate by the women's movement and the gay
movement. From our point of view as black gay men, the most striking
features of these debates is the exclusion and erasure of sex from the
agenda: white women and men, gay and straight, have more or less
colonized cultural debates about sexual representation. While some
feminists have begun to take on questions of race and racism, white gay
men retain a deafening silence on race. In many ways, that's not
surprising given the relative apathy and depoliticized culture of the gay
"scene."

The profound absence of any political awareness of race among
white gays is highlighted by recent trends in gay style. After the clone
imagery in which gays adopted very straight signifiers of masculinity — moustaches, short hair, workclothes — in order to challenge
stereotypes of limp-wristed "poofs," there developed a stylistic flirta-

tion with S&M, leather, quasi-military uniforms, and skinhead styles. The racist and fascist connotations of these new styles escaped gay consciousness, as those who embraced the "threatening" symbolism of the skinhead and tough-guy look were only concerned with projecting an image of gay masculinity. When some gay activists challenged the offensive aspects of this new masculinism it provoked outrage from gays who saw it as an infringement of their right to dress how they liked.

The ignorance of gay men who forget that these styles depend on the connotations of power inscribed in symbols of *white* masculinity is made all the more ironic by the fact that the origins of gay liberation depend on black peoples' struggles. The documentary film *Before Stonewall* shows how gays in America learned tactics for demanding their rights to equality, dignity, and autonomy by studying the civil rights struggles led by figures like Dr. Martin Luther King, Jr. As Audre Lorde points out in the film, the black struggle became the prototype for all the liberation struggles of the late 1960s: gays, women, peace, ecology, and antiestablishment. But, although gays derived inspiration from the symbols of black liberation, they failed to return the symbolic debt, as it were, by proceeding to ignore racism. The exclusion of race from the gay agenda was highlighted around the issue of coming out. As the London-based Gay Black Group has argued, the call by gay activists to reject the heterosexist norms of the nuclear family was totally ethnocentric as it ignored the fact that black lesbians and gay men *need* our families, which offer us support and protection from the racism we experience on the street, at school, from the police, and from the state. Our families are contradictory spaces: Sometimes we cannot afford to live without the support of our brothers and sisters, mothers and fathers, yet we also need to challenge the homophobic attitudes we encounter in our communities. But white gays have passed all this by because race is not an issue for them. Instead, the horizon of their political consciousness has been dominated by concerns with individualized sexuality. Here, other aspects of white gay racism have surfaced, most clearly in debates on desire and pleasure focused around photography.

White power, black sexuality: The debate on pornography

During the 1970s, feminists took the initiative in making sexual representation a political issue. The women's movement condemned pornography for exploiting and objectifying women's bodies. This cultural critique has profound effects; inadvertently, the radical feminist line that "porn is the theory, rape is the practice" found an unconscious alliance with the views on obscenity held by the New Right, where figures like Mary Whitehouse have also politicized representation in terms of citing porn as a cause of violence against women and children.

Gays have defended porn with libertarian arguments that hold the desire of the individual to do what "he" wants as paramount. Such sexual libertarianism and individualism is itself based on certain racial privileges, as it is only whiteness that enables some gay men to act out this "freedom of choice." But from our point of view there is another range of questions brought into view by pornography. As these are the only spaces for us to look at eroticized images of other black men, what interests us are the contradictory experiences that pornography implicates us in.

Our starting point is ambivalence. As black men, we are implicated in the same landscape of stereotypes in the gay subculture, which is dominated by the needs and demands of white males. Black men fit into this territory by being confined to a narrow repertoire of types — the supersexual stud and the sexual savage on the one hand, the delicate and exotic "Oriental" on the other. The repetition of these stereotypes in sexual representations betrays the circulation of "colonial fantasy," and traces the way the contours of this landscape have been shaped by mainstream cultural legacies of slavery, empire, and imperialism. The *Spartacus* guidebook for gay (white) tourists, for example, comments that boys can be bought for a pack of cigarettes in the Philippines.

In this context, Robert Mapplethorpe's catalogue *Black Males* appears doubly interesting. Mapplethorpe appropriates the conventions of porn's racialized codes of representation, and by abstracting its stereotypes into "art," he makes racism's phantasms of desire respectable. The use of glossy photographic textures and surfaces serves to highlight the visible difference of black skin: Coupled with the use of porn conventions in body posture, framing devices like cropping, and the fragmentation of bodies into details, his work reveals an underlying fetishism. In pictures like "Man in a Polyester Suit," the dialectics of fear and fascination in colonial fantasy are reinscribed by the centrality of the black man's "monstrous" phallus. The black subject is objectified into Otherness as the size of his penis symbolizes a threat to the secure identity of the white male ego. Yet, the phobic object is contained by the two-dimensional frame of the photo, thus the white male viewer is made safe in his identification, and at the same time he is able to indulge that commonplace white curiosity about the nature of black sexuality, and black male sexuality in particular. As Frantz Fanon argued in *Black Skin, White Masks*, European myths about the aggressive, violent, and animalistic "nature" of black sexuality were fabricated and fictioned by the phallocentric anxieties and fantasies of the all-powerful white "master." In Mapplethorpe's imagery, the stench of racist stereotypes rotting in the soil of violent history is sanitized and deodorized by the clinical precision of his authoritative, aestheticizing master vision. In reiterating the terms of colonial fantasy, his pictures service the expectations of white desire, but what do they say to our wants and desires as black gay men?

While we recognize the oppressive dimension of these images of black men as Other, we are also attracted: *We want to look but don't always find the images we want to see*. This ambivalent mixture of attraction and repulsion goes for images of black gay men in porn generally, but the inscribed or preferred meanings of these images are not fixed; they can, at times, be pried apart into alternative readings when different experiences are brought to bear on their interpretation. Colonial fantasy can sometimes be reappropriated by black viewers and reconstructed to serve purposes of identity. In seeing images of black gay men there is an affirmation and a validation of a black gay sexual identity. The stereotypes of black men in gay pornography have other meanings for us, because at one level they say "black gays exist." Even more, occasionally "positive" images slip through the net of white-defined codes. The convention in porn is to show single models in solo frames to enable the construction of one-to-one fantasy: Sometimes, when porn models pose in couples or groups, other connotations — friendships, solidarities, collective identities — can struggle to the surface for our recognition.

This ambivalence in our responses to porn embodies aspects of the contradictions we live through in the gay subculture. While few of us actually conform to the stereotypes, some black gays appear to accept and indeed play up to white expectations and assumptions. Certain myths about black male sexuality are maintained not by the imposition of force from above, but by the very people who are dominated by them. More importantly, this subtle dialectic is at play in the broader heterosexual context as well.

Black male gender roles

Our social definitions of what it is to be a "man," about what constitutes "manliness," are not natural, but are historically constructed and culturally variable. The dominant definitions of masculinity, accepted as the social norm, are products of a false consciousness imposed by patriarchal ideology. Patriarchal systems of male power and privilege constantly have to negotiate the meaning of gender roles with a variety of economic, social, and political factors such as class, divisions of labor, and the work/home nexus. So, it's not as if we could strip away the negative stereotypes of black men created by Western patriarchy and discover some natural black masculinity that is good, pure, and wholesome.

The present repertoire of images of black masculinity — from docile Uncle Tom to Superspade heroes like Shaft — have been forged in and through the histories of slavery, colonialism, and imperialism. A central strand of the "racial power" exercised by the white male slave master was the denial of certain masculine attributes to black males, such as authority, dignity, and familial responsibility. Through these collective historical experiences, black men have adopted and used certain patriarchal values such as physical strength, sexual prowess, and being in control to create a system of black male gender roles in which macho tactics are used to cope with the repressive and destructive power of the plantocracy and the state. In contemporary Britain, the predominant stereotype of the black male portrays him as a violent, dangerous threat to white society, its law, and moral order. The contradiction, however, lies in the way that the mythology of "black macho" is maintained by black men who have had to resort to certain forms of force in order to defend themselves and their communities. This cycle between representation and reality makes the fictions of racial ideology empirically "true" — which is to say that the stereotype of black macho is a site of struggle within this "regime of truth." The stereotype of the threatening black "mugger" is paradoxically perpetuated by the way black male youth have had to develop macho behaviors to resist harassment, criminalization, and the coercive intrusions of white male police forces into their communities. The apparent incorporation of patriarchal values into black male gender identities is a contradictory process. In sports, for example, there are concrete advantages to be gained from appearing to play up to white expectations.

Racism defined African peoples as having only bodies and no minds: Black men and women were seen as muscle-machines and thus the superexploitation of slavery could be justified. The logic of this is alive today in schools where teachers encourage black kids to take up sports because they are seen as academic underachievers. But we have also seen how black people have entered sports in order to make economic gains and move out of the ghetto: A figure like Muhammed Ali subverted the image of the "all brawn, no brains" black boxer to become an ambassador of Black Pride. But on the other hand, as Robert Staples shows in his book *Black Masculinity: The Black Man's Role in American Society* the ethos of black machismo leads to disadvantages when the incorporation of patriarchal values turns back on black women, black children, and, indeed, on black men themselves. Staples argues that black men's involvement in crime and drug use in America amounts to a self-destructive "solution" to problems created by racism. Another negative strand in this process, homophobia and anti-gay attitudes, allows us to examine the ways that such definitions of black manhood have limited the agenda of black politics at a collective level.

During the Black Power revolution in the 1960s, slogans such as "black is beautiful" cleared the ground for the cultural reconstruction of a positive black self-image, but this was done at the expense of black women, gays, and lesbians. Because of the hidden sexism and implicit homophobia of the agenda of revolutionary nationalism, as defined by figures like Eldridge Cleaver, black women organized autonomously in the 1970s. Revolutionary black nationalism implied a very male-oriented notion of struggle, which can be seen in Britain, where the term "black youth" really means black *male* youth, and is taken by some black male intellectuals to embody the essence of black resistance. This emphasis on open "racial" confrontation not only ignores the more subtle forms of resistance black people have forged in the African Diaspora, but also depoliticizes the conflicts and contradictions — especially around sexuality and gender — internal to the community. It has only been through black women taking the lead in debates on gender, sexuality, and desire that such issues have entered the agendas of black political discourse. From our point of view, one of the most important consequences of black women's initiatives in this area is to draw attention to the self-destructive aspects of our notions of black masculinity. But equally important, the questions being raised for debate by black women writers, filmmakers, and cultural workers highlight a multiplicity and a diversity of sexual identities that has always existed in the black community. Cheryl Clarke's essay "The Failure to Transform: Homophobia in the Black Community" shows that lesbians and gay men have always been accepted by the community (even though we have been disowned by self-appointed "community leaders") and have always played an integral part in the culture of black people: in politics, in the church, in music and art.

A multiplicity of identities

Sexuality, sexual choices, desires, and identities have always been on the agenda of black politics insofar as our political aspirations for freedom have always found cultural forms of expression. It is in music, above all, that black people's personal and political desires have been articulated. While the music of the Afro-Christian church — hymns, spirituals, gospel — sang of a desire to transcend the misery of the material world, the blues or the "devil's music" of the street sought to find a worldly transcendence here and now through the pleasures of the flesh. In music, black women like Bessie Smith and Gladys Bentley projected strong images of female independence. Bentley, singing in the jazz era of the 1920s, not only openly affirmed her lesbian lifestyle, she also let everybody know she wanted nothing to do with men as far as sex was concerned; she made sexual choices on *her* terms. In the blues sex is celebrated, but it is also problematic: A Billie Holiday song such as "No Good Man" gives a succinct critique of a certain type of black masculinity, but it also acknowledges ambivalence and the "messiness" of desire and intimacy.

Moreover, through black music black men have themselves launched critiques of traditional concepts of masculinity. While "black macho" images were big box-office in the Blaxploitation movies of the early 1970s, Stevie Wonder and Marvin Gaye undercut the braggadocio to reveal a whole range of concerns with caring, responsibility, and sensitivity. In this period, classic Motown like "I'll be There," by the Four Tops, valued reliability and dependability, while "Papa Was a Rolling Stone," by the Temptations, was critical of certain models of black paternity and fatherhood. Today, artists like Luther Vandross, the Chi-Lites, and the much-maligned Michael Jackson disclose the "soft side" of black manliness. As a way forward to debates on race, sexuality, and culture, we need to reclaim these resources to make visible the positive ways black men have been involved in a political struggle around the very meaning of masculinity.

Once we reclaim the camp and crazy "carnivalesque" excesses of Little Richard — the original Queen of Rock 'n' Roll — we can appreciate the way black men in popular music have parodied the stereotypes of black masculinity to "theatricalize" and send up the whole charade of gender roles. Little Richard's "outrageousness," the model for many who have deployed the subversive rhetoric of irony like George Clinton and Parliament-Funkadelic, Cameo, and perhaps even Prince, affirms the plurality of black male identities and draws critical attention to the cultural constructedness of sexual identity. These figures remind us that our pleasures are political and that our politics can be pleasurable.

References

The notion of "colonial fantasy" is developed by Homi Bhabha in "The Other Question: The Stereotype and Colonial Discourse," *Screen*, Vol. 24, No. 4, (November–December 1983).

Clarke, Cheryl. "The Failure to Transform: Homophobia in the Black Community," in *Home Girls: A Black Feminist Anthology*, ed. Barbara Smith, Kitchen Table Press, 1983.

Cleaver, Eldridge. "Notes on a Native Son," in *Soul on Ice*, London: Panther Books, 1969.

The Gay Black Group. "White Racism," *Gay News*, No. 251 (October 1982).

Mapplethorpe, Robert. *Black Males*, Amsterdam: Galerie Jurka, 1980.

Schiller, Greta (director). *Before Stonewall: The Making of a Gay and Lesbian Community*, 1983.

Staples, Robert. *Black Masculinity: The Black Man's Role in American Society*. Black Scholar Press, 1982.

White, Charles. *The Life and Times of Little Richard*. London: Pan Books, 1984.

ESSEX HEMPHILL

Looking for Langston
An interview with
Isaac Julien

L*ooking for Langston* is a visually beautiful and lyric exploration of black gay identities, a meditation on black gay desire in the context of the Harlem Renaissance. The film was funded by Britain's Channel 4. The director, Isaac Julien, created this "controversial" film to explore the role of the black artist in relationship to the black community, and specifically the role of the black gay artist both within the black community and in the context of the larger society as well. The multifaceted complexities that black gay artists face are examined by exploring Langston Hughes and the pivotal role he played in the Harlem Renaissance. For many, Hughes is a "sacred icon," an icon saddled with what Julien astutely refers to as "the burden of representation," a burden that effectively obscured questions of Hughes's sexual identity until Julien chose to gently undress him, or, more appropriately, ease him out of his closet. Julien's actions were not appreciated by the Hughes estate, which engaged Julien in a copyright battle over the use of Hughes's poetry. Ultimately, the estate managed to legally disrupt the original version of the film, requiring deletions of several of Hughes's poems before the film could be screened in America. To date, *Looking for Langston* is perhaps the most controversial film to come from the London-based Sankofa Film and Video Collective of which Julien is a member. The film has won numerous awards and earned critical praise from European and American critics, though some critics attacked it from stances as vehemently homophobic as the stance that drove the estate to fight the film. Presently, there are two versions of *Looking for Langston* — one for the U.S. and one for the world. The following interview was conducted with Julien at his home in London in June of 1989, three months after the film was screened on national British television (Channel 4, in the gay and lesbian series, "Out on Tuesday"), and four months before it was finally screened in the U.S. In the words of James Baldwin, which fittingly describe the challenge Julien undertook creating this film: "A person does not lightly elect to oppose his society. One would much rather be at home among one's compatriots than be mocked and detested by them. And there's a level on which the mockery of the people, even their hatred is moving, because it is so blind."

❂

ESSEX HEMPHILL: What motivated you to create _Looking for Langston_?
ISAAC JULIEN: The idea to make a film about black gay experiences was one that I always wanted to explore, but how one went about it was always the most difficult thing. In a sense, all of the films that I've made have had some kind of "dabbling" with those notions of constructing a black gay identity in some way or the other. Be it in _Territories_ — the two black gays dancing while the Union Jack flag burns, or in _Passion of Remembrance_ — the two black gay characters, Michael and Gary, or in _This is Not an AIDS Advertisement_ which is a much more propagandist-type work. But specifically dealing with black gay experiences was quite difficult. The inspirational things which motivated me to begin to make the film were brought to my attention by a young black man named Derrick McClintoch. Derrick became familiar with black American litera-ture, and although I had heard about Langston Hughes, Derrick was the person responsible for bringing Hughes to my attention. I had also read the gay anthology _Black Men/White Men_, which contained selections of Langston Hughes's poetry. That opened up the space to make some interrogations around Hughes's sexual identity.

Initial ideas came about around a number of things: wanting to do a film about black gay identities that would somehow not be a straight-forward film just about sexuality, because then, to talk about black gay experiences, one had to historically anchor it in a space where one would feel at ease in talking about those experiences, or one would be made uncomfortable. Obviously, trying to talk about black gay history in any way becomes problematic because of the different sequences and hidden nuances in black American history. I had to look to America because that seemed to be where most of the history was located. In trying to talk about black gay identities without compromise, I didn't want to deal with just gay issues. I wanted to talk about the role of the black artist in relationship to the black community and specifically the role of the black gay artist. Those were the kinds of arenas I wanted to dwell in, and Langston Hughes was a perfect subject. There seemed to be so much controversy around him as a person in relationship to his sexual identity. It was a very interesting strategy for me because one could have easily embarked on a project called "Looking for Jimmy," for James Baldwin, but it was obvious the different prices that some black gay artists had to pay for being out or in the closet.

I wanted to unravel the complexities of sustaining black art, for example, in its different forms, while at the same time struggling with any kind of sexual tensions or sexual ambivalences that Hughes may have had toward the black family or black straight society. So if you happened to be gay during the Harlem Renaissance what kind of spaces would you have existed in? These were some of the questions I was thinking about and toying with around the project.

How much time did you put into researching and pulling together the elements that compose your "meditation"?

Serious research for *Looking for Langston* started two years before I began shooting. I correlated all of the Hughes biographies — Arnold Rampersad's *The Life of Langston Hughes* and Faith Berry's *Langston Hughes: Before and Beyond Harlem* — I researched the letters and writings that Hughes had exchanged between different artists, and I also spoke to Rampersad at length. I spoke to Joseph Beam, Jewelle Gomez, and a number of black gay artists. The actual archival research was initiated and organized by Mark Nash and myself. We saw St. Claire Bourne's *The Dreamkeeper* [a documentary on Langston Hughes] and we enjoyed the film a lot. We found it interesting and quite important. We proceeded to contact the researcher on that project, the archivist, Linda Novak. She was very helpful along with Rampersad in giving us information. Novak was our consultant on the project initially. In the winter of 1987, the heavy research was done — heavy in the sense that we had to go to a number of archival sources in Washington and New York and get material, which was very difficult, because we couldn't really obtain a large amount of moving images around that particular period — the twenties. So we put advertisements into newspapers and things like that. The response was quite minimal. It became more difficult once we tried to obtain interviews with different people. We tried but we were unsuccessful in obtaining an interview with Raoul Abdul who was one of Hughes's secretaries. We tried to contact the Hughes estate a number of times but we were unsuccessful. They really weren't helpful at all. They weren't very sympathetic.

On my first visit to the states to begin the research, I ended up going to the Schomburg Library, ordering photographs from their collection, talking with Roy DeCarava (who knew Hughes very well), going to Donna van der Zee to obtain photographs from James van der Zee's collection, and going to Robert Mapplethorpe's agent and getting photographs from him. There was a lot of work done around picture and visual research.

On my second visit to the States, in the spring of 1988, I met a young man named Hilton Als. He is a writer and journalist. He had been the secretary for Owen Dodson, who was a friend of Hughes. Hilton Als was doing research for a book he calls *An Introduction to Negro Faggotry in the Harlem Renaissance*. He gave me a set of the essays from that book, and they later inform the primary voice of the film. I realized that making this film was going to be a dangerous project in the sense that I was always worried about how the film was going to be received in America. We made initial copyright clearances with the British publisher for Hughes's work (Serpent's Tail), and we sought to get the copyright clearances for America from the Hughes estate, which we did not obtain. Hence, the second version of the film.

But the initial research and ideas were propelled by meeting people such as yourself and also by your poems. I wanted to make this relational shift between the past and the present which I was able to do by using your poems and Hughes's poems. I wanted to do the same things visually. The choice to shoot in all black-and-white, and the relationship between the archival and the constructed vignette in the film, help to make it seamless. It was a project that in its making from initial idea to execution, required two and a half to three years of work.

Is that a typical length of time for you to spend with a work? Because of the subject matter — looking at black gay issues, and because Hughes was the key subject, were there additional roadblocks that you faced?

Well, obviously, it was quite expensive. I live in England, and going back and forth between America and England was one reason the film took a while to complete. I was also trying to engage Diaspora-type relationships in the work. I wanted to make the connections between black gay identities in the present and black gay identities in the past, and to also make the film exist in a space somewhere between the two — in mid-Atlantic, as it were. Hence, the British voice-over, the British narration.

You consider *Looking for Langston* to be a "meditation" and I think we need to be clear about that — a meditation as opposed to a documentary which is what St. Claire Bourne created when he presented Hughes in *The Dreamkeeper*. How did you arrive at the concept of a "meditation"?

I agree with you in resisting the notion of classifying the film as a documentary; obviously, the choice I made *not to make a documentary* was important. I did think of constructing a series of interviews with different people who knew Hughes or were around during the Harlem Renaissance, but that became too constricting because the idea was to have desire exist in the construction of images and for the storytelling to actually construct a narrative that would enable audiences to meditate and to think, rather than be told. This was a question I thought about very seriously; and it was a risk, but I think a risk that has paid off. *The Dreamkeeper* already existed; I didn't see any point in duplicating that approach.

Are you satisfied with the outcome of *Looking for Langston* in terms of the issues that you were seeking to address?

Oh, most definitely. In many respects, I feel it is the most satisfying film I've done to date in the sense that the risks I took by following my own intuitive mode of working paid off. I wanted to dwell on the psyche and the imaginary as well as the factual.

***Looking for Langston* is a very sensual film. What inspired you to go with the black-and-white setting? And the fact that the men presented in the film are wearing tuxedos, and the other elements that make the film elegant and stylish — what inspired that?**

There were a number of references that I wanted to appropriate. If one wanted to try to look in an archive to find specific images of black gay dance halls one would be undertaking a journey that would have no beginning because such places didn't exist then. Sensuality and desire were issues that weren't really at stake. But there were issues that were at stake; it was very important to construct images of dreams. One can only view that world [the Harlem Renaissance] or review it from an imaginary position. Once one accepts that there are a number of historical moments that one can grapple with and debate over, the rest is imaginary. I wanted to exploit that.

You created a mosaic of very important historical figures. There is footage of Bessie Smith singing "St. Louis Blues" juxtaposed against "Blues for Langston" sung by Blackberri. There is also footage from the film work of Oscar Micheaux juxtaposed against footage of present-day New York. There are photos of Countee Cullen, James Baldwin, and other historical elements. How did this weaving of audio and visual elements begin for you?

If you are talking about black gay identities, you're talking about identities that are never whole in the sense that there is always a desire to make them whole, but in real life, experiences are always fragmentary and contradictory. So, basically, this is a hybrid of different material coming from different moments in history. You just can't really seriously try to tackle black gay identities and not find yourself drawing from one historical moment to a more contemporary moment. So it is a kind of hybrid. That hybrid dictated the structure of the film, the choice to make everything black-and-white. Around the issues of black gay history, you're going to always have to go into a number of different arenas, areas, and domains to actually get the different materials, that's why all those connections which wouldn't be readily available are made in *Looking for Langston*, because you're drawing on different nuances. For example, blues is very important in relationship to black culture, and specifically in relationship to black gay identities because blues songs were some of the first spaces where one could actually hear black gay desire. That's the reason why there is Bessie Smith juxtaposed to Blackberri, for example.

How has the response been in the United Kingdom and in Europe to *Looking for Langston* — from the general audience as well as from black gay men and women?

In response to its theatrical showings it was very well received. In fact, it won the "Gay Teddy Bear Award" for the best gay film at the Berlin Film Festival. The media coverage has been absolutely phenomenal. In relationship to audiences, I hope that the work isn't just criticized and debated around its author being black and gay. I'd like to reach wider audiences than just black gay audiences. The black gay men who have seen the film have congratulated me on it. I think that very soon in the black gay communities there will be debates about the film because there have not been very many black gay films.

There have been different critiques about the film. There was one review which tried to compare the way Sankofa gets funded and its patrons, Channel 4 (who are indeed white men), to the patronage of some black artists by whites during the Harlem Renaissance. This is what one reviewer put forth, raising questions, as he did, about what that patronage means in relationship to black art. But I'm more interested in questions concerning the commodification of black art and culture. I think questions such as commodification provide a more realistic analysis and critique of black art as we approach the end of the twentieth century. In the film I was pointing out ways in which black artists were taken up and then thrown out like the ever-shifting tastes of fashion.

The legal battle you faced over copyright issues must have been one of the risks you factored into making this film. What you did, by focusing on Langston Hughes, was take a black cultural icon and basically undress him, which goes against the black middle class's belief that it's important to project the *right* image. With *Looking for Langston* you seem to have said, "Yes, the right image must be projected when it can be, but perhaps what's best for us is that we have a more realistic picture of the icons we elect or that come into being."

One of my roles as an artist is to uncover fictional constructs which surround black cultural icons. I think demanding a space for these issues to be debated should be my role as well. Indeed, there had been a lot of controversy surrounding Hughes's sexual identity anyway; it seemed to me to be a very important area to dwell in, even if it meant being at odds with different audiences and different sections of the black community. I thought it was imperative to at least suggest and visualize some of those anxieties.

I was more interested in complementing Langston Hughes's works, poetically speaking, than dealing with his sexual lifestyle. That is the reason it is a poetic, experimental text. There isn't a character in the film called Langston Hughes because, again, I wasn't particularly interested in celebrating his own specific lifestyle. I was trying to comment on how I imagined this lifestyle would have existed. The role of the black artist versus the black community, or the role of the black artist in the black community, and where sexual difference plays itself out either in disowning or accepting the differences. These were the kinds of questions I was interested in portraying.

So in terms of the Hughes estate's response, I was rather surprised. I never really anticipated it to be such a demonstrative one. Although I was wary that the Hughes estate was being extremely sensitive and constructing a number of closures around Hughes's sexual identity, I was rather surprised at the estate's response to the film, and disappointed.

You've created a classic work — time will prove that to be the case. You dared to open up a film dialogue about sexual difference within the black community. Are you going to explore this issue further in future film works?

I am only beginning to deal with questions of the black family.

ESSEX HEMPHILL

Undressing icons

The controversy surrounding *Looking for Langston* has posed far more urgent questions than whether Langston Hughes, black America's best-known poet and writer, practiced an asexual, bisexual, homosexual, or heterosexual lifestyle. Hughes's estate and sacred closet, guarded by the late George Bass, the executor and a former secretary to Hughes, challenged the copyright permissions that Sankofa Film and Video obtained in Europe, which allowed director Isaac Julien to incorporate selections of Hughes's poetry into his "meditation," a meditation on all things Harlem Renaissance, including Hughes, who was one of the Renaissance's most prominent writers. Hughes embodies and is synonymous with the Harlem Renaissance, and thus Julien could not have "meditated" on the issues of homosexuality, race relations, and the role of the Negro artist during that period without encountering the overwhelming icon of Hughes.

The questions that emerge from Bass's attempt to prevent American audiences from viewing *Looking for Langston* emerge directly from the practice among black academicians of ignoring gays and lesbians in almost every articulation and theory concerning matters of race and culture. Additionally, the sexuality of black icons is deemed inappropriate for public discussion, and thus, electric fences are erected around these issues, fences of silence, confoundment, and denial. This is done in an attempt to prevent black icons from being undressed to discover whether they were really kings, queens, or ordinary tramps. And these fences are most surely erected to keep the icons "unsullied" by issues of sexuality, and erected to prevent black gays and lesbians from claiming historical affirmations and references for *our* desires.

The lack of visibility and forthright discussion of gays and lesbians in major publications such as *Jet, Ebony, Ebony Man, Black Scholar, Emerge, Callaloo,* and many other black periodicals and journals is clearly deliberate. These publications make no attempt to bring an understanding of sexual diversity to the black community, which they all claim to be serving.

Who has access to black history? Who is allowed to examine it and interpret it? Who decides what can and cannot be discussed? If one looks to the heterosexual black male writers of the last forty years to read their views and opinions on homosexuality, many of these so-called brilliant thinkers and creative geniuses have responded to the subject of sexual diversity with an array of dysfunctional strains of ignorance. The discussion of the "third sex" is one that has left black heterosexuals speechless, threatened, enraged, or contemptuous. In mockery, hatred, and ridicule they have portrayed homosexuals; they have caricatured, demeaned, and abused us. Their poems, plays, short stories, novels, and essays are the wrong places for black gays and lesbians to seek *true* reflection and affirmation. Their critical analysis of social, cultural, and historic issues is fraudulent when it asserts that black sexuality is monolithic. Black sexuality is considered politically, morally, and spiritually correct only if it expresses itself in patriarchal, religious-based constructions of family, politics, art, and culture. Any variance or transgression can cause one to be burdened with shame. Supposedly, some of these "enlightened" men (and women) speak for the race, but I ask, whose race are they speaking for, and can it really survive if these are its most enlightened thinkers?

The practice of homophobia by black academicians, the sanctioning of it, the deliberate silencing of gay people, begs this simple question: What are they afraid of, they who would deem themselves keepers and historians for the race? After all we've been through, from kidnapping to slavery, from civil rights to assimilation, the achievements and contributions of black gay men and lesbians cannot be denied any longer.

By creating *Looking for Langston,* Julien gives us the first black gay film to articulate black gay desire and assert the experience of black gay men into a "sacred" historic context — the Harlem Renaissance. Julien *dared* to question history for the names and identities of other black gay men — our ancestors. He meditates on the questions of identity and the position of "other" that is occupied by black gays and lesbians in black culture. He made a brave assault on a closet sealed by kisses and semen, a closet where the soul of a black gay man is likely imprisoned.

It was Bass's contention that he was appalled when he saw *Looking for Langston,* and he suggested that Julien should have called the film *Looking for Jimmy,* after the profound black writer, James Baldwin, who was also homosexual. Bass's suggestion was *deliberately* inaccurate in the context of the film, because historically Baldwin's literary significance occurs *after* the Harlem Renaissance. Baldwin was a child during the period Julien selected to examine, but Baldwin would later inherit the legacies of Hughes, Countee Cullen, Alain Locke, Bruce Nugent, Wallace Thurman, and other "Renaissance" homosexuals.

Twice the Hughes estate successfully blocked the screening of *Looking for Langston* in the United States, and when it did finally screen in New York in October of 1989, the estate required that the volume be turned down on the poems by Hughes involved in the copyright dispute. The subsequent irony in the act of forcing the volume down was surely lost on the Hughes estate, but it did not go unnoticed as one more example of silencing the voices of black gays and lesbians. The estate also legally forced Julien to remove several of Hughes's poems from the film's soundtrack, further silencing Hughes's work from being viewed in a homosexual context.

The idea of black solidarity is a fond remembrance of how the race once collectively focused its efforts to achieve this little bit of liberation that we now badger and harm each other with in the name of W.E.B. DuBois, Marcus Garvey, Malcolm X, Dr. King, and God.

Perhaps black assimilation into Western culture is more complete than we realize. It was common at one time to openly silence and intimidate outspoken black people. Now black people practice these tactics against each other — just like white men.

The altered version of *Looking for Langston* is an empty triumph for the Hughes estate. It is a triumph lacking any dignity for the dead or the living. The silence surrounding black gay and lesbian lives is being meticulously dismantled. Meticulously. Every closet *is* coming down — none are sacred — even if our liberation is considered profane, those closets are ancestral burial sites that we rightfully claim and exhume.

JOSEPH BEAM

James Baldwin
Not a bad legacy, brother

Many years ago, while rummaging through cartons in our basement, I found a tattered, coverless copy of James Baldwin's *Giovanni's Room*, which had probably been left behind by one of the roomers with whom we shared our house. I read it, and realized that Joey and David's experience reflected what I felt. I lay among those sweaty, tangled sheets with them. I knew, even at eleven, that it was boys and men to whom I was sexually attracted, but I didn't quite understand what that meant. But those feelings, of both terror and anticipation, informed the earliest of my childhood friendships.

The specifics of *Giovanni's Room* — the white main characters, the strange locales of New York and Paris, even Baldwin's blackness and gayness — seemed incidental. The novel sent deep resonances through me even then, though, I wondered: Could there be happy endings in this kind of love?

Years and circumstances intervened before I returned to Baldwin's work. A white prep school, a predominantly white college experience, and my increased interest in the black civil rights movement made Baldwin essential reading. After all, it was his voice, angry and eloquent, and the voices — and deaths — of many other black people that made possible my attendance at Malvern Prep, an exclusive high school. It was his words and the machinations of other civil rights activists that mandated my nondescript Baptist college in Indiana, in the early seventies, to fund the black student union and offer black studies courses.

I was as amazed then as I am now by how some white people could be so right, while others were so wrong. I wondered why students petitioned against Black Awareness Weekend, specifically the appearances of Gwendolyn Brooks and Julian Bond. What tremors did they create in white knees? I remember turning to *A Rap on Race*, a dialogue between anthropologist Margaret Mead and Baldwin, for answers. Mead had always impressed me as a humane individual who was interested, quite admirably, in the culture and traditions of people of color around the globe. Perhaps these two surveyors of the human psyche and condition might cast some light on the madness of my campus and how the notion of whiteness made so many students so willfully ignorant.

Yet, as I look back on Baldwin's writing, I admire most his wisdom and courage in dealing sensitively with male relationships, and the richness with which he drew black culture. The racial landscape has been the primary domain of black male writers. Amiri Baraka went directly to the bank saying terrible things about white people. But then again, there are writers who offer concepts to ponder and rhetoricians who give us that akimbo warrior stance and a slogan to wail. Baldwin wrote with the delicacy we've come to expect from women writers, yet at times his male characters could be as misogynist and despicable as those of any other male writer.

I would have wished Baldwin to have been pro-feminist. In a dialogue with black lesbian-feminist Audre Lorde which appeared several years ago in *Essence*, he spoke with less surety than Lorde about the mission of black writers. Lorde clearly saw other black women as her audience and issues of concern to black women as her primary subject matter. She pressed Baldwin: "What do you have to say about the sexual violence of black men *in* the black community? Shouldn't you be talking about that? What are you saying to my son Jonathan?" Lorde continued.

The crisis in black male fiction, its lack of emotion and possibility, results from focusing on the racist foot on our necks. But life goes on. How do we interact positively with each other in our communities? The most glorious thing about Zora Neale Hurston's *Their Eyes Were Watching God* is the absence of white people. Indeed, we have our own country, which Baldwin so well described in his fiction.

Just Above My Head, Baldwin's last novel, published in 1979, catapulted black male fiction light-years. Heretofore, black male writers suffered from a kind of "nationalistic heterosexism." Homophobia always limited the depths to which we could relate, reducing us to stereotypes speaking slang and aphorisms. In *Just Above My Head*, in plain view of the black family, it was possible for two black men to be lovers, and be political, and be cherished for who they were. Baldwin had crossed this treacherous terrain decades before. Because he could envision us as lovers, our possibilities were endless. We could be warriors, artists, and astronauts; we could be severe, sensitive, and philosophical.

The first and only time I heard James Baldwin read, I sat perched on the edge of my chair catching every syllable that dropped from his lips. In the too-crowded, too-hot room, I watched him pat beads of perspiration from his forehead with a flourish only a *true diva* could muster. He was a diva, yet up close he seemed quite fragile, having paid the price of the ticket for being arrogant, articulate, and black.

James Baldwin lived as long as he was supposed to live: Sixty-three years is the average life expectancy for black men; white men live seven years longer. He said much more than he was supposed to say: twenty-three works published since 1953. Not a bad legacy for someone whom the Republic wished deaf and dumb by age fourteen. Not a bad legacy at all, brother.

CARLYLE R. BLACK

James Baldwin
(1924–1987)

If Beale Street Could Talk
it would tell you
about a courageous Black man
who often graced its path.

His *Notes of a Native Son*
from Harlem
tells of how he journeyed
to *Another Country*, Paris,
to write most of his books and essays.

Fearing that here in America
he had *No Name in the Street*,
writing in the security
of *Giovanni's Room*,
Jimmy's Blues
made him realize
he had to
Go Tell It on the Mountain,
This *Rap on Race*.

Oh, but tell me
what is *The Price of the Ticket*?
Tell Me
How Long the Train's Been Gone?
Can we discuss
The Evidence of Things Not Seen?

Alas, *The Devil Finds Work*
and our *Little Man,*
Little Man
at the late age of sixty-three
is dead.

The Woman at the Well mourned,
but I cry
No *Blues for Mr. Charlie*
'cause I know
he's *Going to Meet the Man*
Just Above My Head.

I will pray for him
in my *Amen Corner*
and wait
for *The Fire Next Time.*

RON SIMMONS, Ph.D.

Tongues Untied
An interview with
Marlon Riggs

Marlon Riggs was an "army brat" born in Fort Worth, Texas, in 1957. When he was eleven years old, his family moved to Georgia and then to West Germany, where he attended high school. In 1974, he returned to the States to pursue a B.A. in American history at Harvard University.

After graduating, he went to Texas to work at a television station. Frustrated by the racism he encountered there, he decided to go to the University of California at Berkeley for a master's in journalism specializing in historical documentary. His thesis project was *Long Train Running*, a half-hour video on the history of the blues in Oakland, California. Other projects followed: short documentaries on the U.S. arms race, Nicaragua, Central America, sexism, and disability rights.

His first masterpiece, however, dealt with racism. It was the first hour-long video in which he had total control as producer and director. It took him nearly five years to raise the $230,000 budget, but the result was worth every year and every dollar. The winner of a 1989 National Emmy Award, *Ethnic Notions* established Marlon Riggs as one of the foremost contemporary producers of historical video documentary.

Riggs's second masterpiece is *Tongues Untied,* an hour-long video documentary on the black gay experience. Within six months of its premiere in the fall of 1989, it had received four awards. The film version of the video was selected for screening at the Berlin Film Festival as well as the prestigious Cannes Film Festival. *Tongues Untied* was broadcast on WNET, New York City's public television station, during Gay Pride Week in June 1990.

Riggs is already raising funds for the sequel to *Ethnic Notions*, a documentary on the history of blacks in network television called *Color*

Adjustment: Blacks in Prime Time. So far he has received a Rockefeller Foundation grant, a CPB Production grant, and an American Film Institute Independent Film Makers award. He also teaches at the University of California at Berkeley.

In his presence, one is struck by the intensity of Marlon Riggs. It is a quiet intensity that cannot be deflected or ignored. His body language, his facial expressions, his articulate speech — all display a decisiveness, a determination one finds in only the most prolific of media producers.

✪

RON SIMMONS: For some time now there has been speculation about when the black gay male would speak up. For over a decade, black women have been vocal in affirming the strength of lesbianism in their lives. Filmmakers such as Michelle Parkerson, and writers such as Barbara Smith, Audre Lorde, Cheryl Clarke, and Jewelle Gomez have given black people and the world glimpses of women loving women through their works. Gay brothers have hesitated in revealing themselves, for obvious reasons. The black community is so vehement in its denunciation of lesbians and gays that few brothers dare to confess to such "sins." "Faggots" have been ridiculed and spoken of with absolute scorn by some of our most brilliant writers, scholars, and leaders — Amiri Baraka, Haki Madhubuti, Nathan Hare, Robert Staples, Dr. Frances Cress Welsing, Molefi Asante, and Minister Louis Farrakhan — most of whom view homosexuality as one more pathology resulting from white racist oppression. Prisons are pointed to as gay breeding grounds. The fact that most black gay men are introduced to homosexuality by their peers during pre-adolescence is ignored.

This attitude and ignorance is also evident in black films where the racist myth of the super-macho black stud is alive and well. Any character discovered to be gay is ridiculed and ultimately put down. Examples of this can be found in many of the early blaxploitation films such as *Uptight* and *Come Back Charleston Blue*, as well as in contemporary films such as *Beverly Hills Cops* and *School Daze*.

Rejected by the black community, black gay life has become a subculture known but rarely spoken of. As black gays, we often find ourselves leading double lives, suffering the mental anguish caused by false pretense. The silence and secrecy continues as any light generated by the black gay dynamic falls unseen into the void that you often speak of.

MARLON RIGGS: In doing documentary work I noticed there are certain safe political subjects that we as black filmmakers could deal with, such as racism, discrimination, Afro-American history, culture, and community life. Yet, within all of those excellent works there was this glaring void, this glaring absence, as if the subject of homosexuality within the black community didn't exist. All these things we were talking about of our history, our legacy, our culture, excluded any mention of same-sex relations; excluded any mention of those relations within the context of the lives of people we consider heroes. This void was very troubling and it became more troubling as I watched it over time. For me, there is a desperate need to address that absence, to address that void.

The black community is only now beginning to realize the extent of bisexuality and homosexuality within our community, but it's here. It's been here for a long time and it's going to continue to be here. We might as well acknowledge it and move on.

I wanted *Tongues Untied* to show the multiplicity of our conditions within the black community and how we deal with issues of sexuality and race, gender, class, political consciousness, political responsibility, and identity. Identity is a big issue. As some would phrase it: "What are we first — black or gay?" I try to invalidate that argument. Part of the message of the video is that the way to break loose of the schizophrenia in trying to define identity is to realize that you are many things within one person. Don't try to arrange a hierarchy of things that are virtuous in your character and say, "This is more important than that." Realize that both are equally important; they both inform your character. Both are nurturing and nourishing of your spirit. You can embrace all of that lovingly and equally.

Tongues Untied is explicitly a point-of-view work. It does not attempt to address questions of so-called "balance" or "objectivity." I am a black gay man. I made the work from that perspective. There is no debate about whether my life is right or wrong. It is right — period! It is right. It is good. It is affirming. It is life-sustaining. My life is of value and so is the life of my community.

One cannot help but admire your courage. Given the success of *Ethnic Notions*, **few artists would risk a very promising future by producing such a provocative work as** *Tongues Untied*.

My feeling is that there are imperatives in one's life. I think people during the 1960s, more so than now, realized what that meant. There are some things you've got to do. You don't know all the answers. You don't know all of the consequences — but you've got to do something because you know it's right. There is no alternative. You cannot sit in silence. You cannot maintain neutrality. You know it's right and you've got to move.

I felt immensely alienated from myself as a child and as a young adult. I didn't feel that I truly fit in the black community because I was different and I knew it. I didn't fit with the whites at Harvard because they were definitely different. There was no black gay community. No support. Nothing. Even today a number of black gay children grow up not having anybody to look to. What information and images they get are all derogatory put-downs. We go through so much pain, so much alienation.

Tongues Untied tries to provide people growing up with an image of the possibilities of life. I want them to know it is possible to live life fully, happily, and joyfully with the full understanding and the full affirmation of who you are. That's what I wanted *Tongues Untied* to do, so people won't have to go through the pain that we went through in discovering who we are.

For me *Tongues Untied* was a clear answer to the question: "What will you do, as black gay men, to correct the wrong that has been done to our community?"

Given the difficulties and hostilities black filmmakers encounter in the film and video industry in general, you might seem a bit naïve to many people. A large part of the success of *Ethnic Notions* had to do with its being broadcast on public television. The system granted you access to millions of viewers. That same system can just as easily deny that access if they feel a work is too black, too political, or too gay.

I realized that given the subject matter, *Tongues Untied* would not be broadcast on most public broadcast stations. Not because it deals with homosexuality; we have seen works that deal with being gay and lesbian on public television in the last few years. It's more the form and the frankness with which I confront certain issues in the black community, the gay community, and America at large.

In *Tongues Untied* there is anger and there is rage. There is pain and there is a frankness of language that I know is troublesome for television in this country. It's not that you hear or see a lot. It's not a pornographic work, but there is eroticism in that you see two black men touching. For many that in itself is explosive. We can deal with a slap on the back. We can deal with the handshake and the "high five," but when it comes to black men tenderly touching, it's too much. People either laugh or they draw away.

I was not going to sacrifice my work in order to get it on the venue of public television. The distribution has been through colleges and universities. It has been through a number of film festivals, gay and lesbian as well as mainstream; black film and video festivals as well as white. There have been community screenings through organizations like Gay Men of African Descent in New York, the D.C. Coalition of Black Lesbians and Gays, the Black Gay and Lesbian Leadership Forum in L.A., and Black Gay Men United in Oakland, California.

It's interesting to see how the established film community has reacted to *Tongues Untied*. They can't deny the excellence of the work. In the first six months of its release it received four awards and several honorable mentions, but they seem to find it difficult to categorize.

The Black Filmmakers Hall of Fame gave it two awards: "Outstanding Merit" and "Best Experimental Video." The San Francisco Film Festival also gave it a "Best Experimental Video" award. Yet the Atlanta Film Festival gave it an award for "Best Performance," and the Berlin Film Festival selected it as the "Best Documentary." You even refer to it sometimes as a documentary, and at other times as an experimental video.

I call *Tongues Untied* "experimental" video for lack of a better word. It crosses many boundaries of genre. It is documentary. It's personal biography. It's poetry. It's music video. It's "vogue" dance. It's "vérité" footage of people just talking, speaking directly into the camera as if the camera is a person and the audience is right there. It's extremely provocative at times, which is something that I like to do. And something that is new for me — it's humorous too.

Tongues Untied is a documentary in that it tries to undo the legacy of silence about black gay life. It affirms who we are, what our existence is in all of its diversities, and that we are of great value to our community and ourselves. What I wanted to do with *Tongues Untied* was to start the dialogue, and preserve our lives in a form that people can see and address, not only now, but in years to come. People will see there was a vibrant black gay community in these United States in 1989.

Are you surprised that so many people outside of the black gay community have praised the work?

Most of the reactions have surprised me. I thought that *Tongues Untied* was so specific, so particular in its message and focus that a lot of people just wouldn't get it, wouldn't feel what the video was about. But in fact people have. People who don't know much about the black gay experience are impressed with the passion and the honesty of the work. Diverse audiences have been moved by it because it is infused with strong emotions and truth.

Yet ironically, you have been accused by some critics in the black gay community of misleading the audience because you have a white lover. As one reviewer put it: If you state in the video's conclusion that "Black men loving black men is the revolutionary act," then why aren't you "acting?"

It's a tricky question because as another reviewer commented, the issue of interracial love is "unresolved" in the tape. I would say that in some sense that's true. I don't think I mislead though. In the video I didn't say that I left the Castro [district] in search of "someone better" but rather I chose the words "some place better" because what I was looking for was community and home and family. I know it's a small point, but for me it wasn't misleading. My only defense is that what I was searching for at that stage in my life was not so much a lover because I already had a lover at that point who is white.

Was that Jack, the lover you have now?

Yes, we've been lovers for the past ten years.

Many people do interpret "black men loving black men" solely in terms of a sexual, romantic affinity, and love. But what I meant was love in the sense of friendship, community, family, and fraternity, which was far more important, in nurturing me as a black gay man, than the love of a particular lover who is white. It's more important because for black people in this country it's difficult to exist, to flourish, to find sustenance and spiritual strength when you're totally surrounded by whites, or when the source of your support is solely from whites. There are things that white people can't understand, don't feel, and don't know no matter how much they love you.

For a long time, I thought about this question of incorporating my relationship into the video. If in the end I had said, "Black men loving black men is a revolutionary act," and had added, "now I have a white lover," it would have undercut everything unless I went through another half-hour explaining what that means. I didn't have the time or the financial resources to continue what would have been easily another fifteen or twenty minutes to explain all the nuances of what it means to be involved in an interracial relationship, while at the same time feeling that the love of black men for black men is of supreme importance. So I had to jettison that sort of more personal declaration at the end and really look at it in a more communal sense, which is why I ended with the images of civil rights marches and the community of men marching in the street.

I think I understand. When a person has committed themselves to a love relationship, it's not a political act per se. So if that person should change in one respect, it doesn't mean that they must abandon their commitment to that relationship.

Yes, and many people don't understand that. To them it's sort of like "Yes, now I recognize that I love black men, therefore I must jettison all of my relationships with white men — friendships, sexually, whatever." That's just not the case. People's lives don't by and large work that way. And those who try to make them work that way, I find, are usually very unhappy and conflicted because they have deep-seated feelings which they repress and never acknowledge or try to deal with.

How did your lover, Jack, react to *Tongues Untied*?

It was surprising in that he was not threatened. I was careful not to show him, or anyone else, parts of *Tongues Untied* until it was finished because I didn't want to take up time explaining it and reassuring him. I didn't want to change the brutal honesty of the film to protect anyone's feelings, including my own. After *Tongues* premiered, I was expecting to take a good week or two to explain to him that I loved him still, if not more; and that "black men loving black men" was not to be interpreted as my no longer having love for him.

I guess he intrinsically understood that, because he never felt threatened. In fact, he teased me about it and said, "I guess I'm the continuation of the curse of the white boy."

It is surprising that he never felt threatened. Why do you think he was able to handle it so well?

I think partly because he knows what my creative work is about in general; and partly because he's seen the quality of my relationships with other black men, such as the brothers in Black Gay Men United. He could place the idea of "black men loving black men" in a much larger context than just looking for a lover or a boyfriend. He understood what my need for a black man's love is about and my need to love other black men.

How did your family react to the film?

My family lives in Germany, but I knew the film would not be restricted to gay audiences and that eventually it would be seen by mainstream audiences and the mainstream press, so I wanted to prepare them. I also wanted them to see it in the context of an audience and not view it at home in isolation because I knew seeing it alone would be hard since I was confessing many painful things that I had never talked about with them.

I invited my mother to see *Tongues* at the Berlin Film Festival, and I gave her very little preparation. She came to the screening and I sat her with a friend of mine. I sat in a different part of the auditorium because it would have been too much for me to have been beside her during all of it. After it was over, I went over to her and I could tell by the redness of her eyes that she had been crying. She hugged me and told me it was wonderful and brilliant. Then she started crying and said she didn't know how much I had been hurt and how hurt I had felt as a child. She said that she really hurt for me knowing I had gone through so much and wished she could have helped. It was a very moving and heartfelt moment. In fact, friends of mine who were observing us started crying, too. It was a very weepy scene.

But it was a wonderful weekend because not only was she complimentary, but she kept hearing people who didn't know me continuously saying how wonderful and courageous the film was. She was so proud. I have a photo of the two of us that someone took and I have never seen my mother look so proud. She's standing beside me with her hand on my shoulder and there's this sort of matronly pride on her face. It's just amazing to see it so stark, and it lets me know I really do have her support and love and nurturing throughout all of this.

Did she know you were gay before she saw the film?

Yes, I told my mother I was gay when I graduated from the School of Journalism at Berkeley. When she came to Berkeley for the ceremony,

I told her I was gay and my roommate was my lover, that he was Jack, and that he was white.

How did she react?

She was shocked; more though by my being gay than he being white because I had had white friends throughout my adolescent life. She said she had no inkling I was gay but she was very supportive. She had the kinds of questions that I think many of us have heard from our parents when we tell them we're gay: "Are you happy?" "Are you sure?"

I think for many parents it's one thing to accept that your son or daughter is gay individually, but when you see them in the context of their other gay relationships that's another matter. When I was suffering from kidney failure, my mother came to stay with us. She came in contact with my friends on a daily basis when they came to the hospital or to my home to see how I was doing. She saw a tremendously supportive network of friends who were gay and lesbian, and she realized that here was a family — very different than she had ever conceived — but a family very supportive, strong, and intact. I think that reassured her about what gay life is, as well as what it could be.

I was struck by the way you dealt with your HIV status in *Tongues Untied*. To what extent was the realization that you were HIV-positive a motivating factor in doing the video? Did it have any impact on your thinking?

Sure, it made a world of difference. Before I became ill with kidney failure and discovered my sero-positivity, I was really flailing in terms of thinking how to structure and conceive of the film. I knew certain poems I liked. I knew certain voices and poets I liked. There were certain experiences I wanted to get at, but I really didn't have any idea of how to focus it, how to structure it and make it come together.

Becoming seriously ill and discovering that I was HIV-positive sort of kicked me into a totally different gear. I discovered my mortality. It made things much more urgent. *Tongues Untied* became something I couldn't put off and think about ad nauseam until things arrived at me from the muse. I realized time might be very short. And although the work might have been flawed in some ways, it was more important to get it out of the inside of me and put it on tape because *Tongues Untied* could perhaps have been my last gift to the community.

I knew that a lot of my experiences resonated and mirrored the experiences of other black gay men — men who are in interracial relationships, men who are not, black men who are facing racism, who face problems of self-hatred and internalized anger. I knew a lot of what I had been thinking about should be put in a medium so that others could then have their experiences affirmed.

Learning I was HIV-positive just drove me in a far more accelerated manner. The adrenaline was just rushing through me along with images and ideas; and the urgency, the sort of desperate urgency to do something, moved me to finish *Tongues Untied* essentially within four months. I was able to shoot everything over the course of the summer of 1989 and then edit, within two months, an hour-long piece. If someone had told me I was about to do that, I would have said, "You're crazy. That's impossible."

Did knowing your HIV status impact on the style of *Tongues Untied* in terms of putting so much of yourself in it? Did you originally plan to make it so autobiographical?

No, that wasn't just HIV. It was realizing that I would not be able to get other people to confess to the issues and experiences I wanted to talk about. Most black men in interracial relationships won't talk about a past obsession with white men. Most of them won't admit to being called an "Uncle Tom." It's difficult to find someone willing to go on camera and talk in a very personal way about what it means to be HIV-positive and face the prospect of death.

Like most documentary filmmakers, I was first trying to find someone else who would say it for me; someone who would talk about their life and hopefully echo my own. But I found that I had to provide the original voice. I had to be the person, the vehicle, and the vessel for these experiences.

Part of the reason, too, that I wanted to reveal my own HIV status was the realization that some black people had to come forward and combat the stigma of being associated with AIDS. Some of us have to come forward and treat AIDS in a humane fashion like any other infection or disease, and not look at it as a stain upon one's character or a source of shame.

I really wanted to present an image that would de-stigmatize the association of black people with AIDS — especially black gay men with AIDS — and therefore allow other people to talk about their lives truthfully.

Was it hard to relive the memories of your childhood and put them on the screen?

The hardest part of doing *Tongues Untied* was the autobiographical sections — partly because of professional training, but more so because of the kinds of very painful memories I had to delve into. Writing the script about those memories and experiences was a battle in itself, but then to actually have to edit it and select the best takes was very tough. When I came to the first section where you see me talking about my childhood, I couldn't work. I couldn't proceed. I stopped and just looked at the blank screen. This went on for two or three days. I would come in to edit, look at the blank screen, and then leave.

Once I did start editing it, I was sort of on automatic pilot. I would assemble the section a second or two at a time. You know, selecting a little bite here and then choosing the lips to go with it there, then coming back to select the next sentence. Finally when I finished the section, I reviewed it to see if it worked technically and aesthetically. I wasn't looking at it in terms of the emotional impact, just the timing of the edits. When I played it back, I suddenly started crying. It was a very strong, violent, painful kind of sobbing. Thank goodness no one else was in the control room.

I know the crying was cathartic because when I stopped it was as if those memories held no more pain for me. Since that point I've been able to look at that section and it's never affected me again. Nor have the memories seized me the way they used to, when they would render me into a sort of powerless space that many people feel as adolescents when they don't have the emotional tools to combat the horrors of racism and homophobia that they confront as children.

Through *Tongues Untied* I reversed the process. Instead of letting those memories control me, I now control them and use them to illuminate what I chose to illuminate about my life as well as issues in other people's lives. Those memories are no longer the painful horrors that I always tried to run from and find shelter.

For you, being a filmmaker is a means, not an end. You didn't become a filmmaker because you loved films or because you were encouraged to do so as a child. For you, as I guess for so many black filmmakers, filmmaking was simply the best way to say your message.

I didn't know anything about filmmaking when I decided to become a filmmaker. What drew me to film and video was that I wanted to communicate so much of what I was learning at Harvard. I was shocked by all the discoveries I came across when I studied American history, particularly when I found out about race relations and our legacy of black cultural achievement. It was shameful that I had never been exposed to such information before. It was a shock to realize that only a privileged few could get that kind of information, that kind of education.

I didn't want to teach — go to some nice school and just teach a few hundred people each year. That's good work, but I wanted to communicate to the broadest possible audience and for me that was television.

Other than subject matter, does being gay influence your work? Is there a "gay sensibility" that permeates your style or your perspective?

In doing *Ethnic Notions*, I realized that an approach from someone who was part of a more "straight black" perspective would have been angrier in tone, would have been more vehement. You know — "Look at what the white man has done to us! Fucked us over through history!" I didn't want to do that.

The voice that I heard, the voice I embraced as I was writing the script, was a woman's voice. I never ever heard, in my mind, narration for *Ethnic Notions* with a man's voice. Never. It was always a woman's voice.

I don't know if as a straight man I would have heard that voice; or if hearing it I would have accepted it and embraced it. I think I might have responded in a sort of — "No, I need to be much tougher. I need to be firmer. I need a male voice to do the narration, to speak with authority." The voice with which I wanted to speak was much more quiet.

When does your creative ear hear a man's voice?

When I'm feeling certain about something, absolutely certain in a sort of righteous way, a male voice will come to me. When I'm getting vehement, it's definitely a man's voice. And it's a voice reminiscent of a Martin Luther King, Jr., or how I imagine Frederick Douglass must have sounded. It's a resonant voice. A voice that draws on our church tradition. I was trained in that. My parents and grandparents expected me to become a preacher. I didn't. I became a filmmaker and that's my platform, my podium, the pedestal from which I preach these days.

MARLON RIGGS

Tongues untied

I'd heard my calling by age 6.
We had a word for boys like me.
(Punk)
Punk not because I played sex with other boys —
everybody on the block did that.
(Punk)
But because I didn't mind giving it away.
(Punk)
Other boys traded — "You can have my booty
if you gimme yours" —
but I gave it up,
free,
(Punk)

At age 11 we moved to Georgia.
I graduated to new knowledge.
(Homo)
"Don't you know how to kiss?"
my new best friend asked,
(Homo)
shocked, I didn't know what to do with a girl
when I "lost" at spin the bottle.
(Homo)
"No." I answered.
"I'll show you how," he said,
his brown eyes inviting.
(Homo)

We practiced kissing for weeks,
dry, wet, French.
(Homo)
'Til his older brother called us a name.
(Homo)
"What's a 'homo'?" I asked.
"Punk, faggot, freak."
I understood.
We stopped kissing.
Best friend became
worst enemy.

(Muthafuckin coon)
Age 12, they bused me to Hepzibah Junior High
on the outskirts of Augusta.
(Muthafuckin coon)
A spray-painted sign greeted me on the wall.
(Niggers Go Home)
(Muthafuckin coon)
Rednecks hated me
because I was one of only two blacks
placed in 8A, the class for Hepzibah's
best and brightest.
(Muthafuckin Coon Nigger Go Home)

The blacks hated me
because they assumed my class status made me uppity,
assumed my silence as superiority.
(Uncle Tom)
I was shy.
(Uncle Tom Muthafuckin Coon)
I was confused.
(Uncle Tom Muthafuckin Coon Nigger Go Home)
I was afraid and alone.

(Uncle Tom Muthafuckin Coon Punk
Faggot Freak Nigger Go Home)

Cornered
by identities I never wanted to claim,
I ran.
Fast.
Hard
Deep
inside myself

where it was still.
Silent.
Safe:

Deception.

II

A whiteboy came to my rescue.
Beckoned with gray/green eyes, a soft Tennessee drawl.
Seduced me out of my adolescent silence.

He called me friend.
I fell in love.
We never touched, never kissed,
but he left his imprint.
What a blessing
his immaculate seduction.
To feel the beat of life,
to trust passion again.
What a joy.
That it should come from a whiteboy
with gray/green eyes,
what a curse.

III

In California,
I learned the touch and taste of snow.
Cruising whiteboys, I played out
adolescent dreams deferred.
Patterns of black upon white upon black upon white
mesmerized me. I focused hard, concentrated deep.

Maybe from time to time
a brother glanced my way.
I never noticed.
I was immersed in vanilla.
I savored this single flavor,
one deliberately not my own.

I avoided the question, why?

Pretended not to notice
the absence of black images

in this new gay life,
in bookstores
poster shops
film festivals,
my own fantasies.

Tried not to notice
the few images of blacks
that were most popular:
joke
fetish
cartoon caricature
or disco diva adored
from a distance.

Something in Oz, in me, was amiss,
but I tried not to notice.

I was intent on the search
for love, affirmation, my reflection
in eyes of blue, gray, green.

Searching, I found something I didn't expect,
something decades of determined assimilation
could not blind me to:

In this great gay mecca,
I was an invisible man, still
I had no shadow, no substance.
No history, no place.
No reflection.

I was an alien, unseen, and seen, unwanted.
Here, as in Hepzibah,
I was a nigga, still.

I quit the Castro
no longer my home, my mecca
(never was, in fact),
and went in search of something better.

IV

In search of self
I listened

to the beat of my heart,
to rhythms muffled
beneath layers
of delusion, pain,
alienation, silence.

The beat was my salvation.

I let this primal pulse lead me
past broken dreams, solitude
and fragments of identity
to a new place, a home
not of peace, harmony and sunshine.

No.
But truth.

Simple, shameless, brazen truth.

V

And even still,
I follow this beat,
move to the primal pulse,
though lately I've lived with another rhythm.
At first, I thought just time passing.
But I discovered a time bomb
ticking in my blood.

Friends, faces disappear.

I watch.
I wait.
I listen
for my own
quiet
implosion.

But while I wait,
older, stronger rhythms resonate within me,
sustain my spirit, silence the clock.
Rhythms of blood, culture,
history, and race.

–204–

Whatever awaits me,
this much I know:

I was blind to my brother's beauty/my own
but now I see.
Deaf to the voice that believed
we were worth wanting/loving
each other.
Now I hear.
I was mute,
tongue-tied,
burdened by shadows and silence.
Now I speak
and my burden is lightened
lifted
free.

REGINALD T. JACKSON

The absence of fear
An open letter to a brother

Alexis,

How are you, chil'? I'm being "profound" again — or at least thinking I am. I'm worried about our people. I truly believe the time is ripe for black gay brothers and sisters to take our rightful place within this world, and yet, I am terrified that we won't.

I'm sitting here in my bedroom watching a PBS special — *A Conference on Evil*. What else would a young, exciting, contemporary black gay male like myself be doing? Never mind.

"We must have the courage to re-create ourselves daily," are the words just spoken by Maya Angelou, and at this moment they ring most true in my ears. Today, more than ever, we brothers must reach out to one another, accept our faults, bandage each other's wounds, and hold on to each other for dear life. We must have the "courage" to first define ourselves as what we truly are: Then, like caterpillars, we must shed our cocoons with each new season of life. The definitions of ourselves I speak of are drawn from the word "faggot" and the image of the "queen."

I know how you agonized about this, first arguing against the stereotypical image, then for it, and finally against it — yielding in favor of the social norm, only to show your true allegiance by turning into the grandest queen on this planet with the coming of night — your time for mischief. I know, deep in your heart, you loved your total self — faggot, queen, whatever — although you never actually said so; not even on your deathbed, battered and beaten by AIDS. More than anything else I wanted you to embrace your total self before you left this world. But you were unable to do so, even as we sat in your hospital room — the victim and the friend.

I was eleven years old when I was first called "faggot," and although I was ignorant of the total meaning of the word, I was irate, to say the least. Growing up black, and effeminate or androgynous, was no easy achievement. The worst thing you could be called was faggot — it was a red flag to a bull. It was trigger to my deepest fears and growing insecurities, easily tripped by family members who never meant to hurt me, but who knew all too well how to pull my ticket and irk me to death — all with love.

In retrospect, Alexis, I think the cruelest part of being labeled "queer" or "sissy" is the lack of explanation about the meanings of those words. I wanted to understand the totality of my supposed "perversion"; I could count on any and everyone to spit the word faggot at me, but there was no one able to go further and say that along with the daily anguish of disapproving sneers and catcalls, there would also be the love of a man. A black man. If someone had told me then what I now know about being a faggot, I would have gladly withstood the name-calling.

Now, Alexis, though I know you will cringe to hear it, I proudly call myself faggot, but to my surprise, I find it is unfashionable or politically incorrect to do so. It seems some black gays and lesbians believe we must forget about being faggots and other such pejorative terms, and instead, attach to ourselves the labels of "black homosexual" or "black lesbian." Well, I beg to differ. I like faggot. It has served me well in the past and I have no need to trade it in for something else. I understand where those opposed to its use are coming from. Faggot can be a negative term used not to describe, but to degrade and terrorize, and in that sense, it should not be tolerated; however, hiding it in the closet or burying it in the past won't get rid of it. As you know, Alexis, I live an extremely "out" life daily, and therefore I feel sufficiently qualified to determine how I will identify myself.

On any "typical" day, on my way to my nine-to-five, as I step aboard the uptown number 4 or 5 to ride to the upper east side of New York City, I am immediately confronted — sometimes by chapter and verse from the Bible — with exactly how almost everyone on the train feels about who they *think* I am and what they *think* I do in bed. At which time, usually adorned with my "Silence=Death" and "In the Life — Lesbian and Gay Pride" buttons, I look each and every one of my fellow commuters in the eye and say — either with my body language or verbally — "Yes, you have guessed right. I am a faggot, and I am ecstatic to be so." Then, standing five feet ten and a half inches and weighing all of 120 pounds, I stare down even the roughest looking homeboy, while he and the rest of the passengers return to reading hemorrhoid ads, staring blankly in front of themselves, or hiding behind a newspaper.

Having been the victim of an attack by three young homophobes on the D train to Harlem two years earlier, one of the B-Boys — probably a banshee (a street-tough type that in reality is just as gay as I) — taunted me about looking like Michael Jackson. He accused me of spreading AIDS and perverting other decent homeboys with my "homo shit." He then, quite angrily, threatened to smash my face in with a bottle and take my Sony Walkman. To have stated: "I am a black homosexual male — politically correct and well-read" — would have done little to prevent him from rearranging my facial structure. I withstood the insults and escaped serious injury by mere luck. I was shaken to my very core. The truth about who I was echoed through me and terrified me more than the B-Boys. I was not terrified because I had a problem with being gay. Being gay wasn't the horror — being a faggot was.

I knew what it would mean to be labeled faggot. The thoughts, expectations, and denigrations that would be associated with my every move. I, like you, had refrained from snapping my fingers or speaking too stereotypically — though it is my truest nature to do so. Sitting there, wondering whether I was to escape with my facial structure intact, I was nothing. I refused to be who I was — homosexual, faggot, queen — and attached myself to a lie even I didn't believe. Therefore, deliberately cut off from myself, in bed with a lie, I was nothing.

Shortly thereafter, I asked myself, what was the big deal? What would it really mean to my life to be labeled a faggot? I finally decided that if being judged and misunderstood were to be the conditions of my existence, I would exist, knowing it would not be easy or fun to fight daily battles to be who I am. "You must pay the cost to be the boss," my mother would often say. I am more than willing to pay the cost. I realized I had better decide who I am and more importantly, determine what I'm willing to do to be me. I'm willing to be judged and called names because I am, at the very least, a faggot, and that's all right. In fact, it's the way I want it, and the thoughts, expectations, and denigrations are nothing compared to that. I'm a relatively intelligent, progressive, sensitive, and funny human being, well worth knowing, and if someone is ignorant enough to attack me or dismiss me because of who they think I am or what they think I do in bed, then they aren't worth my time.

Fortunately, the B-Boy incident shook me up enough to pull me out of my confusion. With enthusiasm and pride I claimed my true homosexual self. I wonder if it would have done the same for you, Alexis? Is that really what it takes? Since then, I have faced down anyone with a problem with my sexual preference or color. Not as a black homosexual male, but as a proud black faggot. It wasn't *homosexual male* that was yelled at me as I walked down school hallways or city streets. It wasn't *black homosexual male* that started the numerous cat fights between me and others, including family members. It wasn't *black homosexual male* that made me cry when I was eleven. It was *faggot*. And it's *faggot* that I now embrace.

We must disarm the word *faggot* in order to move closer to our true selves. Whether we like it or not, we are the faggots we were cruelly called in grammar school: That's why we're so bothered by the word even now. We give the word — and more importantly, the people who use it against us — greater power over us. The power to frighten or anger us, or to trigger our deepest fears and insecurities. We have to endow faggot with alternative meanings that empower us. Nothing is more disarming than taking an attacker's insults and reversing them, using them as a part of your own assault or defense. We cannot continue to give others the power to hurt us by calling us a faggot. It has gone on long enough. I have been hurting too long and need no one to add to my burden. I will not continue to give some stranger the power to — with one word — hurt me. We must stop being victims. I know this won't be easy. Not everyone can or wants to stare down homeboys or fools, but we must help each other over the hump. We have so much work to do. This or other problems must not keep us down.

Alexis, though I have your picture on my mantle, so I can view it every morning, I have you — in the form of memories — with me all day. The most touching memories are those of you being the last bitch or very queenly. Times when you were threatening to throw out your roommate — our dear friend and "sister" — or your sharp verbal response to your father's snide comments — "It smells like fish in here." Those were the best times. You were indeed fierce, and I'm sure you continue to be so. You were a martyr, a hero, one of many who continue to be denied their just honor, but I will never forget you, though some would want me to. As you know, the image of the queen as hero is not something a large number of macho, butch, or boy-next-door-type, we're-just-like-you-looking black gay brothers want to see, but it is a reality. It pains me (as I suspect it did you) that so many of my fellow *brothers* look down on me for being a "Queen," snapping my fingers, and adding a "Girlfriend" to the end of my sentences. These brothers suffer from selective amnesia, it would seem. You see, it was queens, in high heels and chiffon, who fought cops for Stonewall; sissies who had bottles and billy clubs wailed at and on them as they marched down city streets for "our" rights. It was drag queens who patrolled the docks and piers with straight razors, fighting and dying at the hands of joyriding homophobes. We queens have been shouted at, stalked, stabbed, and all but stuffed as some Muslim's or redneck's trophy.

Yes, we shimmer in the glitter of expensive fashions, but we also get down and dirty for the cause, allowing our other brothers — who aren't ready to make "the statement" yet, or who can't be identified as queer "Uptown" — to lead reasonably comfortable lives enjoying gay rights, the pride parades, the bars, parks, baths, and movies.

It is downright tragic to think that the *brother* giving me a dirty look is a fellow black gay man. As you know, nothing hurts more or longer than being sneered at by a fellow sissy or given that "You're a disappointment" or "Butch-up" look from another faggot. It's family that we must fear the most, because family knows our weaknesses and therefore can hurt us the most. I only ask these brothers and sisters that the next time they see a queen — be it a femme queen, referring to himself as a woman, complete with genitalia and mannerisms; or a corporate queen, with a briefcase dangling from his arched wrists, swishing through Wall Street; or a church queen, star of the choir, pulpit, or congregation; or a butch queen, in full leather, cowboy, or construction drag; or a Banshee queen, in B-Boy drag, complete with sneakers and gold chain; or an African queen, in African drag, complete with dreadlocks, napps, and authentic African jewelery; or a drag queen, in women's clothes; or a therapy queen, with the latest self-help book and natural herbs; or a movement queen, adorned in politically correct clothes and buttons with an overworked schedule book; or a disco diva, dressed to kill with face and hair beat severely (done up), and an extra pair of clothes for the ride home — you think twice about looking down your nose at him. Before you turn your head, *remember that our true heroes were proud queens who died for your right not to be a queen,* and out of respect for your true ancestors — who probably go back as far as an African queen lounging beside the Congo, well attended by the fiercest warriors — support the brother in front of you. Don't dismiss our past as fluff because of misguided pride or nouveau intellect. This one time, all that glitters is gold.

Well, Alexis, I don't know what will come of this letter, but I do know writing it — talking to you — has helped calm my anxieties for now. Before I collapse into bed, I must end with this thought: Remember how we talked, often into the early morning hours, about how we, descendants of Mother Africa, must remember who we really are. How we are the past, future, and present all at once — the circle, the sphere that encompasses all. How we, unlike those of many other cultures on this planet, do not move on a single plane leaving parts of ourselves behind as antiquity. We, more intensely than others, constantly collide with and re-create ourselves. We began as a myriad of forms, including faggots and queens, and we must learn to exist as such. We must not break the circle, but protect it. It is what continues to make us great.

On this note, Alexis, I will stop, because as I look out my window, I see how beautiful the night is, and know somewhere out there you are off to find mischief. Perhaps I will join you, someday.

Much love and faith,
Reggie

RON SIMMONS, Ph.D.

Some thoughts on the challenges facing black gay intellectuals

One of the most serious challenges facing black gay intellectuals is the development of a progressive view of homosexuality in the African American community. Such a perspective is needed to assist the larger African American community's struggle for self-determination by freeing it from the limitations of homophobia, as well as to liberate and self-actualize black gay genius. Unfortunately, the black gay scholar is faced with a unique burden when intellectualizing with his or her racial peers.[1] Because we are gay, they believe our lives are invalid and our knowledge irrelevant. The insight black gay scholars may provide on the critical problems confronting the African American community is ignored by our heterosexual brothers and sisters who are attempting to solve those problems. Indeed, they often think of homosexuality as one more problem caused by white oppression.

In the African American community, "homophobia" is not so much a fear of "homosexuals" but a fear that homosexuality will become pervasive in the community. Thus, a homophobic person can accept a homosexual as an individual friend or family member, yet not accept homosexuality. This is the attitude that predominates in the African American community. The motivation for homophobia is "heterosexism" — the belief that heterosexual sex is good and proper, and homosexual sex is bad and immoral.

Historically, discussions and theories on homosexuality in the African American community have been offered by scholars who have little, if any, understanding of the homosexual experience. Homophobic and heterosexist viewpoints are espoused by some of our most respected leaders, writers, and scholars, such as Nathan Hare, Jawanza Kunjufu,

Robert Staples, Louis Farrakhan, Molefi Asante, Haki Madhubuti, Amiri Baraka, and Yosuf Ben-Jochannan.

There are three basic challenges facing black gay intellectuals. First, we must develop an analysis and understanding of homosexuality in the African American community that is affirming and constructive. Second, we must correct the bias and misinformation put forth by black homophobic and heterosexist scholars. Third, we must not allow the hurt and anger we may feel toward such scholars to cause us to dismiss them or their ideas on other issues that we may agree on.

Black homophobic literature

In reviewing African American literature, one finds that black homophobic and heterosexist scholars believe homosexuality in the African American community is the result of: (1) the emasculation of black men by white oppression (e.g., Staples, Madhubuti, Asante, Farrakhan, and Baraka); (2) the breakdown of the family structure and the loss of male role models (e.g., Kunjufu, Madhubuti, Farrakhan, and Hare); (3) a sinister plot perpetuated by diabolical racists who want to destroy the black race (e.g., Hare); and (4) immorality as defined in biblical scriptures, Koranic suras, or Egyptian "Books of the Dead" (e.g., Farrakhan and Ben-Jochannan).

In their 1984 book, *The Endangered Black Family: Coping with the Unisexualization and Coming Extinction of the Black Race*, Nathan Hare and his wife, Julia, cite ancient Greece and the modern Western world as examples of societies in a "state of decay" where norms and values are confused, and

> people are alienated and set apart from their natural origins. [In such societies] there emerges a breakdown in childrearing and socialization... Without a solid core to their personalities, children — grow up confused — develop[ing] problems of identity, most notably that of gender confusion. Homosexuality accordingly will proliferate.[2]

The Hares' view of black homosexuality is a simple one in which "homosexuality," "gender confusion," and "sex-change operations" are synonymous. To them, homosexuality, along with "unisexualization," "feminism," and "birth control," are all part of a genocidal plot masterminded by the "white liberal-radical-moderate-establishment coalition." The Hares feel "no need to engage in endless debates about the pros and cons of homosexuality... Homosexuality does not promote black family stability and — historically has been a product largely of European society."[3]

The Hares are what Jawanza Kunjufu calls "traditionalists."[4] They long for a primal past in which the male role was "protection [and] providing" while the female attended to "nurturing and gathering."[5]

They lament, "Where once there were pretty women and working men, there now are pretty men and working women."[6]

Both the Hares and Kunjufu believe that black boys become homosexuals because of the preponderance of white female schoolteachers; the Hares, in particular, claim that "white teachers infiltrate black child centers, nurseries and primary schools, compelling black boys to play with blonde dolls in the name of progress."[7]

Nathan and Julia Hare's homophobic raving does not negate the fact that there may be racist genocidal plots against the black community, or that black men are systematically destroyed. Our homosexuality, however, is not a part of such plots and our love is not genocidal. It is their divisive homophobic and heterosexist reactions to our natural sexual expression that play into the plot of divide and conquer.

Robert Staples, in his book *Black Masculinity*, asserts that the "nation's prisons are the main places where homosexual preferences are evident — because of the unavailability of women."[8] He goes on to allege that some black men continue the "homosexual lifestyle" after being released for various reasons, "ranging from a desire to escape family responsibilities to acquiring money through prostitution." The increasing visibility of black lesbians, according to Staples, is a result of "the shortage of Black men or — the conflict in male/female relationships." He also contends that black homosexuals are "deeply involved in the white homosexual community."[9]

In a 1983 speech at Morgan State University, Minister Louis Farrakhan cited incarceration and the lack of positive male role models as causes of homosexuality among black men, stating:

Those of you — who are homosexual — you weren't born [that] way brother — You never had a strong male image... [These] are conditions that are forced on black men. You're filling up the jails and they're turning [you] into freaks in the jails.[10]

In his book *Afrocentricity*, Molefi Asante also blames "prison breeding" for the "outburst of homosexuality among black men." He is particularly outraged that "black gays are often put in front of white or integrated organizations to show the liberalism of the group." To Asante, homosexuality is a "white decadence" that cannot be condoned or accepted. It can, however, be "tolerated until such time as our families and schools are engaged in Afrocentric instruction for males."[11]

Asante suggests that gay brothers submerge their homosexuality to satisfy what he terms the "collective will," stating:

Afrocentric relationships are based upon ... what is best for the collective imperative of the people... All brothers who are homosexuals should know that they too can become committed to the collective will. It means the submergence of their own wills into the collective will of our people.[12]

Haki Madhubuti claims in his book *Enemies: The Clash of Races* that there is a preponderance of black homosexuals in the higher socio-economic groups. He believes that homosexuality is backward, abnormal, and "rampant in significant parts of the black community":

> It is a profound comment on the power of the system that [it] is able to transform black men into sexual lovers of each other... On many black college campuses [and in] the black church, homosexuality and bisexuality [have become] an accepted norm. And far too often these homosexual Black men, because of their *sensitivity, talent and connections* are found in the most sensitive positions of responsibility in the ... working world ... actually directing many community, political and educational programs [emphasis added].[13]

Ironically, in a footnote, Madhubuti presents a voice of reason about the "human complexity of homosexuality." Calling for understanding and dialogue, he states that:

> Black homosexuality is on the rise and the question becomes do we enlist them into our struggle, or do we continue to alienate and make enemies of them?... If we are truly conscious adults we have to show a sensitivity to their personal differences as well as the political and cultural differences of our people.[14]

That such logic and compassion would be relegated to a footnote might indicate a fear on Madhubuti's part of appearing soft on homosexuality. In the black community, a male is often forced to denounce homosexuality in order to avoid suspicion. Calls for understanding and dialogue must be posed as tactical maneuvers, not strategic goals. Nathan and Julia Hare present a similar stance in *The Endangered Black Family*. After claiming that homosexuality does not promote black family stability, they state:

> On the other hand — and this is crucial — we will refuse to embark on one more tangent of displaced contempt and misdirected scorn for the homosexualized [*sic*] black brothers or sisters and drive them over to the camp of the white liberal-radical-moderate-establishment coalition. What we must do is offer the homosexual brother or sister a proper compassion and acceptance without advocacy... Some of them may yet be saved. And yet, we must declare open warfare upon the sources of [their] confusion.[15]

Haki Madhubuti published *Enemies* in 1978. Twelve years later, he published another book titled *Black Men. Obsolete, Single, Dangerous? The Afrikan American Family in Transition. Essays in Discovery, Solution and Hope.* Despite the intriguing title, Madhubuti is hopeless in discovering or understanding black men who are gay. In fact, he regresses on the gay issue. Whereas a footnote in *Enemies* called for "dialogue" and "sensitivity," in *Black Men*, Madhubuti offers no insight whatsoever on homosexuality. He does not even categorize gays as black men, stating, "Much of the current Black studies have focused on either the Black family, Black women, Afrika, the Black homosexual community or Europe's and America's influence on the Black world. Few Black scholars or activists have given serious attention to the condition of Black men."[16]

In analyzing homosexuality, Madhubuti returns to the "white oppression" model. In a listing of the "most prevalent tactics [used by the] U.S. white supremacy system to disrupt black families and neutralize black men," he states that one tactic is to make black men into "so-called 'women,' in which case homosexual and bisexual activity becomes the norm rather than the exception. Men of other cultures do not fear the so-called 'woman-like' men of any race."[17]

Madhubuti seems incapable of envisioning black gay men as anything other than effeminate men who pretend to be women. He doesn't realize that black men who are soft and feminine are still a threat to the system if they are politically conscious. Loving each other as men does not make black gays any less dangerous to the racist status quo. As a group, black gays can only be accused of being as politically "unconscious" as our heterosexual peers.

The lack of insight about African American homosexuality displayed by some of our heterosexual intellectuals is tragic. Their simplistic and shortsighted analyses promote ignorance and confusion in the African American community, and the oppression of black gays and lesbians. This oppression cripples the vital resources of the community insomuch as it requires a tremendous amount of energy to hate one another, as opposed to utilizing our differences constructively toward empowerment of the African American community.

Respond with love, not anger

Confronted by racial oppression in the larger society and sexual oppression in our own community, black gay intellectuals face formidable challenges. As stated earlier, we must not allow ourselves to be paralyzed by the hurt, anger, and rage we may feel toward homophobic and heterosexist scholars. Rejecting us is their loss — and it comes back to haunt us *all*. We have the right to criticize their erroneous ideas and to help build a better world for everyone. We know the reality of our lives. We know that we are not gay because of "prison." The vast majority of black gay men have never been near a prison. For Staples, Farrakhan, and Asante to suggest that most black gay men are gay because of prison shows a serious lack of competent insight and scholarship.

We know we are not gay because of "white oppression." Too many of us realized we were "different" during preadolescence before we knew what racism was or who white people were. Our feelings for other males were not taught by white schoolteachers or white dolls. America has done everything in its power to make black men hate themselves. Black men have been taught for hundreds of years that they are worthless. Yet despite this, black gay men love each other. We have protected, comforted, and cared for ourselves, and for thousands of our brothers, in a white society that despises our "blackness" and in a black community that condemns our love. When black men love each other in an environment that negates them, it is not a sign of sickness. It is a sign of health.

As gay men, we know that our desire to love each other is not wrong. There is a sacredness in the act of men loving men. We have experienced the exultation of brothers bonding together. Countless precious moments we have shared with friends and lovers validate the value of our lives. The sacredness of our love is our strength. It gives us the courage to challenge the homophobia and heterosexism of our brothers and sisters, and sustains us in the face of their rejection and ridicule.

It is our task to provide an understanding and a vision of homosexuality motivated by our love and not our anger. Anger eats within. It destroys the person who is angry more often than the subject of the anger. Love nurtures and strengthens us to challenge our brothers and sisters because we love them too much to allow their ignorance to continue.

We must help Haki Madhubuti see that his homophobia and heterosexism kept him separated from Max Robinson, his "friend and brother in the struggle." Robinson's death had a great impact on Madhubuti's feelings about AIDS. Before Robinson's death, Madhubuti was "convinced that AIDS was a white middle-class homosexual disease that, at worse, would only touch Black homosexuals." The first time he saw Robinson in the hospital, Madhubuti was "inwardly crushed" by Robinson's emaciated look and found it difficult to "keep back the tears." He states:

> Max did not tell me that he had AIDS... According to him, he was improving quickly and would be able to go home soon. I let it go at that, and two months later — without my seeing him again — Max was dead. It was his wish that people know he died of AIDS and did not contract it through the *assumed avenues* of drug use or homosexual activity. Max was a woman's man to the bone (one of his problems), and he did drink a great deal.[18]

Madhubuti's tale of Max Robinson's death is tragic in so many ways. It is a tragedy that on his deathbed Max Robinson had to lie to his friend. He did not tell Madhubuti the nature and extent of his illness, nor the nature and extent of his sexuality because he probably knew that Madhubuti viewed AIDS as something that "at worse, would only touch black homosexuals." Members of the black gay community knew that Robinson was more complex than simply being a "woman's man to the bone," and perhaps this pretense, that people like Madhubuti forced upon him, contributed to Robinson's three divorces and his drinking problem.

Baraka's dilemma: To be or not to be?

Too often the homophobia and heterosexism within the African American community forces men to be the "hardest hard." They must nullify any feelings and emotions others may consider unmanly. To prove their manhood, they will often attack that which they fear in themselves. Amiri Baraka (born Everett Leroy Jones) constantly denounces homosexuality in his writings. He despises "faggots" and believes being called one is the worst insult a man can suffer. In "A Poem For Black Hearts," Baraka praises the late Malcolm X as a "black god" whose death black men must avenge or be called "faggots till the end of the earth."[19]

Faggots are the epitome of what Baraka opposes. "Faggot" is the description he uses to insult black leaders he disagrees with. In the poem "Black Art," he speaks of the "negroleader on the steps of the white house — kneeling between the sheriff's thighs negotiating cooly for his people."[20] In "Civil Rights Poem," Baraka begins by stating, "Roywilkins is an eternal faggot. His spirit is a faggot."[21] In the poem "The Black Man Is Making New Gods," he refers to the crucifixion of Christ as "The Fag's Death they give us on a cross."[22] For Baraka, faggots have no redeeming qualities and should be persecuted as a matter of principle. In the poem "Hegel," he states, "I am not saying 'Let the State fuck its faggots,' only that no fag go unfucked, for purely impersonal reasons."[23]

In plays such as *The Baptism* and *The Toilet*, Baraka portrays homosexuals as degenerates and cowards.[24] They are weak, soft, and unmanly. Gay men are the antithesis of what he idealizes as the "Black man," and they become synonymous with his image of white men. In an essay titled "American Sexual Reference: Black Male," he writes "Most American white men are trained to be fags... [T]heir faces are weak and blank ... that red flush, those silk blue faggot eyes."[25]

According to Baraka, since white men have black men doing their manual labor, white men have become "estranged from ... actual physical work." As a consequence, white men are alienated from reality and nature. They have no real "claim to manhood." He states:

[A] people who lose their self-sufficiency because they depend on their "subjects" to do the world's work become effeminate and perverted... Do you understand the softness of the white man, the weakness ... the estrangement from reality? Can you for a second imagine the average mid-dle-class white man able to do somebody harm? Alone? Without the technology that at this moment [allows] him [to] rule the world.[26]

Baraka characterizes white men as spineless, middle-class bureaucrats, and black men as natural super-strong studs. To support his position, he points with pride to the fact that blacks dominate the "manly art" of boxing.[27]

Amiri Baraka is a fascinating study of the homosexual-heterosexual conflict among African American males, for the tragic irony is that the "faggot" Baraka attacks so viciously is in reality himself. He has never reconciled his homosexual past with his persona as the clenched-fist black militant leading mass movements, the perfect example of the black warrior. This conflict is alluded to in "Tone Poem" in which he writes:

Read this line young colored or white and know I felt the twist of dividing memory. Blood spoiled in the air, caked and anonymous. Arms opening, opened last night, we sat up howling and kissing. Men who loved each other. Will that be understood? That we could, and still move under cold nights with clenched-fists.[28]

Perhaps it is the homosexual desires Baraka had as an adolescent and young adult that motivate his homophobia. His homosexual desires are not revealed in *The Autobiography of LeRoi Jones*. No, to truly understand the paradox of Baraka's need to denounce faggots while at the same time suppressing his attraction, one must read an auto-biographical novel he wrote twenty years earlier, *The System of Dante's Hell*.[29] It is a story many gay brothers can relate to. After reading it, one's anger toward Baraka's homophobia is replaced with sympathy. We understand the pain and the fear.

Before he deemed himself Imamu Amiri Baraka, before he divorced his white wife, before he changed the spelling of his name from Leroy, to LeRoi, Baraka was a "short ... skinny ... runt [with] big bulbous eyes." He felt inadequate because of his size and was obsessed with growing taller. In grade school, his peers told him about "dicks and pussies and fags and bulldaggers." He saw how people reacted to "cocksuckers," and he grew to understand "what fucking was and what it had to do with sucking."[30]

As a teenager Baraka pretended to have only heterosexual desires, for he understood the penalty for being a faggot. "We did a lot of things, [those] years... We [told] lies to keep from getting belted, and [watched] a faggot take a beating in the snow from our lie. Our fear."[31]

As an undergraduate at Howard University, Baraka saw gay men harassed and ridiculed.[32] He felt alienated. It was at Howard that he changed his name to LeRoi, and began to read Gertrude Stein.[33] Poor grades, however, forced him to leave Howard in his junior year. He joined the Air Force and was stationed at various bases, including one in Rantoul, Illinois, near Chicago. It was in Chicago that he again engaged in homosexuality. In *The System of Dante's Hell*, he writes:

> In Chicago I kept making the queer scene. Under the "El" with a preacher... [He] held my head under the quilt. The first guy ... spoke to me grinning and I said my name was Stephen Dedalus... One more guy and it was over. On the train, I wrote all this down. A journal now sitting in a tray on top the closet... The journal says "Am I like that?"[34]

Once more, Baraka found himself disconnected and alienated.[35] His homosexual desires would not cease. He felt guilty and frightened of himself. "My cold sin in the cities," he writes, "My fear of my own death's insanity, and an actual longing for men that brooked in each finger of my memory."[36]

One night in the "Bottom," a poor black ghetto in Shreveport, Louisiana, the shame Baraka feels as a homosexual reaches a climax when he finds himself drunk in a whorehouse, dancing with a prostitute named Peaches. He becomes ill and attempts to leave, but she prevents him.

> She came around and rubbed my tiny pecker with her fingers. And still I moved away. I saw the look she gave me and wanted somehow to protest, say, "I'm sorry. I'm fucked up. My mind, is screwy, I don't know why. I can't think. I'm sick. I've been fucked in the ass. I love books... You don't want me. Please, Please, don't want me."[37]

Outside, Peaches and her friends tease Baraka like some "fag" by taking his cap and tossing it amongst themselves.[38] To get his hat back, Baraka agrees to buy Peaches another drink. He, too, has more to drink and becomes more intoxicated. Overwhelmed with shame, he longs to be "Some other soul, than the filth I feel. Have in me. Guilt like something of God's. Some separate suffering self."[39] Voices begin to haunt him. "You've got to like girls. Say something... Move. Frightened bastard. Frightened scared sissy motherfucker."[40]

Delirious, Baraka reminisces about his cold sin in the cities.

> It was Chicago. The fags and the winter. Sick thin boy, come out of those els... To go back. To sit lonely. Need to be used, touched ... I hate it... To feel myself go soft and want some person not myself... That I walked the streets hunting for warmth. To be pushed under a quilt, and call it love. To shit water for days and say I've been loved. Been warm.[41]

After dragging Baraka back to her house, Peaches strips him and grabs his penis. He is unable to get an erection. She chastises him and becomes violent.

She pulled, breathing spit on my chest. "Comeon, Baby, Comeon... Get hard... Get hard." And she slapped me now, with her hand. A short hard punch... She cursed. & pulled as hard as she could. [She said] "You don't like women, huh?... No wonder you so pretty ... ol bigeye faggot... Goddam punk, you gonna fuck me tonight or I'm gonna pull your fuckin dick aloose."

I was crying now. Hot hot tears and trying to ... say to Peaches, "Please, you don't know me. Not what's in my head. I'm beautiful. Stephen Dedalus... Feel my face, how tender. My eyes..."

And I [thought] of a black man under the el who took me home ... I remembered telling him all these things ... And [crawling] out of bed morning... Loved. Afraid.

[Peaches] started yelling. Faggot. Faggot. Sissy Motherfucker. And I pumped myself. Straining. Threw my hips at her. And she yelled, for me to fuck her. Fuck her. Fuck me, you lousy fag. And I twisted, spitting tears, and hitting my hips on hers, pounding my flesh in her, hearing myself weep.[42]

After fucking Peaches, Baraka dresses and leaves. He stumbles through the streets, lost and intoxicated. A gay man approaches him in the darkness saying, "Lemme suck yo dick, honey..." Once again Baraka is confronted with homosexual desire. The man begs him, but Baraka won't give in. Peaches has freed him of his past. He walks away as the gay man screams behind him like "some hurt ugly thing dying alone."[43]

Baraka returns to Peaches's house to sleep. He awakes a new man, a heterosexual man.

I woke up... And I felt myself smiling... [It] seemed that things had come to order... It seemed settled... I thought of black men sitting on their beds this saturday of my life listening quietly to their wives' soft talk. And felt the world grow together as I hadn't known it. All lies before, I thought. All fraud and sickness. This was the world... I cursed Chicago, and softened at the world. "You look so sweet," [Peaches] was saying. "Like you're real rested."[44]

Understanding Baraka's life turns our anger toward him to sympathy; indeed, pity. That he would feel so much guilt and shame for desiring male love is the lesser tragedy. The greater tragedy is that once he claims "heterosexuality," perhaps as a disguise, he then denounces and ridicules "faggots" so vehemently. How could a factor of life affording him the opportunity to be understanding and compassionate become one of pathetic hypocrisy? Baraka is not the first man to become a homophobe after experiencing homosexuality or repressing homosexual desire. We have encountered his kind before. Have taken them to our beds and soothed their fears. Made them feel whole in our arms. Our anger will not help these brothers to understand that they fear themselves. We must show them through compassion and understanding that one can be gay and be a socially, culturally and politically useful man. We can be gay and committed to "Blackness," committed to the liberation of black people. We can be clenched-fist militants no matter what gender we love.

Clap if you believe

We can specifically reject the homophobia and heterosexism of writers and scholars such as Madhubuti, Asante, and others, but we should not allow our rejection of their ideas and opinions in regard to those issues to prevent us from supporting them on issues we agree on. We cannot totally reject them. Our common problems as African Americans are too immense and our common resources too scarce. We may all agree with Madhubuti when he observes that:

> [M]any Black men have defined their lives as Black duplicates of the white male ethos... Black men, acting out of frustration and *ignorance*, adopt attitudes that are not productive or progressive... The political and sexual games that ... are demeaning and disrespectful ... become, due to a lack of *self-definition*, Black men's games also.[45]

We should also include homophobia as another attitude that black males have adopted largely from the white culture.

If Madhubuti is sincere in his call for "sensitivity [to the] personal differences as well as the political and cultural differences" of black people, we can indeed achieve understanding and dialogue. We can work with him if he truly believes that:

> *The search for truth* should always be our guiding force... Always be willing to question past actions as well as accept constructive criticism. Advocating an Afrikan American cultural movement doesn't mean being dogmatic and insensitive to other positions. Good is good, no matter where it comes from.[46]

If we, as African American people, join together in a "search for truth" that is mutually respectful of our differences, we will all benefit from the insights uncovered and the constructive criticism offered by each other. As black gays and lesbians, we must develop alliances with progressive black groups, organizations, and individuals to work together for the common good of the black community.

Developing an alliance with an organization such as the Nation of Islam, however, may not be as simple. Minister Farrakhan is undoubtedly becoming one of the great African American orators of this century in the tradition of Dr. King, Malcolm X, DuBois, and others. Millions of people listen to his speeches and respect what he says. He has an ability to communicate ideas that is exciting to behold. Unfortunately, Farrakhan's homophobic and heterosexist comments contribute to the oppression of black gays, lesbians, and women.

In 1990, members of the Nation of Islam began to run for political office in Washington, D.C., and in Maryland. If Farrakhan or his followers were to gain political power in the community, to what extent would their policies be secular rather than religious? Would they advocate that all issues in the black community be decided by the Koran?

Why should Africa's descendents base their lives and their future on the Koran, or the Bible? With all due respect, the Koran is not an artifact of African culture, it is Arabian. And the Bible in its present form was given to us by white slavemasters. Indeed, both books were introduced to Africa by people more interested in increasing their wealth than in Africa's well-being. Europeans and Arabs enslaved Africans. We don't owe them anything, so why should we be subservient to their books?

On May 20, 1990, Minister Farrakhan gave a speech in Oakland entitled, "The Time and What Must Be Done," in which he stated that African Americans are "polluted" by the decadence of white society. He advocated the strict enforcement of Old Testament and Koranic laws to force black people out of their wickedness and degeneracy. As the audience cheered, Farrakhan proclaimed that to save the nation, "the punishment for sleeping with your daughter — is death" and "the punishment for rape is death." He also included adultery and homosexuality as crimes that should be punished by death, stating:

> God is no respecter of persons — [Y]our mother is not above the law. Your brother, your sister, your friend — nobody is above God's law.
>
> Do you know why [in biblical times] they [stoned you to death] for adultery? Because there is nothing more sacred than marriage and family. Nothing... [applause] And every time you stone [an adulterer] you're killing the thought in your own mind... You make an example [by stoning someone] because the individual is not more important than the community [or the] nation. So you sacrifice the individual for the preservation of a nation. [applause]
>
> Now brothers, in the Holy world you can't switch. [Farrakhan walks across the stage like an effeminate man] No, no, no ... in the Holy world you better hide that stuff 'cause see if God made you for a woman, you can't go with a man... You know what the penalty of that is in the Holy land? Death... They don't play with that... [he laughs] Sister get to going with another sister — Both women [are decapitated.][47]

It is dangerous and unwise for Farrakhan to equate homosexuality and adultery with rape and child molestation. The former are victimless activities between consenting adults. The latter are acts of victimization using force and coercion. Has Farrakhan forgotten the dilemma he and Malcolm X faced when they discovered that the Honorable Elijah Muhammad was a *repeated* adulterer? On page 295 of his autobiography, Malcolm states:

> As far back as 1955, I had heard hints... [My] mind simply refused to accept anything so grotesque as adultery mentioned in the same breath with Mr. Muhammad's name...
>
> [In April 1963,] I told Mr. Muhammad what was being said... Elijah Muhammad [replied,] "When you read about how David took another man's wife, I'm that David. You read about Noah, who got drunk — that's me. You read about Lot, who went and laid up with his own daughters. I have to fulfill all of those things."
>
> I found — some [Muslim officials] had already heard [the rumors.] One of them, Minister Louis [Farrakhan] of Boston, as much as seven months before. They had been living with the dilemma themselves.[48]

Farrakhan did not call for the death penalty to punish the Honorable Elijah Muhammad's adultery. No, he remained silent. And after Malcolm X left the Nation of Islam, Farrakhan was given Malcolm's former position as the head of the New York City Mosque.

It is a mistake, tactically and strategically, to advocate the killing of black gays and lesbians. Why encourage more death in the African American community? Too many black men are being killed daily. Farrakhan's statements against homosexuality give the men who follow him a license to harass black men and women who they think are gay. Persecuting gays reinforces a false sense of manhood. Rather than confront the real enemy — those who actually cause and control the oppression — their frustrations caused by powerlessness are soothed by intimidating those who they consider weak. It's easy to prove your manhood by putting down "faggots." Baraka did it for years.

The Bible and the Koran are not the only holy books used to defend heterosexism and homophobia. Egyptologists and African historians, such as Yosef Ben-Jochannan, refer to the *Book of Coming Forth by Day and by Night* (better known as the Egyptian Book of the Dead) as an Egyptian spiritual text that condemns homosexuality. Ben-Jochannan is clearly one of the foremost African scholars of the twentieth century. Thus, his claims that the ancient Egyptians forbade homosexuality must be investigated seriously by black gay scholars.

In his book *The Black Man's Religion*, Ben-Jochannan lists twenty-nine of the forty-two "Negative Confessions" that a departed Egyptian soul had to affirm on the Day of Judgment. The Negative Confessions are rules to live by, similar to the Ten Commandments. Two of the confessions he cites refer to sexual activity: number 19 — "I have not defiled the wife of a man" — and number 27 — "I have not committed acts of impurity or sodomy."[49]

For a reference, Ben-Jochannan cites E.A. Wallis Budge's *The Egyptian Book of The Dead*. Budge, however, does not use the word "sodomy." According to Budge, three of the forty-two Negative Confessions stated in the hieroglyphic text refer to sexual activity: number 11 — "I have not committed fornication"; number 21 — "I have not defiled the wife of a man"; and number 22 — "I have not polluted, or defiled, myself."[50] It is the latter confession that Ben-Jochannan misinterpreted as forbidding homosexuality. A study of the actual hieroglyph with the assistance of a hieroglyphic dictionary reveals that the Negative Confession of "polluting or defiling" oneself actually refers to "masturbation [or the] irregular emission of semen," not sodomy.[51] Within the dictionary, there is a hieroglyphic symbol that means "sodomy" and it is not used anywhere in the Negative Confessions.

Redefining ourselves and our future

While it is critically important to rebut homophobia and heterosexism, the most crucial challenge facing black gay scholars is to develop an affirming and liberating philosophical understanding of homosexuality that will self-actualize black gay genius. Such a task requires a new epistemology, a new way of "knowing," that incorporates the views our African ancestors had about the material and the metaphysical world. We can no longer accept American society's views of us and the purpose of our lives. We should see ourselves as "geniuses" in the root sense of the word, i.e., *genii* — divine spirits that have a higher purpose to manifest on the physical plane.

In some African cultures, gays were considered blessed because the Creator had endowed them with both male and female principles. Often they served as the spiritual advisors for the community.[52] In light of this should we be surprised that so many gay men are active in the black church?

Another important issue we must address is the role that gay men will play in the socialization of black males. Our younger brothers desperately need an outlook on life that goes beyond the world of Hollywood or Madison Avenue. They need role models and rituals that symbolize rites of passage from childhood to adulthood. Young gay males, in particular, and black males generally, need a definition of "manhood" radically different from the one adopted through assimilation. Such a definition must liberate and empower us, enhance our self-esteem and stimulate the manifestation of creative potential. Black male youth need to know that the measure of a man should be based not on the gender of his sex partner, but on his contribution to the community.

The argument that homosexuality threatens black male-female relationships and the black family lacks credibility. Homosexual love does not destabilize true heterosexual love relationships, the black family, or the black community. If a man is sexually attracted to other men, but community homophobia forces him to hide his feelings, he might marry a woman who then bears their children. Should that man one day be unable to sustain the psychic pain of ignoring his true sexual feelings and leave his family, the fault lies not in his homosexuality but in the community's homophobia that forced him to live a lie.

Our straight brothers and sisters need to be more honest and to admit that their relationships are falling apart even when both parties are staunch heterosexuals. The sisters are constantly complaining about "niggers," while the brothers complain about "bitches." Between them there's an abundance of blame, anger, distrust, and hatred, but little love.

Gay men *do* contribute to the black family. A significant number of us are fathers who support our children. Many of us have nieces and nephews whom we advise, guide, and watch out for. We send money to our parents and give shelter to cousins. Unfortunately, homophobia in the black community forces many of us into "closets." We don't say we're gay, thus our families and the community do not realize the significant contributions we make as gay and lesbian members of the family and the community.

The freeing of black gay genius requires that we develop institutions to secure the foundation of the black gay community. Madhubuti's call for "dialogue" notwithstanding, homophobic statements such as his, and those of Molefi Asante and Nathan Hare, indicate that their tolerance for homosexuality is one of expediency. The reality of our situation dictates that we negotiate with them, and others like them, from a position of cultural, economic, and political strength in the mutual understanding of needing each other.

To achieve the goals outlined herein, the political consciousness of black gay men will have to be raised. Too often, we are narrowly focused on fabulous parties, fierce clubs, fashion, face, and fun. There is a desperate need for organizations to provide social activities that are culturally, educationally, and politically constructive. Organizations such as Gay Men of African Descent (GMAD) in New York City, and Adodi and Unity, Inc., in Philadelphia, should be commended for their efforts in this area.

The tasks faced by black gay intellectuals are formidable. The problems we confront are complex and intertwined. To the extent that our people are homophobic and heterosexist, our tasks become more difficult. We should acknowledge the "sensitivities" and "talents" within us, the root of which is black gay genius. We have been blessed with gifts to share in a society that views love and tenderness between men as a weakness. As we balance and synthesize the male and female energy within our souls, we come closer to the Supreme Being. The inner Voice tells us that our feelings of love are righteous. Black men loving black men is indeed a sacred act.

Notes

1. This essay focuses on black gay males. It does not address the experiences of black lesbians. Thus, the masculine pronoun and possessive will be used in most cases.

2. Nathan Hare and Julia Hare, *The Endangered Black Family: Coping with the Unisexualization and Coming Extinction of the Black Race* (San Francisco: Black Think Tank, 1984), p. 64.

3. Ibid., p. 65.

4. See Jawanza Kunjufu, "Not Allowed to Be Friends and/or Lovers," in *Crisis in Black Sexual Politics,* ed. Nathan Hare and Julia Hare (San Francisco: Black Think Tank, 1989), p. 110.

5. Hare and Hare, *The Endangered Black Family*, p. 151.

6. Nathan Hare and Julia Hare, eds., *Crisis in Black Sexual Politics* (San Francisco: Black Think Tank), p. 2.

7. Hare and Hare, *The Endangered Black Family*, p. 66.

8. Robert Staples, *Black Masculinity: The Black Man's Role in American Society* (San Francisco: Black Scholar Press, 1982), p. 88.

9. Ibid., p. 90.

10. Joseph Eure and Richard Jerome, eds., *Back Where We Belong: Selected Speeches by Minister Louis Farrakhan* (Philadelphia: PC International Press, 1989), p. 138.

11. Molefi Keke Asante, *Afrocentricity: The Theory of Social Change* (Buffalo: Amulefi, 1980), p. 65. Apparently, Asante is so homophobic that he uses "Homosexuality" as a section heading, yet he doesn't list the section in the table of contents.

12. Ibid.

13. Haki R. Madhubuti (Don L. Lee), *Enemies: The Clash of Races* (Chicago: Third World Press, 1978), p. 148.

14. Ibid.

15. Hare and Hare, *The Endangered Black Family*, p. 65.

16. Haki R. Madhubuti, *Black Men: Obsolete, Single, Dangerous? The Afrikan American in Transition: Essays in Discovery, Solution, and Hope* (Chicago: Third World Press, 1990), p. 60.

17. Ibid., pp. 73–74.

18. Ibid., p. 52.

19. LeRoi Jones (Amiri Baraka), *Black Magic* (New York: Bobbs-Merrill, 1969), p. 112.

20. LeRoi Jones (Amiri Baraka) and Larry Neal, *Black Fire* (New York: Morrow, 1968), p. 302.

21. Jones (Baraka), *Black Magic,* p. 140.

22. Ibid., pp. 205–206.

23. Ibid., pp. 23–24.

24. LeRoi Jones (Amiri Baraka), *The Baptism* and *The Toilet* (New York: Grove Press, 1966).

25. LeRoi Jones (Amiri Baraka), *Home: Social Essays* (New York: Morrow, 1966), p. 216.

26. Ibid., pp. 217 and 220.

27. Ibid., p. 217.

28. Jones (Baraka), *Black Magic*, p. 28.

29. LeRoi Jones (Amiri Baraka), *The System of Dante's Hell* (London: MacGibbon & Kee, 1966). The thesis of this essay regarding Baraka's former homosexuality rests primarily on the premise that *The System of Dante's Hell* is an autobiographical novel. This researcher believes such a premise to be correct for several reasons. First, *The System of Dante's Hell* is written in the first person. It is set in Newark, New Jersey, and many of the names of characters and places, as well as sequences of events, in *The System of Dante's Hell* parallels Baraka's own life as stated in his autobiography. See Imamu Amiri Baraka, *The Autobiography of LeRoi Jones* (New York: Freundlich Books, 1984). Second, Baraka has cited *The System of Dante's Hell* in an autobiographical context. In his *Autobiography*, Baraka refers the reader to *The System of Dante's Hell* and the incident involving Peaches for details about his once being AWOL while in the military. On page 12 of the *Autobiography*, he states: "In Shreveport ... I ended up two days AWOL. I had gotten lost and laid up with a sister down in the Bottom (one black community of Shreveport — see *The System of Dante's Hell*) and finally came back rumpled and hung over and absolutely broke." Third, Baraka's homosexuality is referred to by his first wife, Hettie Jones, in *How I Became Hettie Jones* (New York: Dutton, 1990), p. 86. She states: "[Roi] once confessed to me some homosexual feelings, though never any specific experiences."

30. Baraka, *The Autobiography of LeRoi Jones*, pp. 1 and 12.

31. Jones (Baraka), *The System of Dante's Hell*, p. 65. In his play *The Toilet*, Baraka writes of a similar incident in high school where one boy, "Karolis," is beaten by a boy named Ray and his friends. Ray is described as "short, intelligent," and "popeyed." Karolis is attacked for writing Ray a love letter. Ray watches silently as his friends beat Karolis unconscious, but at the end of the play it is clear that Ray lied about not having had a homosexual encounter with Karolis.

32. See LeRoi Jones (Baraka), "The Alternative," in *Tales* (New York: Grove Press, 1967).

33. Baraka, *The Autobiography of LeRoi Jones*, pp. 87–88.

34. Jones (Baraka), *The System of Dante's Hell*, pp. 57–58.

35. Baraka, *The Autobiography of LeRoi Jones*, p. 100.

36. Jones (Baraka), *The System of Dante's Hell*, pp. 125 and 127.

37. Ibid., p. 131.

38. Ibid., p. 132.

39. Ibid., p. 134.

40. Ibid., pp. 134 and 135.

41. Ibid., pp. 138–139.

42. Ibid., pp. 139–141.

43. Ibid., p. 142.

44. Ibid., pp. 147–148.

45. Madhubuti, *Black Men*, p. 61.

46. Ibid., p.111.

47. Louis Farrakhan, *The Time and What Must Be Done*, a videotape of a speech delivered in Oakland, California, May 20, 1990. The videotape was produced by the Final Call, Inc., Chicago, Illinois.

48. Malcolm X and Alex Haley, *The Autobiography of Malcolm X* (New York: Grove Press, 1966), pp. 295–299.

49. Yosef Ben-Jochannan, *The Black Man's Religion and Extracts and Comments from the Holy Black Bible* (New York: Alkebu-lan Books Associates, 1974), p. 46.

50. E.A. Wallis Budge, *The Egyptian Book of the Dead* (New York: Dover, 1967), pp. 196–201. It's interesting to note that Ben-Jochannan did not include in his list the Negative Confession, "I have not committed fornication." To have done so would have implied that the Egyptians forbade sexual activity between unmarried persons — a commandment few heterosexual cultural nationalists would ever consider obeying.

51. E.A. Wallis Budge, *An Egyptian Hieroglyphic Dictionary*, vol. 2 (New York: Dover, 1978), p. 818.

52. See Judy Grahn, *Another Mother Tongue* (Boston: Beacon Press, 1984), pp. 120–126; Arthur Evans, *Witchcraft and the Gay Counterculture* (Boston: Fag Rag Books, 1978), pp. 106–107; Esther Newton, "Of Yams, Grinders, and Gays," *Outlook: National Lesbian and Gay Quarterly* 1 (Summer 1988): 28–37; and Cary Alan Johnson, "Inside Gay Africa," *Black/Out: The Magazine of the National Coalition of Black Lesbians and Gays* 1, no. 2 (Fall 1986): 18–21, 30–31.

CHARLES I. NERO

Toward a black gay aesthetic
Signifying in contemporary black gay literature

Western literature has often posited the heterosexual white male as hero, with Gays, Blacks and women as Other... The development of Black literature, women's literature, Gay literature, and now Black Gay literature is not so much a rewriting of history as an additional writing of it; together these various literatures, like our various selves, produce history... Our past as Black Gay men is only now being examined.

—Daniel Garrett, "Other Countries: The Importance of Difference"[1]

Much of the Afro-American literary tradition can be read as successive attempts to create a new narrative space for representing the recurring referent of Afro-American literature, the so-called Black Experience.

—Henry Louis Gates, Jr., *The Signifying Monkey*[2]

All I can say is — if this is my time in life ... goodbye misery.

—Lorraine Hansberry, *A Raisin in the Sun*[3]

Introduction

With only a few exceptions, the intellectual writings of black Americans have been dominated by heterosexual ideologies that have resulted in the gay male experience being either excluded, marginalized, or ridiculed.[4] Because of the heterosexism among African American intellectuals and the racism in the white gay community, black gay men have been an invisible population. However, the last five years have seen a movement characterized by political activism and literary production by openly gay black men. Given their invisibility by both black heterosexism and white gay racism, two questions emerge: How have black gay men created a positive identity for themselves and how have they constructed literary texts which would render their lives visible, and therefore valid? I propose in this essay to answer the former by answering the latter, i.e., I will focus on the strategies by black men who have either identified themselves as gay or who feature black gay characters prominently in their work. The writers I examine will be Samuel Delany, George Wolfe, Billi Gordon, Larry Duplechan, Craig R. Harris, and Essex Hemphill.

The critical framework that I use is strongly influenced by my reading of Mary Helen Washington's *Invented Lives* and Henry Louis Gates, Jr.'s critical method of signifying. In *Invented Lives*, Washington brilliantly analyzes the narrative strategies ten black women have used between 1860 and 1960 to bring themselves into visibility and power in a world dominated by racism and sexism.[5] Like Washington, Gates's concern is with the paradoxical relationship of African Americans with the printed text, i.e., since Eurocentric writing defines the black as "other," how does the "other" gain authority in the text? To resolve this, Gates proposes a theory of criticism based upon the African American oral tradition of signifying. Signifying is, for Gates, "the black term for what in classical European rhetoric are called the figures of signification," or stated differently, "the indirect use of words that changes the meaning of a word or words."[6] Signifying has numerous figures which include: capping, loud-talking, the dozens, reading, going off, talking smart, sounding, joaning (jonesing), dropping lugs, snapping, woofing, styling out, and calling out of one's name.

As a rhetorical strategy, signifying assumes that there is shared knowledge between communicators and, therefore, that information can be given indirectly. Geneva Smitherman in *Talkin and Testifyin* gives the following examples of signifying:

- Stokely Carmichael, addressing a white audience at the University of California, Berkeley, 1966: "It's a privilege and an honor to be in the white intellectual ghetto of the West."
- Malcolm X on Martin Luther King, Jr.'s nonviolent revolution (referring to the common practice of singing "We Shall Overcome" at civil rights protests of the sixties): "In a revolution, you swinging, not singing."
- Reverend Jesse Jackson, merging sacred and secular siggin in a Breadbasket Saturday morning sermon: "Pimp, punk, prostitute, preacher, Ph.D. — all the P's — you still in slavery!"
- A black middle-class wife to her husband who had just arrived home several hours later than usual: "You sho got home early today for a change."[7]

Effective signifying is, Smitherman states, "to put somebody in check ... to make them think about and, one hopes, correct their behavior."[8] Because signifying relies on indirection to give information, it requires that participants in any communicative encounter pay attention to, as Claudia Mitchell-Kernan states, "the total universe of discourse."[9]

Gates's theory of signifying focuses on black forms of talk. I believe that identifying these forms of talk in contemporary black gay literature is important for two reasons. First, the use of signifying by black gay men places their writing squarely within the African American literary tradition. Second, signifying permits black gay men to revise the "Black Experience" in African American literature and, thereby, to create a space for themselves.

The remainder of this essay is divided into two parts. The first part examines the heterosexist context in which black gay men write. Examined are heterosexism and homophobia in the writings of contemporary social scientists, scholars, and, in a longer passage, the novels of Toni Morrison. The last section discusses black gay men's attempts to revise the African American literary tradition. Specifically examined are the signifying on representations of desire, the black religious experience, and gender configurations.

Heterosexism and African American intellectuals

Some social scientists have claimed that homosexuality is alien to the black community. Communication scholar Molefi Asante has argued in *Afrocentricity: A Theory of Social Change* that homosexual practices among black men were initially imposed on them by their white slave owners and that the practice is maintained by the American prison institution.[10] Asante has attributed homosexuality to Greco-Roman culture, with the added assertion that "homosexuality does not represent an Afrocentric way of life."[11] Likewise, in *Black Skin, White Masks*, Frantz Fanon, the widely read Martiniquois psychiatrist and freedom-fighter, declared that "Caribbean men never experience the Oedipus complex," and therefore, in the Caribbean, "there is no homosexuality, which is, rather, an attribute of the white race, Western civilization."[12]

Other scholars and writers have contended that homosexuality is a pathology stemming from the inability of black men to cope with the complexities of manhood in a racist society. Alvin Poussaint, the noted Harvard psychiatrist and adviser to the *Cosby Show*, stated in a 1978 *Ebony* article that some black men adopt homosexuality as a maneuver to help them avoid the increasing tension developing between black men and women.[13] "Homosexuality," according to black writer and liberationist Imamu Amiri Baraka, "is the most extreme form of alienation acknowledged within white society" and it occurs among "a people who lose their self-sufficiency because they depend on their subjects to do the world's work," thus rendering them "effeminate and perverted."[14] According to Eldridge Cleaver, homosexuality among black men is a "racial death wish," and a frustrating experience because "in their sickness [black men who practice homosexuality] are unable to have a baby by a white man."[15] In *The Endangered Black Family*, Nathan Hare and Julia Hare view homosexuals as confused but worthy of compassion because, they state, "Some of them may yet be saved."[16] The Hares seem to imply that black gay and lesbian people require treatment for either illness or brainwashing: "What we must do is offer the homosexual brother or sister a proper compassion and acceptance without advocacy. We might not advocate, for instance, the religion of Mormonism, or venereal disease, laziness or gross obesity..."[17]

The acclaimed writer Toni Morrison has woven into her novels these ideas of homosexuality as alien to African cultures, as forced upon black men by racist European civilizations, and as the inability to acquire and sustain manhood. In her first novel, *The Bluest Eye*, she played on the stereotype of the "light-skinned" black man as weak, effeminate, and sexually impotent. Soaphead Church, "a cinnamon-eyed West Indian with lightly browned skin," limited his sexual interests to little girls because, Morrison wrote, "he was too diffident to confront homosexuality" and found "little boys insulting, scary, and stubborn."[18] In *Tar Baby*, black homosexual men were self-mutilating transvestites who had dumped their masculinity because they "found the whole business of being black and men at the same time too difficult."[19]

In her 1988 Pulitzer Prize–winning *Beloved*, Morrison surpassed her earlier efforts in using homophobia with the creation of the five heroic black men of the Sweet Home plantation. Sweet Home men were unlike slaves on nearby plantations, as their owner Mr. Garner bragged to other farmers: "Y'all got boys. Young boys, old boys, picky boys, stroppin boys. Now at Sweet Home, my niggers is men every one of em. Bought um thataway, raised em thataway. Men every one."[20] Although deprived of sex with women, Sweet Home men were capable of enormous restraint and for sexual relief they either masturbated or engaged in sex with farm animals. When Mr. Garner added to his plantation a new slave, the thirteen-year-old "iron-eyed" Sethe, the Sweet Home men "let the girl be" and allowed her to choose one of them despite the fact that they "were young and so sick with the absence of women they had taken to *calves*" (emphasis added).[21] Sethe took over a year to choose one of the Sweet Home men. Morrison described that year of waiting: "[It was] a long, tough year of thrashing on pallets eaten up with dreams of her. A year of yearning, when rape seemed the solitary gift of life. The restraint they had exercised possible only because they were Sweet Home men..."[22]

Yet Morrison's description of the restrained Sweet Home men does a great disservice to the complexity of men's lives. Her description reinforces a false notion of a hierarchy of sexual practices in which masturbation is only a substitute for intercourse. Morrison's description is homophobic because it reveals her inability to imagine homosexual relationships among heroic characters. By implication, sex with farm animals is preferable to homoerotic sex, which is like a perverse reading of a spiritual: "Before I practice homosexuality, I'll practice bestiality, and go home to my Father and be free."

Morrison rejects from her fiction the idea that homosexual desire among slave men could actually lead to loving relationships. This, in fact, did happen. Autobiographical evidence exists that slave men in the Americas practiced and even institutionalized homosexuality. Esteban Montejo, the subject of *The Autobiography of a Runaway Slave*, twice discusses the prevalence of homosexuality among Cuban slave men in his comments on the sexual customs of the plantation. The first incident refers to physical abuse and possibly the rape of young black boys. Montejo states:

> If a boy was pretty and lively he was sent inside, to the master's house. And there they started softening him up ... well, I don't know! They used to give the boy a long palm-leaf and make him stand at one end of the table while they ate. And they said, "Now see that no flies get in the food!' If a fly did, they scolded him severely and even whipped him.[23]

The second incident is discussed within the context of the scarcity of women on the plantation. "To have one [a woman] of your own," Montejo writes, "you had either to be over twenty-five or catch yourself one in the fields."[24] Some men, however, he states, "had sex among themselves and did not want to know anything of women."[25] Montejo's comments include observations about the economics of homosexual households. He notes that the division of labor in these households resembled male–female roles in which the "effeminate men washed the clothes and did the cooking too, if they had a husband."[26] The men in these relationships also benefited financially from the existence of the "provision grounds," lands allocated to slaves in the Caribbean to grow crops to sell in the local markets on Sunday. Montejo writes: "They [effeminate men] were good workers and occupied themselves with their plots of land, giving the produce to their husbands to sell to the white farmers."[27]

Most interesting in Montejo's narrative is the reaction of other slaves to their homosexual brethren. The older men hated homosexuality, he states, and they "would have nothing to do with queers."[28] Their hatred leads Montejo to speculate that the practice did not come from Africa. Unfortunately, Montejo limits his speculations on homosexuality to origins and not to prohibitions. Thus, another speculation could be that homosexuality was prohibited, but that the practice itself was neither unknown nor undreamt. Montejo's narrative suggests that the influence of the old men over the feelings and attitudes of other slaves about homosexuality was limited. The slaves did not have a pejorative name for those who practiced homosexuality and it was not until "after Abolition that the term [effeminate] came into use," Montejo states.[29] Montejo, himself, held the view that the practice of homosexuality was a private matter: "To tell the truth, it [homosexuality] never bothered me. I am of the opinion that a man can stick his arse where he wants."[30] Montejo's narrative challenges the heterosexist assumptions about the sexualities and the family life of blacks before abolition in the Americas. At least in Cuba, homoerotic sex and exclusively male families were not uncommon.

In the United States, accounts of homosexuality among blacks before abolition are scanty. This is because accounts of slaves' sexuality are sparse and, until recently, social customs in the United States and Great Britain proscribed public discussions of sexuality.[31] Homosexuality, however, did occur during the colonial period among black men because laws forbidding the practice were created and sentences were carried out. These laws and sentences are discussed in A. Leon Higginbotham, Jr.'s *In the Matter of Color: Race and the American Legal Process* and Jonathan Katz's two documentary works *Gay/Lesbian Almanac* and *Gay American History*. Katz documents the case of Jan Creoli, identified as a "negro," who in 1646 in New Netherland (Manhattan) was sentenced to be "choked to death, and then burnt to ashes" for committing the act of sodomy with ten-year-old Manuel Congo.[32] Congo, whose name suggests that he was black, was sentenced "to be carried to the place where Creoli is to be executed, tied to a stake, and faggots piled around him, for justice sake, and to be flogged..."[33] In a second case, "Mingo alias Cocke Negro," a Massachusetts slave, was reportedly executed for "forcible Buggery," a term that Katz suggests is a male–male act, rather than bestiality.[34] Both Katz and Higginbotham discuss the development of sexual crime laws in Pennsylvania between 1700 and 1780 that carefully distinguished between blacks and whites: Life imprisonment was the penalty for whites and death was for blacks convicted of buggery which, Katz notes, probably meant bestiality and sodomy.[35]

Although the evidence for homosexual practices among black male slaves is small, it does suggest that we do not exclude homoeroticism from life on the plantation. The gay Jewish historian Martin Bauml Duberman's words are most appropriate here:

> After all, to date we've accumulated only a tiny collection of historical materials that record the existence of *heterosexual* behavior in the past. Yet no one claims that that minuscule amount of evidence is an accurate measure of the actual amount of heterosexual activity which took place.[36]

Duberman's words and the evidence we have suggest that, at best, our understanding of the sexuality of our slave ancestors is fragmentary. We need to uncover more and to reread diaries, letters, and narratives to gain a greater understanding of the sexuality of our forebears. At the very least, we need to revise our models of the black family and of homosexuality as alien to black culture.

Morrison's homophobia, as that of so many other black intellectuals, is perhaps more closely related to Judeo-Christian beliefs than to the beliefs of her ancestors. Male homosexuality is associated with biblical ideas of weakness as effeminacy.[37] Many of these intellectuals would also argue that the Judeo-Christian tradition is a major tool of the Western-Eurocentric view of reality that furthers the oppression of blacks. Paradoxically, by their condemnation of homosexuality and lesbianism, these intellectuals contribute to upholding an oppressive Eurocentric view of reality.

Enter black gay men

It should be obvious that black gay men must look at other black intellectuals with great caution and skepticism because the dominant view of reality expressed is oppressively heterosexist. Black gay men must also be cautious of looking for an image of themselves in white gay men because the United States is still a racist society. For example, even though one in five homosexual or bisexual men with AIDS is black, it can be argued that Larry Kramer's searing AIDS polemic, *The Normal Heart*, is about gay people, *not* black people. The characters in the drama are from the "fabled 1970s Fire Island/*After Dark* crowd," which tended to be white, middle-class, and very exclusionary on the basis of race, unless one counts the occasional presence of the reigning "disco diva" — who was usually a black woman or the wonderful African American gender-blurring singer Sylvester. In addition, Kramer makes several remarks in *The Normal Heart* that imply that he accepts certain historically racist ideas about blacks.[38] With a critical eye, one can also find occurrences of racism in works ranging from literature to visual pornography created by or aimed at gay men that employ a racist vision of reality.[39]

Partly as a reaction to racism in gay culture, but mostly in response to the heterosexism of black intellectuals and writers, African American gay men signify on many aspects of the "Black Experience" in their literature. The areas discussed in this section are representations of sexual desire, the black religious experience, and gender configurations.

Representing sexual desire

Because of the historical and often virulent presence of racism, black literature has frequently had as its goal the elevation of "the race" by presenting the group in its "best light." The race's "best light" often has meant depicting blacks with those values and ways that mirrored white Americans and Europeans. For black writers this has usually meant tremendous anxiety over the representation of sexuality. An excellent example of this anxiety is W.E.B. DuBois's reaction to Claude McKay's 1920 novel *Home to Harlem*. In the novel, McKay, gay and Jamaican, wrote about much of the night life in Harlem, including one of the first descriptions of a gay and lesbian bar in an African American work of fiction. DuBois wrote:

> ...Claude McKay's *Home to Harlem* for the most part nauseates me, and after the dirtier parts of its filth I feel distinctly like taking a bath ... McKay has set out to cater for that prurient demand on the part of white folks for a portrayal in Negroes of that utter licentiousness ... which a certain decadent section of the white world ... wants to see written out in black and white and saddled on black Harlem ... He has used every art and emphasis to paint drunkenness, fighting, lascivious sexual promiscuity and utter absence of restraint in as bold and bright colors as he can ... As a picture of Harlem life or of Negro life anywhere, it is, of course, nonsense. Untrue, not so much as on account of its facts, but on account of its emphasis and glaring colors.[40]

The anxiety that DuBois felt was as acute for black women. Mary Helen Washington comments that this anxiety about the representation of sexuality "goes back to the nineteenth century and the prescription for womanly 'virtues' which made slave women automatically immoral and less feminine than white women," as in the case of the slave woman Harriet Jacobs, who considered not publishing her 1860 narrative *Incidents in the Life of a Slave Girl* because she "bore two children as a single woman rather than submit to forced concubinage."[41] The representation of sexuality is even more problematic for black gay men than for heterosexual African Americans because of societal disapproval against impersonal sex, in which gay men frequently engage, and because gay sex is not connected in any way with the means of reproduction.

Black gay science fiction writer Samuel Delany, in his autobiography *The Motion of Light in Water*, takes particular delight in signifying on society's disapproval of impersonal homoerotic sex. His signifying is greatly aided by using the autobiographical form, a successful mode for black Americans, as Michael Cooke maintains, because "the self is the source of the system of which it is a part, creates what it discovers, and although it is nothing unto itself, it is the possibility of everything for itself."[42] By using himself as the source of the system, Delany is able to signify on ideas about impersonal sex. Delany imbues situations involving impersonal sex with social and political significance in the context of the repressive 1950s and early 1960s. Contrary to stereotypes that group sex is wild and out of control, the situation on the piers at the end of Christopher Street "with thirty-five, fifty, a hundred all-but-strangers is," Delany states, "hugely ordered, highly social, attentive, silent, and grounded in a certain care, if not community."[43] At the piers, when arrests of eight or nine men occurred and were reported in the newspapers without mentioning the hundreds who had escaped, it was a reassurance to the city fathers, the police, the men arrested, and even those who escaped "that the image of the homosexual as outside society — which is the myth that the outside of language, with all its articulation, is based on — was, somehow, despite the arrests, intact."[44] Delany's first visit to the St. Mark's Baths in 1963 produced a Foucault-like revelation that the legal and medical silences on homosexuality was "a huge and pervasive discourse" which prevented one from gaining "a clear, accurate, and extensive picture of extant public sexual institutions."[45] The result of Delany's signification is that his participation in impersonal sex in public places is given a political and social importance much like the significance given to ordinary, day-to-day acts of resistance recounted by the subjects of African American autobiographies from Frederick Douglass's *My Bondage and My Freedom* to Maya Angelou's *I Know Why the Caged Bird Sings*.

Just as Delany seeks to revise attitudes about impersonal sex, Larry Duplechan signifies on both black middle-class and gay stereotypes of interracial love and lust. On the one hand the black middle class and the mental health professions have conspired together to label a black person's sexual attraction to a white as pathology.[46] On the other, gay men have created a host of terms to denigrate participants in black/white sexual relationships, e.g.: *dinge queen, chocolate lover*, and *snow queen*. In *Blackbird* and *Eight Days a Week*, we are introduced to Duplechan's protagonist, Johnnie Ray Rousseau, as a senior in high school in the former, and as a 22-year-old aspiring singer living in Los Angeles in the latter. In Duplechan's first novel, *Eight Days a Week*, he summarizes both the gay and the black middle-class stereotype: "I was once told by a black alto sax player named Zaz (we were in bed at the time, mind you) that my preference for white men (and blonds, the whitest of white, to boot) was the sad but understandable end result of 300 years of white male oppression."[47] Contrary to Zaz's opinion, Johnnie Ray's sexual attraction to white men is anything but the result of 300 years of white male oppression, and if it is, it allows Duplechan a major moment of signifying in African American literature: the sexual objectification of white men by a black man.

Revising our culture's ideas about male–male sexual desire and love is a major concern in Essex Hemphill's collection of poems *Conditions*.[48] In particular, "Conditions XXIV" signifies on heterosexual culture's highly celebrated "rite of passage," the marriage ceremony. Hemphill signifies on the marriage ceremony in an excellent example of "capping," a figure of speech which revises an original statement by adding new terms. Hemphill honors the bonds created from desire by capping on the exchange of wedding bands. In the opening and closing sentences, fingers are not the received place for wedding rings:

> In america
> I place my ring
> on your cock
> where it belongs...
>
> In america,
> place your ring
> on my cock
> where it belongs.

Vows are also exchanged in the poem, but they do not restrict and confine. Instead, these vows are "What the rose whispers/before blooming..." The vows are:

> I give you my heart,
> a safe house.
> I give you promises other than
> milk, honey, liberty.
> I assume you will always
> be a free man with a dream.

Implicitly, "Conditions XXIV" strips away the public pomp and spectacle of the wedding ceremony to reveal its most fundamental level: desire. By capping on the wedding ceremony, Hemphill places homoerotic desire on an equal plane with heterosexuality.

Signifying on the church

Historically religion has served as a liberating force in the African American community. Black slaves publicly and politically declared that Christianity and the institution of slavery were incompatible as early as 1774, according to Albert Raboteau in *Slave Religion*. "In that year," Raboteau notes, "the governor of Massachusetts received 'The Petition of a Grate Number of Blacks of this Province who by divine permission are held in a state of slavery within the bowels of a free and Christian Country.'"[49] In the petition slaves argued for their freedom by combining the political rhetoric of the Revolution with an appeal to the claims of Christian fellowship. Christian churches were some of the first institutions blacks created and owned in the United States. From 1790 to 1830 ambitious northern free black men like Richard Allen and Absalom Jones circumvented racism by creating new Christian denominations, notably the African Methodist Episcopal and the African Methodist Episcopal Zion churches.

The organized black church, however, has not been free from oppressing its constituents. Historically, the black church has practiced sexism. In her 1849 narrative, Jarena Lee, a spiritual visionary and a free black woman, reported having her desire to preach thwarted by her husband and Rev. Richard Allen.[50] Lee, however, overcame the objections of men by claiming that her instructions came directly from God; thus, those instructions superseded the sexist prohibitions of men. Some contemporary black churches and their ministers have adopted heterosexist policies and have openly made homophobic remarks. In an essay which appeared in the gay anthology *Black Men/White Men*, Leonard Patterson, a black gay minister, movingly wrote about how he was forced to leave Ebenezer Baptist Church in Atlanta, Georgia. Patterson's troubles at Ebenezer began when Reverend Joseph Roberts replaced Reverend Martin L. King, Sr. Roberts objected to the fact that Patterson's white lover also attended Ebenezer. Moreover, Patterson was guilty of not playing the game: "I was told, in effect, that as long as I played the political game and went with a person who was more easily passed off as a 'cousin,' I would be able to go far in the ministry. Perhaps I should even marry and have someone on the side. Apparently these arrangements would make me more 'respectable.'"[51] For refusing to play the political game, Patterson states that he was "attacked verbally from the pulpit, forbidden to enter the study for prayer with the other associate ministers, and had seeds of animosity planted against [him]... in the minds of certain members so that in meetings with them the subject of homosexuality would inevitably be brought up."[52] Patterson recounts an extremely offensive remark made to him by a church member one Sunday: "If you lie down with dogs, you get up smelling like dirt."[53] Patterson and his lover finally left Ebenezer. Although disillusioned with organized religion, Patterson writes encouragingly that what he and his lover experienced at Ebenezer has "given us more strength to love each other and others."[54]

Exorcism is a practice used to oppress gays in the church. The late Pentecostal minister and professor, Reverend James Tinney, underwent an exorcism when he came out as a gay man. Tinney briefly mentions the experience in his essay "Struggles of a Black Pentecostal," which was originally published in a 1981 issue of *Insight*. Five years later in *Blackbird* Duplechan signifies on Tinney's reflections on exorcism. It should be noted that Duplechan was probably familiar with Tinney's essay. Both that essay and Duplechan's short story "Peanuts and the Old Spice Kid" appeared in Michael Smith's anthology *Black Men/White Men*.

The events which precipitate the exorcism are similar in *Blackbird* and in Tinney's essay. Both Tinney and Duplechan's protagonist, Johnnie Ray Rousseau, are aware of their sexual identity. Tinney writes that he was aware of his homoerotic feelings "even at the age of four."[55] Johnnie Ray's exorcism is preceded by an enjoyable first sexual experience with the older bi-ethnic Marshall Two Hawks McNeil, a college student. Publicly stating and affirming their sexual identity actually causes the exorcisms. Put another way, their exorcisms are punishments for stating that they practice "the love that dares not speak its name." Tinney announced to his wife of three years that he was gay. Her reaction set into motion the events that caused the exorcism: "She immediately called the pastor and his wife and other close confidants to pray for me."[56] Johnnie Ray's exorcism was set into motion by two events. First, his confidential confession to Daniel Levine, the youth minister, that he had gay feelings. Then, Levine's betrayal of the confidential confession to Johnnie Ray's parents provoked the second event: the teenager's affirmation of his sexual identity to his parents in the presence of the minister.

Tinney does not discuss the events of his exorcism. In fact, he limits the actions of his wife, minister, and church members to one sentence: "Pray and talk and counsel they did."[57] Tinney's description of the exorcism is brief, but the event left him traumatized. The exorcism, he wrote, "was extremely painful to my own sense of worth and well-being. It was an experience I would not wish upon anyone ever."[58]

Duplechan signifies explicitly and implicitly on Tinney's remark "Pray and talk and counsel they did." Explicitly Duplechan "reads" Tinney by giving a fuller narrative description of the praying, talking, and counseling of the church people. Implicitly, Duplechan's "reading" of Tinney is a critique of the clergy and the values of the middle class. Further, Duplechan's "reading" is an example of what Smitherman calls heavy signifying, "a way of teaching or driving home a cognitive message but ... without preaching or lecturing."[59]

Let us consider Duplechan's "read" or "heavy signifying" of each of the three terms — pray, talk, and counsel — as they occur in the confrontation between Johnnie Ray and the church people — his parents and the youth minister. The confrontation about Johnnie Ray's homosexuality happens at his home. Duplechan shows that prayer is often a means of ensuring conformity. In an emotional outburst Johnnie Ray's mother asks the teen: "Have you asked him? Have you asked the savior to help you?... Have you prayed every day for help? Every day?"[60] When Johnnie Ray answers no, his mother incredulously asks him, "Don't you want to be normal?"[61] Normality, which is conforming to existing value structures, is believed by the middle classes to be what will guarantee them success in the world. Johnnie Ray's mother reveals that she is less concerned with his happiness than she is with his possibilities of success. To insure his success, she and her husband must use talk to force Johnnie Ray to become normal. Talk, thus, is a means of intimidation. When Johnnie Ray claims that he has accepted it as a fact that he is gay, his mother intimidates him by "loud talking":

You probably think you're real cute ... going to Daniel [the youth minister] with this 'I think I'm a homosexual' crap, and now sittin' here and tellin' us you've *accepted* that you're gay ... Lord ha' mercy today! I don't know what I coulda done to give birth to a *pervert*.[62]

While Johnnie Ray's mother uses "loud talking" to intimidate her son, his father cries. When his father finally talks, it is a mixture of intimidation and compassion: "You're no pervert," he says. "No son of mine is gonna be a pervert. You're just a little confused." Finally, there is the expert, Reverend Levine, who offers counsel. Levine, however, is a scoundrel. Although he has betrayed Johnnie Ray's confidence, he sits throughout the entire family crisis "looking as holy and righteous at having done so as my parents looked utterly devastated at the news."[64] Levine is able to sit "in beatific calm" because of the family's unhappiness.[65] In other words, the family crisis that Levine has provided proves that the ministry is necessary. Levine's expert counsel to the family, which they reluctantly agree upon, is an exorcism — "a deliverance from unclean spirits."[66]

By signifying on Tinney, Duplechan exposes an unholy alliance between the church and the middle classes. The church is eager to oppress gay people to prove its worth to the middle classes. For the sake of conformity which, with hope, leads to success, the middle class is willing to oppress its children. The middle class, thus, is denounced for its willingness to use the church to further its ambitions.

In the short story "Cut Off from among Their People," Craig G. Harris does a "heavy sig" on the black family which also signifies on strategies from slave narratives. The story takes place at the funeral of Jeff's lover, who has died of complications from AIDS. Both the family and the church, two major institutions in the heterosexual African American community, are allied against Jeff. The lover's biological family has "diplomatically" excluded Jeff from the decisions about the funeral. At the funeral Jeff is ignored by the family and humiliated by the church. The lover's mother stares at him contemptuously. Jeff is not allowed to sit with the family. The minister chosen by the family only adds to Jeff's humiliation. The minister is asked not to wear his ceremonial robes but instead to wear an ordinary suit.

The "heavy sig" is done by using irony. The minister is exposed as a scoundrel, similar to Levine in *Blackbird*. At the funeral he delivers a homophobic sermon from the book of Leviticus:

> In Leviticus, Chapter 20, the Lord tell [*sic*] us: If a man lie with mankind as he lieth with a woman, both of them have committed an abomination: they shall surely be put to death; their blood shall be upon them. There's no cause to wonder why medical science could not find a cure for this man's illness. How could medicine cure temptation? What drug can exorcise Satan from a young man's soul? The only cure is to be found in the Lord. The only cure is repentance, for Leviticus clearly tells us, "...whoever shall commit any of these abominations, even the souls that commit them shall be cut off from among their people."[67]

After the funeral Jeff is abandoned and left to his own devices to get to the burial site. His humiliation is relieved by a sympathetic undertaker who offers Jeff a ride to the burial site. Ironically, it is the undertaker, the caregiver to the dead — not the minister, who is the caregiver to the living — who offers Jeff the compassion he so desperately needs. Denouncing both the family and the church, the undertaker's remarks to Jeff become the authentic sermon in the story:

> I lost my lover to AIDS three months ago. It's been very difficult — living with these memories and secrets and hurt, and with no one to share them. These people won't allow themselves to understand. If it's not preached from a pulpit and kissed up to the Almighty, they don't want to know about it. So, I hold it in, and hold it in, and then I see us passing, one after another — tearless funerals, the widowed treated like nonentities, and these 'another faggot burns in hell' sermons. My heart goes out to you brother. You gotta let your love for him keep you strong.[68]

As a result of Harris's use of ironic signifying, one is left to ponder the meaning of the story's title, "Cut Off from among Their People." Who is cut off from their people? The story immediately implies that black gays are oppressed because they are alienated from their families. The opposite, however, is also true: Black families are oppressors, are alienated from their gay children, and thus, suffer. Black families suffer because their oppression robs them of a crucial sign of humaneness: compassion. By their oppression, the family of Jeff's deceased lover has lost the ability to be compassionate.

Harris's strategy — the cost of oppression is the loss of humanity — signifies on slave narratives by authors such as Frederick Douglass. Slave owners' loss of compassion, the sign of humaneness, is a recurring theme in Frederick Douglass's 1845 narrative. Slavery, Douglass contended, placed in the hands of whites "the fatal poison of irresponsible power."[69] Douglass gives numerous grisly examples of his contention: murderous overseers, greedy urban craftsmen, and raping masters. But perhaps none of his examples is meant to be as moving as that of his slave mistress, Mrs. Auld. Originally a woman of independent means, Douglass describes her before "the fatal poison of irresponsible power" took full control of her:

> I was utterly astonished at her goodness. I scarcely knew how to behave towards her. She was entirely unlike any other white woman I had ever seen. I could not approach her as I was accustomed to approach other white ladies. My early instruction was all out of place. The crouching servility, usually so acceptable a quality in a slave, did not answer when manifested toward her. Her favor was not gained by it; she seemed to be disturbed by it. She did not deem it impudent or unmannerly for a slave to look her in the face. The meanest slave was put fully at ease in her

presence, and none left without feeling better for having seen her. Her face was made of heavenly smiles, and her voice of tranquil music.[70]

Mrs. Auld even disobeyed the law and taught Douglass some rudiments of spelling. However, Douglass states, "Slavery proved as injurious to her as it did to me ... Under its influence, the tender heart became stone, and the lamblike disposition gave way to one of tiger-like fierceness."[71]

"Cut Off from among Their People" is an extraordinary act of "heavy signifying." By using a strategy similar to Frederick Douglass's, Harris equates heterosexism and homophobia with slavery. For upholding heterosexism and homophobia, the church and the black family are oppressors. As rendered by Harris, they are like the Mrs. Auld of Douglass's narrative. They are kind to the black gay man when he is a child, and corrupted by intolerance years later. Their oppression has robbed them of compassion. The black family and their church, thus, have lost the sign of humanity.

Gender configurations

The last section of this essay examines gay men and the problem of gender configurations. Specifically, in the black literary tradition gay men have been objects of ridicule for not possessing masculine-appearing behaviors. This ridicule was especially evident in the militant Black Power movement of the 1960s and 1970s. The militancy that characterized that movement placed an enormous emphasis on developing black "manhood." Manhood became a metaphor for the strength and potency necessary to overthrow the oppressive forces of a white racist society. Images of pathetic homosexuals were often used to show what black manhood was not or to what it could degenerate. For example, Haki Madhubuti (Don L. Lee) wrote in "Don't Cry Scream":

> swung on a faggot who politely
> scratched his ass in my presence.
> he smiled broken teeth stained from
> his over-used tongue, fisted-face.
> teeth dropped in tune with ray
> charles singing "yesterday."[72]

Concurrent with the Black Power movement's image of manhood was the development of the urban tough, loud, back-talking gay black man. This stereotype was seen on the Broadway stage in Melvin Van Peebles's *Ain't Supposed to Die a Natural Death*, but it was most clearly articulated by Antonio Fargas's character, Lindy, in the film *Car Wash*. When the black militant Abdullah accused Lindy of being another example of how the white man has corrupted the black man and robbed him of his masculinity, Lindy responded, "Honey, I'm more man than you'll ever be and more woman than you'll ever get." Lindy was a gratifying character because he was tough and articulate, yet his character was not revolutionary. Vito Russo comments in *The Celluloid Closet:* "Lindy is only a cartoon — [his] effect in the end was just that of the safe sissy who ruled the day in the topsy-turvy situations of Thirties comedies."[73] But the stereotype of the tough, loud, back-talking effeminate black gay man as an object of ridicule is revised in works by Samuel Delany, George Wolfe, and Billi Gordon.

Delany signifies on such a stereotype in a section of *The Motion of Light in Water* called "A black man...? A gay man...?" The section's title itself suggests the dilemma of a bifurcated identity that Julius Johnson discusses in his doctoral dissertation "Influence of Assimilation on the Psychosocial Adjustment of Black Homosexual Men."[74] Johnson documented the fact that some African American brothers become "black gay men" while others become "gay black men"; the designation often underscores painful decisions to have primary identities either in the black or in the gay community.

Delany's first memory of a gay black man was Herman, an outrageously effeminate musician who played the organ in his father's mortuary. As a child, Delany admits that he was as confused as he was amused by Herman's aggressive antics. When a casket delivery man asked Herman if he was "one of them faggots that likes men," Herman quickly signified on the man:

> "Me? Oh, chile', chile', you must be ill or something!... I swear, you must have been workin' out in the heat too long today. I do believe you must be sick!" Here he would feel the man's forehead, then removing his hand, look at the sweat that had come off on his own palm, touch his finger to his tongue, and declare, "Oh, my lord, you are tasty!... Imagine, honey! Thinkin' such nastiness like that about a woman like me! I mean, I just might faint right here, and you gonna have to carry me to a chair and fan me and bring me my smellin' salts!" Meanwhile he would be rubbing the man's chest and arms.[75]

Ultimately Delany's attitude toward Herman was one of ambivalence. Delany's sig on the stereotype was his recognition of its artifice. He recognized that there were many unanswered questions about Herman's sexual life: "Had he gone to bars? Had he gone to baths?... Had there been a long-term lover, waiting for him at home, unmet by, and unmentioned to, people like my father whom he worked for?"[76] Herman had played a role to survive in a heterosexist and homophobic world. In that role "Herman had a place in our social scheme," Delany wrote, "but by no means an acceptable place, and certainly not a place I wanted to fill."[77] Thus, as a teen, Delany remembered that he did not see Herman as a role model for a man. As an adult, however, Delany's opinion of Herman changed. He did not see Herman as a role model, but, he stated, "I always treasured the image of Herman's outrageous and defiant freedom to say absolutely anything ... Anything except, of course, I am queer, and I like men sexually better than women."[78]

In *The Colored Museum*, George Wolfe introduces Miss Roj, a black transvestite "dressed in striped patio pants, white go-go boots, a halter and cat-shaped sunglasses."[79] Wolfe makes it clear that Miss Roj is a subject most appropriate for African American literature by signifying, perhaps deliberately, on Ralph Ellison's *Invisible Man*. In particular, he signifies on its prologue, to create a powerful social comment on the alienation of the black urban poor. Wolfe's character, Miss Roj, comments that she "comes from another galaxy, as do all snap queens. That's right," she says, "I ain't just your regular oppressed American Negro. No-no-no! I am an extra-terrestrial, and I ain't talkin none of that shit you seen in the movies."[80] Compare that with the first two sentences in the prologue of *Invisible Man*: "I am an invisible man. No, I am not a spook like those who haunted Edgar Allan Poe; nor am I one of your Hollywood-movie ectoplasms."[81] Ellison's nameless protagonist lives in a hole lit by 1,369 bulbs; Miss Roj, whose real name the audience never learns, inhabits every Wednesday, Friday, and Saturday night a disco with blaring lights called the Bottomless Pit, "the watering hole for the wild and weary which asks the question, 'Is there life after Jherri-curl?'"[82] In Ellison's prologue the protagonist gets high on marijuana; Miss Roj gets drunk on Cuba libres [perhaps a veiled reference to popular drinks in the early 1950s, which is when *Invisible Man* was written] and proceeds *to snap*, that is, "when something strikes ... [one's] fancy, when the truth comes piercing through the dark, well you just can't let it pass unnoticed. No darling. You must pronounce it with a snap [of the fingers]."[83]

Ellison's protagonist almost beats a man to death for calling him a nigger. Of course, one wonders how one can be beaten by invisibility. In a scene with a provocation and an outcome similar to Ellison's, Miss Roj "snaps" (signifies) on an assailant. She states:

> Like the time this asshole at Jones Beach decided to take issue with my culotte-sailor ensemble. This child, this muscle-bound Brooklyn thug in a skin tight bikini, very skin-tight so the whole world can see that instead of a brain, God gave him an extra-thick piece of sausage. You know the kind who beat up on their wives for breakfast. Well he decided to blurt out while I walked by, "Hey look at da monkey coon in da faggit suit." Well, I walked up to the poor dear, very calmly lifted my hand and ... (rapid snaps) A heart attack, right there on the beach. You don't believe it?[84]

Ellison's prologue ends with the protagonist listening to Louis Armstrong's "What Did I Do to Be So Black and Blue?"; the lights fade on Miss Roj dancing to Aretha Franklin's "Respect." As white Americans must have been puzzled, outraged, and even guilt-stricken after reading Ellison's *Invisible Man*, so too is the effect Miss Roj has had on the assimilated blacks Wolfe chose to confront. During performances of *The Colored Museum*, black audience members have verbally attacked the actor playing Miss Roj and African American intellectuals have lambasted Wolfe for either not portraying blacks in their "best light" or for demeaning women.[85]

One of the oddest works to appear in black gay culture is Billi Gordon's cookbook, *You've Had Worse Things In Your Mouth*. The title itself is an act of signifying. While one may think it odd to include a cookbook here, it is important to keep in mind that that mode of presentation has been used to create social history in two other books by Afro-Americans. National Public Radio commentator and self-styled writing griot Vertamae Smart Grosvenor came to public prominence in her 1970 *Vibration Cooking; or the Travel Notes of a Geechee Girl.* The format of the book itself was signifying on the published travel narratives of eighteenth- and nineteenth-century whites such as Frederick Law Olmsted, whose observations on slavery have been treated by some historians as more reliable than artifacts actually left by the slaves. Norma Jean and Carole Darden's 1978 *Spoonbread and Strawberry Wine* was as much a family history of North Carolina middle-class blacks as it was a compendium of recipes.

Like George Wolfe, Gordon signifies repeatedly on racial stereotypes and on middle-class culture. On the cover of his cookbook, Gordon, a three-hundred-pound-plus dark-skinned black man, appears in drag. But not just any drag. He is wearing a red kerchief, a red-and-white checkered blouse, and a white apron, calling to mind some combination of Aunt Jemima and Hattie McDaniel in *Gone With the Wind*. As if that were not enough, Gordon signifies in every way imaginable on the American cultural stereotype of mammies as sexless, loyal, no-nonsense creatures. Gordon's character is lusty, vengeful, and flirtatious. Gordon appears in pictures surrounded by adoring muscled, swimsuit-clad white men; she wears bikini swimsuits, tennis outfits, long blond wigs, huge rebellious Afro-wigs, and shocking lamé evening wear. As for recipes, one is quite reluctant to try any of them, particularly those from the section called "Revenge Cooking" in which the ingredients include laxatives, seaweed, and entire bottles of Tabasco sauce. Billi Gordon signifies on the American stereotype of the mammy by reversing it and turning it upside down: His depiction of a mammy with a sex life is far from loyal, and certainly his character cannot and/or does not want to cook.

Conclusion: Toward a black gay aesthetic

Restricted by racism and heterosexism, writers such as Samuel Delany, Larry Duplechan, Essex Hemphill, Craig G. Harris, George

Wolfe, and Billi Gordon have begun to create a literature that validates our lives as black and as gay. My critical reading of this literature relied upon techniques based in the African American tradition of signifying. The writers discussed in this essay are some of the newest members of the African American literary tradition. Clearly, they also seek to revise the aesthetics of that tradition. Homophobia and heterosexism are oppressive forces which must be eliminated from the social, scientific, critical, and imaginative writings within the African American literary tradition.

Notes

1. Daniel Garrett, "Other Countries: The Importance of Difference," in *Other Countries: Black Gay Voices*, ed. Cary Alan Johnson, Colin Robinson, and Terence Taylor (New York: Other Countries, 1988), p. 27.

2. Henry Louis Gates, Jr., *The Signifying Monkey: A Theory of African American Literary Criticism* (New York: Oxford University Press, 1988), p. 111.

3. Lorraine Hansberry, *A Raisin in the Sun* (New York: New American Library, 1958), p. 79.

4. Cogent discussions of homophobia among Black American intellectuals can be found in Cheryl Clarke, "The Failure to Transform: Homophobia in the Black Community," in *Home Girls: A Black Feminist Perspective*, ed. Barbara Smith (New York: Kitchen Table Press, 1983), pp. 197–208; Ann Allen Shockley, "The Illegitimates of Afro-American Literature," *Lambda Rising Book Report* 1, no. 4: 1+.

5. Mary Helen Washington, *Invented Lives* (Garden City, N.Y.: Doubleday, 1987).

6. Gates, *The Signifying Monkey*, p. 81.

7. Geneva Smitherman, *Talkin and Testifyin* (Boston: Houghton Mifflin, 1977), p. 120.

8. Smitherman, *Talkin and Testifyin*, p. 121.

9. Claudia Mitchell-Kernan, "Signifying as a Form of Verbal Art," in *Mother Wit from the Laughing Barrel: Readings in the Interpretation of Afro-American Folklore*, ed. Alan Dundes (Englewood Cliffs, N.J.: Prentice-Hall, 1973), p. 314.

10. Molefi Kete Asante, *Afrocentricity: A Theory of Social Change* (Buffalo, N.Y.: Amulefi, 1980), p. 66.

11. Asante, *Afrocentricity*, p. 64.

12. Frantz Fanon, *Black Skin, White Masks*, trans. Constance Farrington (New York: Grove Press, 1963), p. 84.

13. Alvin Poussaint, "What Makes Them Tick," *Ebony*, October 1978, p. 79.

14. Quoted in Georges-Michel Sarotte, *Like a Brother, Like a Lover: Male Homosexuality in the American Novel and Theatre from Herman Melville to James Baldwin*, trans. Richard Miller (New York: Doubleday, 1978), p. 94.

15. Eldridge Cleaver, *Soul on Ice* (New York: Random House, 1969), p. 174.

16. Nathan Hare and Julia Hare, *The Endangered Black Family: Coping with the*

Unisexualization and Coming Extinction of the Black Race (San Francisco: Black Think Tank, 1984), p. 65.

17. Hare and Hare, *The Endangered Black Family*, p. 65.

18. Toni Morrison, *The Bluest Eye* (New York: Holt, Rinehart & Winston, 1970), p. 132.

19. Toni Morrison, *Tar Baby* (New York: Random House, 1981), p. 216.

20. Toni Morrison, *Beloved* (New York: Random House, 1988), p. 10.

21. Ibid.

22. Ibid.

23. Esteban Montejo, *The Autobiography of a Runaway Slave*, trans. Jocasta Innes, ed. Miguel Barnet (New York: Random House, 1968), p. 21.

24. Ibid., p. 41.

25. Ibid.

26. Ibid.

27. Ibid.

28. Ibid.

29. Ibid.

30. Ibid.

31. On the social practices surrounding the sexuality of slaves, see: John Blassingame, *The Slave Community: Plantation Life in the Antebellum South* (New York: Oxford University Press, 1979), pp. 154–191; Eugene Genovese, *Roll, Jordan, Roll: The World the Slaves Made* (New York: Random House, 1974), pp. 458–475; Mary Helen Washington, *Invented Lives: Narratives of Black Women: 1860–1960* (New York: Doubleday, 1987), pp. 4–8; Deborah Gray White, *Ar'n't I a Woman? Female Slaves in the Plantation South* (New York: Norton, 1985), pp. 142–160.

32. Jonathan Ned Katz, *Gay American History: Lesbians and Gay Men in the U.S.A.* (New York: Avon Books, 1976), p. 35; Jonathan Ned Katz, *Gay/Lesbian Almanac: A New Documentary* (New York: Harper & Row, 1983), p. 61.

33. Katz, *Gay American History*, pp. 35–36.

34. Ibid., p. 61.

35. A. Leon Higginbotham, Jr., *In the Matter of Color: Race and the American Legal Process: The Colonial Period* (New York: Oxford University Press, 1978), pp. 281–282; Katz, *Gay/Lesbian Almanac*, p. 61.

36. Martin Bauml Duberman, "Writhing Bedfellows," in *About Time: Exploring the Gay Past* (New York: Gay Presses of New York, 1986), pp. 13–14.

37. Tom Horner, *Jonathan Loved David: Homosexuality in Biblical Times* (Philadelphia: Westminster Press, 1978), pp. 91–99.

38. For example, toward the end of *The Normal Heart*, one of the indignities that befall a deceased person with AIDS is to be cremated by a black undertaker "for a thousand dollars, no questions asked" (p. 106). The implication here is that the deceased was unable to have a decent or respectable burial, which would, of course, be by a white undertaker. This is significant because it is part of a tradition

in Western aesthetics that associates blacks and Africans with indignity. This also reflects an instance of racism by the author.

39. An interesting case occurred in a serious article in the gay male pornography magazine *Stallion*. The author, Charles Jurrist, criticized the gay literary establishment for its exclusion of or, when included, stereotypical depiction of black men. However, the article perpetuated a stereotype by featuring a series of pictures of a spectacularly endowed Black man.

40. W.E.B. DuBois, review of *Quicksand* by Nella Larson and *Home to Harlem* by Claude McKay, *Crisis* 35 (June 1928): 202; quoted in Lovie Gibson, "DuBois' Propaganda Literature: An Outgrowth of His Sociological Studies," doctoral dissertation, State University of New York at Buffalo, 1977, p. 21.

41. Washington, *Invented Lives*, pp. xxiii–xxiv.

42. Michael G. Cooke, *Afro-American Literature in the Twentieth Century: The Achievement of Intimacy* (New Haven: Yale University Press, 1984), p. 95.

43. Samuel R. Delany, *The Motion of Light in Water* (New York: Morrow, 1988), p. 129.

44. Ibid., p. 175.

45. Ibid., p. 176.

46. William H. Grier and Price M. Cobbs, *Black Rage* (New York: Basic Books, 1968), pp. 91–100.

47. Larry Duplechan, *Eight Days a Week* (Boston: Alyson Publications, 1985), p. 28.

48. Essex Hemphill, *Conditions* (Washington, D.C.: Be Bop Books, 1986).

49. Albert Raboteau, *Slave Religion: The "Invisible Institution" in the Antebellum South* (New York: Oxford University Press, 1978), p. 290.

50. Jarena Lee, *Religious Experience and Journal of Mrs. Jarena Lee, Giving an Account of Her Call to Preach the Gospel* (Philadelphia, 1849); found in Ann Allen Shockley, *Afro-American Women Writers, 1746–1933* (New York: New American Library, 1988).

51. Leonard Patterson, "At Ebenezer Baptist Church," in *Black Men/White Men*, ed. Michael Smith (San Francisco: Gay Sunshine Press, 1983), p. 164.

52. Ibid., pp. 164–165.

53. Ibid., p. 165.

54. Ibid., p. 166.

55. James S. Tinney, "Struggles of a Black Pentecostal," in *Black Men/White Men*, ed. Michael Smith (San Francisco: Gay Sunshine Press, 1983), p. 167.

56. Ibid., p. 170.

57. Ibid.

58. Ibid., pp. 170–171.

59. Smitherman, *Talkin and Testifyin*, p. 120.

60. Larry Duplechan, *Blackbird* (New York: St. Martin's, 1986), p. 152.

61. Ibid., p. 153.

62. Ibid., p. 151.

63. Ibid., p. 153.

64. Ibid., p. 150.

65. Ibid., p. 152.

66. Ibid., p. 155.

67. Craig G. Harris, "Cut Off from among Their People," in *In the Life*, ed. by Joseph Beam (Boston: Alyson Publications, 1986), p. 66.

68. Ibid., p. 67.

69. Frederick Douglass, *Narrative of the Life of Frederick Douglass: An American Slave* (1845; New York: New American Library, 1968), p. 48.

70. Ibid.

71. Ibid., pp. 52–53.

72. Haki Madhubuti, "Don't Cry Scream," quoted in Smitherman, *Talkin and Testifyin*, p. 142.

73. Vito Russo, *The Celluloid Closet: Homosexuality in the Movies* (New York: Harper & Row, 1981), p. 229.

74. Julius Marcus Johnson, "Influence of Assimilation on the Psychosocial Adjustment of Black Homosexual Men," doctoral dissertation, California School of Professional Psychology at Berkeley, 1981.

75. Delany, *Motion of Light*, p. 219.

76. Ibid., p. 221.

77. Ibid., p. 220.

78. Ibid., p. 223.

79. George Wolfe, *The Colored Museum*, in *American Theatre*, ed. James Leverett and M. Elizabeth Osborn, February 1987, p. 4.

80. Ibid.

81. Ralph Ellison, *Invisible Man* (New York: New American Library, 1952), p. 7.

82. Wolfe, *Colored Museum*, p. 4.

83. Ibid.

84. Ibid.

85. See Thulani Davis, "Sapphire Attire: A Review," *Village Voice*, Nov. 11, 1986, p. 91; Roger Fristoe, "George C. Wolfe," *Louisville Courier-Journal*, p. I1; Jack Kroll, "Zapping Black Stereotypes," *Newsweek*, Nov. 17, 1986, p. 85.

Works cited

Asante, Molefi. *Afrocentricity: A Theory of Social Change*. Buffalo, N.Y.: Amulefi, 1980.

Beam, Joseph. *In the Life: A Black Gay Anthology*. Boston: Alyson Publications, 1986.

Blassingame, John W. *The Slave Community: Plantation Life in the Antebellum South.* Rev. ed. New York: Oxford University Press, 1979.

Clarke, Cheryl. "The Failure to Transform: Homophobia in the Black Community." In *Home Girls: A Black Feminist Perspective*, ed. Barbara Smith, pp. 197–208. New York: Kitchen Table Press, 1983.

Cleaver, Eldridge. *Soul on Ice.* New York: Random House, 1969.

Darden, Norma Jean and Carole. *Spoonbread and Strawberry Wine.* New York: Fawcett, 1978.

Delany, Samuel R. *The Motion of Light in Water: Sex and Science Fiction Writing in the East Village, 1957–1965.* New York: Morrow, 1988.

Douglass, Frederick. *Narrative of the Life of Frederick Douglass: An American Slave.* 1845. New York: New American Library, 1968.

Duberman, Martin Bauml. *About Time: Exploring the Gay Past.* New York: Gay Presses of New York, 1986.

Duplechan, Larry. *Blackbird.* New York: St. Martin's, 1986.

———. *Eight Days a Week.* Boston: Alyson Publications, 1985.

Ellison, Ralph. *Invisible Man.* New York: Signet, 1952.

Fanon, Frantz. *Black Skin, White Masks.* Trans. Constance Farrington. New York: Grove Press, 1963.

Garrett, Daniel. "Other Countries: The Importance of Difference." In *Other Countries: Black Gay Voices*, ed. Cary Alan Johnson, Colin Robinson, and Terence Taylor, pp. 17–28. New York: Other Countries, 1988.

Gates, Henry Louis, Jr. *Figures in Black: Words, Signs, and the "Racial" Self.* New York: Oxford University Press, 1987.

———. *The Signifying Monkey: A Theory of Afro-American Literary Criticism.* New York: Oxford University Press, 1988.

Genovese, Eugene. *Roll, Jordan, Roll: The World the Slaves Made.* New York: Random House, 1974.

Gibson, Lovie. "DuBois' Propaganda Literature: An Outgrowth of His Sociological Studies." Doctoral dissertation, State University of New York at Buffalo, 1977.

Gordon, Billi. *You've Had Worse Things In Your Mouth.* San Francisco: West Graphics, 1985.

Grier, William H., and Cobbs, Price M. *Black Rage.* New York: Basic Books, 1968.

Hare, Nathan, and Hare, Julia. *The Endangered Black Family: Coping With the Unisexualization and Coming Extinction of the Black Race.* San Francisco: The Black Think Tank, 1984.

Hemphill, Essex. *Conditions.* Washington, D.C.: Be Bop Books, 1986.

Higginbotham, A. Leon. *In the Matter of Color: Race and The American Legal Process: The Colonial Period.* New York: Oxford University Press, 1978.

Horner, Tom. *Jonathan Loved David: Homosexuality in Biblical Times.* Philadelphia: Westminster Press, 1978.

Johnson, Julius Maurice. "Influence of Assimilation on the Psychosocial Adjustment of Black Homosexual Men." Doctoral dissertation, California School of Professional Psychology at Berkeley, 1981.

Jurrist, Charles. "Black Image." *Stallion*, December 1987, pp. 34–45.

Katz, Jonathan Ned. *Gay American History*. New York: Avon Books, 1976.

——. *Gay/Lesbian Almanac: A New Documentary*. New York: Harper & Row, 1983.

Kernan-Mitchell, Claudia. "Signifying as a Form of Verbal Art." In *Mother Wit From the Laughing Barrel: Readings in the Interpretation of Afro-American Folklore*, ed. Alan Dundes. Englewood Cliffs, N.J.: Prentice-Hall, 1973.

Kramer, Larry. *The Normal Heart*. New York: New American Library, 1985.

Montejo, Esteban. *The Autobiography of a Runaway Slave*. Trans. Jocasta Innes. Ed. Miguel Barnet. New York: Random House, 1968.

Morrison, Toni. *The Bluest Eye*. New York: Holt, Rinehart & Winston, 1970.

——. *Tar Baby*. New York: Random House, 1981.

——. *Beloved*. New York: Random House, 1987.

Poussaint, Alvin. "What Makes Them Tick?" *Ebony*, October 1978, p. 79+.

Raboteau, Albert J. *Slave Religion: The "Invisible Institution" in the Antebellum South*. New York: Oxford University Press, 1978.

Russo, Vito. *The Celluloid Closet: Homosexuality in the Movies*. New York: Harper & Row, 1981.

Scroggs, Robin. *The New Testament and Homosexuality: Contextual Background for Contemporary Debate*. Philadelphia: Fortress Press, 1983.

Shockley, Ann Allen. *Afro-American Women Writers, 1746–1933: An Anthology and Critical Guide*. New York: New American Library, 1988.

——. "The Illegitimates of Afro-American Literature." *Lambda Rising Book Report* 1, no. 4: 1+.

(Smart-Grosvenor), Vertamae. *Vibration Cookin; or The Travel Notes of a Geechee Girl*. New York: Doubleday, 1970.

Smith, Michael J. *Black Men/White Men: A Gay Anthology*. San Francisco: Gay Sunshine Press, 1983.

Smitherman, Geneva. *Talkin and Testifyin: The Language of Black America*. Detroit: Wayne State University Press, 1986.

Washington, Mary Helen. *Invented Lives: Narratives of Black Women, 1860–1960*. New York: Doubleday, 1987.

White, Deborah Gray. *Ar'n't I a Woman? Female Slaves in the Plantation South*. New York: Norton, 1985.

Wolfe, George. *The Colored Museum*. In *American Theatre*. Supplement, February 1987, pp. 1–11.

MARLON RIGGS

Black macho revisited
Reflections of a SNAP! queen

Negro faggotry is in fashion.
SNAP!
Turn on your television and camp queens greet you in living color.
SNAP!
Turn to cable and watch America's most bankable modern minstrel
expound on getting "fucked in the ass" or his fear of faggots.
SNAP!
Turn off the TV, turn on the radio: Rotund rapper Heavy D, the
self-styled "overweight lover MC," expounds on how *his* rap will make
you "happy like a faggot in jail." Perhaps to preempt questions about
how he would know — you might wonder what kind of "lover" he
truly is — Heavy D reassures us that he's just "extremely intellectual,
not bisexual."

Jelly-roll SNAP!

Negro faggotry is in vogue. Madonna commodified it into a com-
mercial hit. Mapplethorpe photographed it and art galleries drew fire
and record crowds in displaying it. Black macho movie characters
dis' — or should we say dish? — their antagonists with unkind references to it. Indeed references to, and representations of, Negro faggotry
seem a rite of passage among contemporary black male rappers and
filmmakers.

Snap-swish-and-dish divas have truly arrived, giving Beauty Shop
drama at center stage, performing the read-and-snap two-step as they
sashay across the movie screen, entertaining us in the castles of our
homes — like court jesters, like eunuchs — with their double entendres

and dead-end lusts, and above all, their relentless hilarity in the face of relentless despair. Negro faggotry is the rage! Black gay men are not. For in the cinematic and television images of and from black America as well as the lyrics and dialogue that now abound and *seem* to address my life as a black gay man, I am struck repeatedly by the determined, unreasoning, often irrational desire to discredit my claim to blackness and hence to black manhood.

In consequence the terrain black gay men navigate in the quest for self and social identity is, to say the least, hostile. What disturbs — no, enrages me, is not so much the obstacles set before me by whites, which history conditions me to expect, but the traps and pitfalls planted by my so-called brothers, who because of the same history should know better.

I am a Negro faggot, if I believe what movies, TV, and rap music say of me. My life is game for play. Because of my sexuality, I cannot be black. A strong, proud, "Afrocentric" black man is resolutely heterosexual, not *even* bisexual. Hence I remain a Negro. My sexual difference is considered of no value; indeed it's a testament to weakness, passivity, the absence of real guts — balls. Hence I remain a sissy, punk, faggot. I cannot be a black gay man because by the tenets of black macho, black gay man is a triple negation. I am consigned, by these tenets, to remain a Negro faggot. And as such I am game for play, to be used, joked about, put down, beaten, slapped, and bashed, not just by illiterate homophobic thugs in the night, but by black American culture's best and brightest.

In a community where the dozens, signifying, dis'ing, and *dishing* are revered as art form, I ask myself: What does this obsession with Negro faggotry signify? What is its significance?

What lies at the heart, I believe, of black America's pervasive cultural homophobia is the desperate need for a convenient Other *within* the community, yet not truly *of* the community, an Other to which blame for the chronic identity crises afflicting the black male psyche can be readily displaced, an indispensable Other which functions as the lowest common denominator of the abject, the base line of transgression beyond which a Black Man is no longer a man, no longer black, an essential Other against which black men and boys maturing, struggling with self-doubt, anxiety, feelings of political, economic, social, and sexual inadequacy — even impotence — can always measure themselves and by comparison seem strong, adept, empowered, superior.

Indeed the representation of Negro faggotry disturbingly parallels and reinforces America's most entrenched racist constructions around African American identity. White icons of the past signifying "Blackness" share with contemporary icons of Negro faggotry a manifest dread of the deviant Other. Behind the Sambo and the SNAP! Queen lies a social psyche in torment, a fragile psyche threatened by deviation from its egocentric/ethnocentric construct of self and society. Such a psyche systematically defines the Other's "deviance" by the essential characteristics which make the Other distinct, then invests those differences with intrinsic defect. Hence: Blacks are inferior because they are not white. Black gays are unnatural because they are not straight. Majority representations of both affirm the view that blackness and gayness constitute a fundamental rupture in the order of things, that our very existence is an affront to nature and humanity.

From black gay men, this burden of (mis)representation is compounded. We are saddled by historic caricatures of the black male, now fused with newer notions of the Negro faggot. The resultant dehumanization is multilayered, and profound.

What strikes me as most insidious, and paradoxical, is the degree to which popular African American depictions of us as black gay men so keenly resonate American majority depictions of us, as black people. Within the black gay community, for example, the SNAP! contains a multiplicity of coded meanings: as in — SNAP! — "Got your point!" Or — SNAP! — "Don't even try it." Or — SNAP! — "You *fierce!*" Or — SNAP! — "Get out my face." Or — SNAP! — "Girlfriend, *pleeeease.*" The snap can be as emotionally and politically charged as a clenched fist, can punctuate debate and dialogue like an exclamation point, a comma, an ellipse, or altogether negate the need for words among those who are adept at decoding its nuanced meanings.

But the particular appropriation of the snap by Hollywood's Black Pack deflates the gesture into rank caricature. Instead of a symbol of communal expression and, at times, cultural defiance, the snap becomes part of a simplistically reductive Negro faggot identity: It functions as a mere signpost of effeminate, cute, comic homosexuality. Thus robbed of its full political and cultural dimension, the snap, in this appropriation, descends to stereotype.

Is this any different from the motives and consequences associated with the legendary white dramatist T.D. Rice, who more than 150 years ago appropriated the tattered clothes and dance style of an old crippled black man, then went on stage and imitated him, thus shaping in the popular American mind an indelible image of blacks as simplistic and poor yet given, without exception, to "natural" rhythm and happy feet?

A family tree displaying dominant types in the cultural iconography of black men would show, I believe, an unmistakable line of descent from Sambo to the SNAP! Queen, and in parallel lineage, from the Brute Negro to the AIDS-infected Black Homo-Con-Rapist.

What the members of this pantheon share in common is an extreme displacement and distortion of sexuality. In Sambo and the SNAP! Queen sexuality is repressed, arrested. Laughter, levity, and a certain childlike disposition cement their mutual status as comic eunuchs. Their alter egos, the Brute Black and the Homo Con, are but psychosocial projections of an otherwise tamed sexuality run amuck — bestial, promiscuous, pathological.

Contemporary proponents of black macho thus converge with white supremacist D.W. Griffith in their cultural practice, deploying similar devices toward similarly dehumanizing ends. In their constructions of "unnatural" sexual aggression, Griffith's infamous chase scene in *Birth of a Nation*, in which a lusting "Brute Negro" (a white actor in blackface) chases a white Southern virgin to her death, displays a striking aesthetic kinship to the homophobic jail rap — or should I say, attempted rape? — in Reginald and Warrington Hudlin's *House Party*.

The resonances go deeper.

Pseudoscientific discourse fused with popular icons of race in late nineteenth-century America to project a social fantasy of black men, not simply as sexual demons, but significantly, as intrinsically corrupt. Diseased, promiscuous, destructive — of self and others — our fundamental nature, it was widely assumed, would lead us to extinction.

Against this historical backdrop consider the highly popular comedy routines of Eddie Murphy, which unite Negro faggotry, "Herpes Simplex 10" — and AIDS — into an indivisible modern icon of sexual terrorism. Rap artists and music videos resonate this perception, fomenting a social psychology that blames the *victim* for his degradation and death.

The sum total of primetime fag pantomimes, camp queens as culture critics, and the proliferating bit-part swish-and-dish divas who like ubiquitous black maids and butlers in fifties Hollywood films move along the edges of the frame, seldom at the center, manifests the persistent psychosocial impulse toward control, displacement, and marginalization of the black gay Other. This impulse, in many respects, is no different than the phobic, distorted projections which motivated blackface minstrelsy.

This is the irony: There are more black male filmmakers and rap artists than ever, yet their works display a persistently narrow, even monolithic, construction of black male identity.

"You have to understand something," explained Professor Griff of the controversial and highly popular rap group Public Enemy, in an interview. "In knowing and understanding black history, African history, there's not a word in any African language which describes homosexual, y'understand what I'm saying? You would like to make them part of the community, but that's something brand new to black people."

And so black macho appropriates African history, or rather, a deeply reductive, mythologized view of African history, to rationalize homophobia. Pseudoacademic claims of "Afrocentricity" have now become a popular invocation when black macho is pressed to defend its essentialist vision of the race. An inheritance from Black Cultural

Nationalism of the late sixties, and Negritude before that, today's Afrocentrism, as popularly theorized, premises an historical narrative which runs thus: Before the white man came, African men were strong, noble, protectors, providers, and warriors for their families and tribes. In precolonial Africa, men were truly men. And women — were women. Nobody was lesbian. Nobody was feminist. Nobody was gay.

This distortion of history, though severe, has its seductions. Given the increasingly besieged state of black men in America, and the nation's historic subversion of an affirming black identity, it is no wonder that a community would turn to pre-Diasporan history for metaphors of empowerment. But the embrace of the African warrior ideal — strong, protective, impassive, patriarchal — has cost us. It has sent us down a perilous road of cultural and spiritual redemption, and distorted or altogether deleted from the historical record the multiplicity of identities around color, gender, sexuality, and class, which inform the African and African American experience.

It is to me supremely revealing that in black macho's popular appropriation of Malcolm X (in movies, music, rap videos), it is consistently Malcolm *before Mecca* — militant, macho, "by any means necessary" Malcolm — who is quoted and idolized, not Malcolm *after* Mecca, when he became more critical of himself and exclusivist Nation of Islam tenets, and embraced a broader, multicultural perspective on nationalist identity.

By the tenets of black macho, true masculinity admits little or no space for self-interrogation or multiple subjectivities around race. Black macho prescribes an inflexible ideal: Strong black men — "Afrocentric" black men — don't flinch, don't weaken, don't take blame or shit, take charge, step-to when challenged, and defend themselves without pause for self-doubt.

Black macho counterpoises this warrior model of masculinity with the emasculated Other: the Other as punk, sissy, Negro faggot, a status with which any man, not just those who in fact are gay, can be, and are, branded should one deviate from rigidly prescribed codes of hyper-masculine conduct.

"When I say Gamma, you say Fag. Gamma. Fag. Gamma. Fag." In the conflict between the frat boys and the "fellas" in Spike Lee's *School Daze*, verbal fag-bashing becomes the weapon of choice in the fellas' contest for male domination. In this regard Lee's movie not only resonates a poisonous dynamic in contemporary black male relations but worse, Lee glorifies it.

Spike Lee and others like him count on the complicit silence of those who know better, who know the truth of their own lives as well as the diverse truths which inform the total black experience.

Notice is served. Our silence has ended. SNAP!

ESSEX HEMPHILL

In an afternoon light

On a recent afternoon in Philadelphia I walked to the corner of 63rd and Malvern Streets to catch a number 10 trolley, *my* imaginary streetcar named Desire. Waiting, when I arrived at the stop was another black man, sipping a bottle of beer and smoking a cigarette. He wore sunshades and was built three sizes larger than my compact frame. I guessed him to be in his thirties though his potbelly suggested an older age or the consumption of too much beer and soul food. A blue hand towel was tossed over his right shoulder. A baseball jacket was draped across his left thigh. He was sitting on the wall I sit on when I wait here. Since there was no trolley in sight, I guardedly walked over and sat at the far end of the wall. He continued to drink his beer as I observed him from the corner of my eye. I pretended to occupy myself with looking for an approaching trolley. He abruptly ended our brief interlude of silence. For no apparent reason he blurted out, "Man, the women's movement is ruling the world. It's turning our sons into faggots and our men into punks."

"What do you mean?" I asked, raising my voice as loudly as he had raised his. Indignation and defensiveness tinged my vocal cords. I thought his remarks were directed specifically at me.

"You see all the cars going by?" he asked, gesturing at the traffic.

"Yeah, so what about it?"

"Well, can't you see that all the drivers in the cars are women—"

"Which only means more women are driving," I interjected.

"—because women have caused major changes in society, brother. Women are ruling more things now. That's why I don't want my son to spend all his time with his mother, his grandmother, and those aunts of his. His mother and I don't live together, but I go visit him and take him downtown or to the movies or down to the Boys' Club to watch basketball games. I think that's important, so he'll know the difference."

"The difference in what?" I asked.

"The difference between a woman and man. You know..."

"Which is supposed to be determined by what — how they use their sex organs? What I do know, brother, is that thirteen and fourteen-year-old black children are breeding babies they can't care for — crack babies, AIDS babies, accidental babies, babies that will grow up and inherit their parents' poverty and powerlessness. The truth is, young people are fucking because they want to fuck. They're encouraged to fuck. Yet we don't talk to them frankly and honestly about sex, sexuality, or their responsibility."

"Okay, brother, hold that thought. You're moving too fast. See, this is what I mean. Suppose you grow up in a home with your father being a minister and your mother is there all the time taking care of the house and kids. You grow up, go off to college, and get a good education. Then you decide you gonna be gay. You like men. I say you learned that. Education did that. Your folks didn't teach you that."

"That's bullshit, and you know it," I insisted. "It's stupid to suggest that women or education can make a man gay. What you fail to understand is that this is the natural diversity of human sexuality no matter what we call it. Also, my father is a minister, my mother was at home raising us before they divorced, and I went to college. And you know what? I'm a faggot."

"No you ain't!" .

"Yes I am. In fact, I'm becoming a well-known faggot."

"I don't believe you."

"Why not?"

"Because you ain't switching and stuff."

"Yeah, all you think being gay is about is men switching — but you're wrong. I'm a faggot because I love *me* enough to be who I am. If your son grows up to be a faggot, it won't be because of the way you or his mother raised him. It will be because he learns to trust the natural expression of his sexuality without fear or shame. If he learns anything about courage from you or his mother, then he'll grow up to be himself. You can't blame being straight or gay on a woman or education. The education that's needed should be for the purpose of bringing us all out of sexual ignorance. It's just another tactic to keep us divided — these sex wars we wage. Our sexuality is determined by the will of human nature, and nature *is* the will of God..."

He sat there for a moment staring at me, sipping his beer. He lit another cigarette. I realized then that he could beat me to a pulp if he chose to impose his bigger size, his vociferous masculinity on me. But I wasn't afraid for what I had said and revealed. On too many occasions, I have sat silently as men like him mouthed off about gays and women, and I said nothing because I was afraid. But not today. Not this afternoon. The longer I sit silently in my own community, my own home, and say nothing, I condone the ignorance and its by-products of violence and discrimination. I prolong my existence in a realm of invisibility and complicity. I prolong our mutual suffering by saying nothing.

Neither of us spoke another word. In this tense interlude, a bus and trolley approached. I was angry with having to encounter him on such a glorious spring day, but this is the kind of work social change requires. I consoled myself believing this.

When he rose I immediately rose too — a defensive strategy, a precaution.

"It's been good talking to you, brother. I'll think about what you've said." He extended his hand to me just as the bus and the trolley neared. I looked at his hand, known and unknown to me, offered tenuously, waiting to clasp my hand.

"Yeah, it was cool talking to you, too," I returned, as I hesitantly shook his hand. He swaggered to the bus and boarded with his beer hidden under the jacket he carried. I walked into the street to meet the trolley in an afternoon light devoid of shame.

JOSEPH BEAM

Making ourselves from scratch

E ach morning as I wipe the sleep from my eyes, don the costume that alleges my safety, and propel myself onto the stoop, I know with the surety of the laws of gravity that my footsteps fall in a world not created in my image. It is not in the newspapers, in store windows, nor is it on the television screen. Too often, it is not in the eyes of my sisters who fear my crack, nor is it present in the countenance of my brothers who fear the face that mirrors our anger. At day's end, having done their bidding, I rush home to do my own: creating myself from scratch as a black gay man.

My desk and typing table anchor the northeast corner of my one-room apartment. There are days that I cling to both objects as if for sanity. On the walls surrounding me are pictures of powerful people, mentors if you will. Among them are: Audre Lorde, James Baldwin, John Edgar Wideman, Essex Hemphill, Lamont Steptoe, Judy Grahn, Tommi Avicolli, Charles Fuller, Toni Morrison, and Barbara Smith. These writers, of local and international fame, are connected by their desire to create images by which they could survive as gays and lesbians, as blacks, and as poor people. Their presence in my writing space bespeaks what another writer, Samuel Delany, calls "the possibility of possibilities."

But it has not always been this way. I have not always known of the possibilities. In the winter of '79, in grad school, in the hinterlands of Iowa, I thought I was the first black gay man to have ever lived. I knew not how to live my life as a man who desired emotional, physical, and spiritual fulfillment from other men. I lived a guarded existence: I watched how I crossed my legs, held my cigarettes, the brightness of the colors I wore. I was sure that some effeminate action would alert the world to my homosexuality. I spent so much energy in self-observation that little was left for classwork and still less to challenge the institutionalized racism I found there. I needed heroes, men and women I could emulate. I left without a degree; the closet door tightly shut.

Several years passed before I realized that my burden of shame could be a source of strength. It was imperative for my survival that I did not attend to or believe the images that were presented of black people or gay people. Perhaps that was the beginning of my passage from passivism to activism, that I needed to create my reality, that I needed to create images by which I, and other black gay men to follow, could live this life.

The gay life is about affectation, but style is not imagemaking. Style, at best, is an attitude, a reaction to oppression, a way of being perceived as less oppressed, a way of feeling attractive when we are deemed unattractive. The most beleaguered groups — women, people of color, gays, and the poor — attend most intently to style and fashion. But is it important to know who tailored the suit Malcolm X wore when he was killed? For a people who fashioned beautiful gowns and topcoats from gunnysack, it's nothing, nothing at all, that we can work some leather, fur, or gold. The lives we lead are richer than Gucci or Waterford; our bodies more fit than Fila or Adidas; our survival more real than Coca-Cola.

As African Americans, we do not bequeath dazzling financial portfolios. We pass from generation to generation our tenacity. So I ask you: What is it that we are passing along to our cousin from North Carolina, the boy down the block, our nephew who is a year old, or our sons who may follow us in this life? What is it that we leave them beyond this shadow-play: the search for a candlelit romance in a poorly lit bar, the rhythm and the beat, the furtive sex in the back street? What is it that we pass along to them or do they, too, need to start from scratch?

ROBERT REID-PHARR

Books, journals, and periodicals by black gay authors and publishers

The following listing of books, journals, and periodicals represents a partial gathering of black gay literature. The list is a beginning for those interested in becoming familiar with the works of black gay authors. It includes works of fiction, nonfiction, anthologies, and collections of poetry. The list also includes anthologies edited by white gay men and lesbians that contain works by black gay men. The listing is prepared alphabetically by author, followed by journals and periodicals published by black gay men, anthologies, and miscellaneous items. The works listed are by self-identified black gay men or men known to have been homosexual. This listing does not contain work appearing in periodicals, such as individual essays, poems, or interviews. Such a listing is presently being compiled. This bibliography may not be complete in every detail, but it is a beginning for assessing the development of a black gay literary sensibility, and as such, it should be a useful tool for those studying black gay literature.

The following designations appear at the end of each author's entry: F = fiction; NF = non-fiction; P = poetry; and T = theater.

Baldwin, James

Go Tell it On the Mountain. New York: Alfred A. Knopf, 1953. F

Notes of a Native Son. Boston: Beacon Press, 1955. NF

Giovanni's Room. New York: Dial, 1956. F

Another Country. New York: Dial, 1960. F

Nobody Knows My Name. New York: Dial, 1961. NF

The Fire Next Time. New York: Dial, 1963. NF

Blues for Mister Charlie. New York: Dell, 1964. T

Nothing Personal. Collaboration with photographer Richard Avedon. New York: Atheneum, 1964. NF

Going to Meet the Man. New York: Dell, 1965. NF

Tell Me How Long the Train's Been Gone. New York: Dial, 1968. F

The Amen Corner. New York: Dial, 1968. T

A Rap on Race (with Margaret Mead). Philadelphia: Lippincott, 1971. NF

No Name in the Street. New York: Dial, 1972. NF

One Day, When I Was Lost. New York: Dial, 1973. T

The Devil Finds Work. New York: Laurel, 1976. NF

Little Man, Little Man: A Story of Childhood. New York: Dial, 1976. F

If Beale Street Could Talk. New York: Dial, 1979. F

Just Above My Head. New York: Dial, 1979. F

The Evidence of Things Unseen: An Essay. New York: Holt, Rinehart & Winston, 1985. NF

Jimmy's Blues. New York: St. Martin's, 1985. P

The Price of the Ticket: Collected Nonfiction 1948-1985. New York: St. Martin's, 1985. NF

Beam, Joseph

In the Life: A Black Gay Anthology. Boston: Alyson Publications, 1986. NF

Bellegarde-Smith, Patrick

Haiti: The Beached Citadel. Boulder: Westview Press, 1990. NF

Corbin, Steven

No Easy Place to Be. New York: Simon & Schuster, 1989. F

Delany, Samuel

The Jewels of Aptor. New York: Ace Books, 1962. F

Captives of the Flame. New York: Ace Books, 1963. F

The Ballad of Beta-2. New York: Ace Books, 1965. F

Babel-17. New York: Ace Books, 1966. F

Empire Star. New York: Ace Books, 1966. F

Nova. New York: Doubleday, 1968. F

The Einstein Intersection. London: V. Gollancz, 1968. F

City of a Thousand Suns. London: Sphere Books, 1969. F

The Fall of the Towers. New York: Ace Books, 1970. F

Driftglass. Garden City: Doubleday, 1971. F

The Tides of Lust. New York: Lancer Books, 1973. F

Triton: An Ambiguous Heterotopia. New York: Bantam, 1976. F

Jewel-Hinged Jaw: Notes on the Language of Science Fiction. Elizabethtown: Dragon Press, 1977. NF

Empire: A Visual Novel. New York: Berkeley Publishing, 1978. F

The American Shore: Meditations on a Tale of Science Fiction by Thomas M. Disch Angouleme. Elizabethtown: Dragon Press, 1978. NF

Starboard Wine: More Notes on the Language of Science Fiction. Pleasantville: Dragon Press, 1984. NF

Heavenly Breakfast: An Essay on the Winter of Love. New York: Bantam, 1979. NF

Tales of Neveryon. New York: Bantam, 1979. F

Distant Stars. New York: Bantam, 1981. F

Dhalgren. New York: Bantam, 1981. F

Neveryona, Or the Tale of Signs and Cities. New York: Bantam, 1983. F

Stars in My Pocket Like Grains of Sand. New York: Bantam, 1984. F

Flight from Neveryon. New York: Bantam, 1985. F

The Bridge of Lost Desire. New York: Arbor House, 1987. F

Wagner/Artaud: A Play of 19th and 20th Century Critical Factors. New York: Ansatz Press, 1988. NF

The Motion of Light in Water: Sex and Science Fiction Writing in the East Village, 1957-1965. New York: Plume, 1988. NF

Straits of Messina. Seattle: Zirconia Press, 1989. NF

Dixon, Melvin

Change of Territory. Lexington: University of Kentucky Press, 1983. P

Ride Out the Wilderness: Geography and Identity in Afro-American Literature. Urbana: University of Illinois Press, 1987. NF

Trouble the Water. Boulder: University of Colorado Press, 1989. F

The Collected Poems: Léopold Sédar Senghor (Translations). Charlottesville: University Press of Virginia, 1990. P

Duplechan, Larry

Eight Days a Week. Boston: Alyson Publications, 1985. F

Blackbird. New York: St. Martin's, 1986. F

Tangled Up in Blue. New York: St. Martin's, 1989. F

Fleming, Mickey C.

About Courage. Los Angeles: Holloway House, 1989. NF

Gonsalves, Roy

Evening Sunshine. New York: Renaissance Books, 1988. P

Hall, Noel Nantambu

Songs, Reflections, and Poetry. New York: Noel Hall, 1974. P

Hemphill, Essex

Earth Life. Washington, D.C.: Be Bop Books, 1985. P

Conditions. Washington, D.C.: Be Bop Books, 1986. P

Jolly, Doyle F.

Day Dreams. Washington, D.C.: Doyle F. Jolly, 1983. P

Kenan, Randall

A Visitation of Spirits. New York: Grove Press, 1989. F

Miller, Alan

At the Club. Oakland, Calif.: Grand Entrances Press, 1988. P

Mitchell, Lionel

Traveling Light. New York: Seaview Books, 1980. F

Nugent, Richard Bruce

"Smoke, Lilies and Jade," in *Fire!!*, ed. Wallace Thurman. New York: Fire!! Press, vol. 1, no. 1, November 1926. Facsimile printed by Fire!! Press. P.O. Box 327, Metuchen, NJ 08840. "Smoke, Lilies and Jade" is possibly the first piece of black literature to openly deal with gay desire. F

"Cavalier," in *Caroling Dusk*, ed. Countee Cullen. New York: Harper, 1927. P

Artists and Influences: 1982, ed. James Hatch. New York: Hatch-Billops Collection Corp., 1982. NF

You Must Remember This: An Oral History of Manhattan from the 1890s to World War II, ed. Jeff Kisseloff. New York: Harcourt, Brace & Jovanovich, 1989. NF

Robinson, Philip

Secret Passages: A Trilogy of Thought. New York: Vantage Press, 1987. P

Rustin, Bayard

Interracial Primer. New York: Fellowship of Reconciliation, 1943. NF

Down the Line: The Collected Writings of Bayard Rustin. Chicago: Quadrangle Books, 1971. NF

Strategies for Freedom: The Changing Patterns of Black Protest. New York: Columbia University Press, 1976. NF

Saint, Assoto

Stations. New York: Galiens Press, 1989. P

Stanford, Adrian

Black and Queer. Boston: Good Gay Poets, 1977. P

Sur, Sur Rodney

Selected Poetry. New York: Sur Rodney Sur, 1981. P

Thurman, Wallace

Fire!! New York: Fire!! Press, vol. 1, no. 1, November 1926.

Infants of the Spring. New York: Macaulay, 1952. F

The Blacker the Berry (with A.C. Furman). New York: Arno Press, 1969. F

The Interne. Ann Arbor: University Microfilms International, 1980. (reprint) F

Tinney, James

Black Pentecostalism: An Annotated Bibliography. Washington, D.C.: James Tinney, 1979. NF

Issues and Trends in Afro-American Journalism (with Justin J. Rector). Lanham, Md.: University Press of America, 1980. NF

Vega

Men of Color. Sicklerville, N.J.: Vega Press, 1989. P

Woods, Donald

The Space. Brooklyn, N.Y.: Vexation Press, 1989. P

JOURNALS, PERIODICALS, NEWSLETTERS
(Some dates of publication were not available)

Attaché. Washington: Diplomat Communications, 1983.

B: The International Newsletter of Black Men Who Love Black Men. New York: B. Nia Ngulu.

B & G. New York: BG Publishing, vol. 1, no. 1, February 1990–.

Black and White Men Together. New York: Black and White Men Together, vol. 1, no. 1, 1972–. Succeeded by *Men of All Colors Together*, April 1985–.

Blackheart: A Journal of Writing and Graphics by Black Gay Men. New York: Blackheart Collective, no. 1, 1982 – no. 3, 1985.

BGM. Washington: Blacklight, vol. 1, no. 1, May/June 1987–.

Blacklight. Washington: Blacklight, vol. 1, no. 1, 1979–1985.

Black/Out: The Magazine of the National Coalition of Black Lesbians and Gays. Washington, D.C.: National Coalition of Black Lesbians and Gays. vol. 1, no. 1, Summer 1986–.

BLK. Los Angeles: *BLK* Publishing, vol. 1, no. 1, 1988–.

Brother to Brother: Newsletter of the Brother to Brother Organization. San Francisco: Brother to Brother, vol. 1, no. 1, September 1982 – vol. 3, no. 2, Summer 1984.

Diplomat Magazine. Washington: Diplomat Communications, vol. 1, no. 1, 1983–1984.

Drum. Austin: Ebony Connection, vol. 1, no. 1, 1987–.

Gay Men of African Descent Newsletter. New York: Gay Men of African Descent, vol. 1, no. 1, October 3, 1987–.

Habari-Daftari: The NCBG Newsmagazine. Washington: National Coalition of Black Gays, no. 1, December 1983 – no. 5, July 1984.

Moja: Black and Gay. New York: Calvin Lowery.

Other Countries: Black Gay Voices. New York: Other Countries, vol. 1, no. 1, Spring 1988–.

The Pyramid Periodical, New York: Rodney G. Dildy and Charles Pouncy, vol. 1, no. 1, Fall 1988.

The Pyramid Poetry Periodical, Bronx, N.Y.: Roy Gonsalves, vol. 1, no. 1, April/May 1986 – vol. 2, no. 2, October/December 1987.

Rafiki: The Journal of the Association of Black Gays. Van Ness, Calif.: Association of Black Gays, vol. 1, no. 1, Fall 1976–.

The Real Read. Los Angeles: Ron Grayson and Cleo Manago, vol. 1, no. 1, April 1989–.

Zami Newsletter. Toronto, vol. 1, no. 1, 1986–.

ANTHOLOGIES

After You're Out, ed. Karla Jay and Allen Young. New York: Links Books, 1975.

Lavender Culture, ed. Karla Jay and Allen Young. New York: Jove, 1979.

Black Men/White Men: A Gay Antholog, ed. Michael J. Smith. San Francisco: Gay Sunshine Press, 1983.

Not Love Alone: A Modern Gay Anthology, ed. Martin Humphries. London: Gay Men's Press, 1985.

In the Life: A Black Gay Anthology, ed. Joseph Beam. Boston: Alyson Publications, 1986.

Gay Life: Leisure, Love and Living for the Contemporary Gay Male, ed. Eric Rofes. Garden City, N.Y.: Doubleday, 1986.

Worlds Apart: An Anthology of Lesbian and Gay Science Fiction and Fantasy, ed. Camilla Decarnin, Eric Garber, and Lyn Paleo. Boston: Alyson Publications, 1986.

New Men, New Minds: Breaking Male Tradition, ed. Franklin Abbott. Freedom, Calif.: Crossing Press, 1987.

Tongues Untied, ed. Martin Humphries. London: Gay Men's Press, 1987.

Gay and Lesbian Poetry in Our Time, ed. Joan Larkin and Carl Morse. New York: St. Martin's, 1988.

Shadows of Love: American Gay Fiction, ed. Charles Jurrist. Boston: Alyson Publications, 1988.

Men on Men 2: An Anthology of Gay Fiction, ed. George Stambolian. New York: New American Library, 1988.

Poets for Life: 76 Poets Respond to AIDS, ed. Michael Klein. New York: Crown Books, 1989.

Men & Intimacy: Personal Accounts Exploring the Dilemmas of Modern Male Sexuality, ed. Franklin Abbott. Freedom, Calif.: Crossing Press, 1990.

MISCELLANEOUS

Gordon, Billi

You've Had Worse Things in Your Mouth (Cookbook). San Francisco: West Graphics, 1985. NF

Fani-Kayode, Rotimi

Black Male/White Male (Photographs). London: Borderline, 1988.

CONTRIBUTORS

CARLYLE R. BLACK is a 24-year-old native of Washington, D.C., who is inspired by the insight of black authors and their interpretations of "our" lives. He hopes to continue along their gilded path and help pave a road to a beautiful future for us all.

RORY BUCHANAN is thirty-four years old and lives in Brooklyn, New York with his sixteen-year-old son. His work has appeared in the *Pyramid Periodical*. He is an AIDS educator with the Minority Task Force on AIDS in New York City.

WALTER RICO BURRELL was a native of Compton, California. He died in the fall of 1990 as a result of complications related to AIDS. Burrell held an A.A. from Compton College, a B.A. from Hampton Institute, and an M.A. from UCLA. He was a journalist, writer, and publicist. He worked for Universal Studios, Motown, Twentieth Century Fox, MGM, and ABC during the course of his career, and he contributed to numerous publications, including *Ebony, Essence,* the *Los Angeles Times,* the *New York Times, Black Stars,* and *Rolling Stone.* Prior to his death, he was a manager and writer in the Public Affairs Office at California State University, Los Angeles, where he also taught classes in composition and journalism.

DON CHARLES, twenty-nine, lives in Kansas City, Missouri, where he was born and raised. "My poetry reflects my personal experience as an unemployed gay black man trying to survive in a hostile society. I'm sexually attracted to other men of color, and not ashamed to say so."

DAMBALLAH is a Washington-based visual artist. His work has been presented in numerous solo and group exhibitions including the National Exhibition of Contemporary African American Art as part of the National Black Arts Festival. His work has been collected by the Afro-American Museum of History and Culture (Philadelphia), the U.S. Public Information Agency, the African American Scholars Council, and numerous private collections. His works have been published in *Black Artists on Art, Mid-Atlantic Center for Race Equity, Art Papers,* and *Selected Essays: Art and Artists from the Harlem Renaissance to the 1980s.*

DERYL K. DEESE was born in Port Arthur, Texas, in 1961. At the age of four he moved to Los Angeles with his mother. He attended Santa Monica High School and excelled in both academics and wrestling. After graduating from high school, he attended the University of Southern California, where he pledged a prominent black fraternity, Alpha Phi Alpha, and graduated with a bachelor of science degree in finance. During college, Deryl finally gave in to his needs and desires for men.

MELVIN DIXON is the author of two novels, *Red Leaves* (New American Library, 1990) and *Trouble the Water* (Fiction Collective Two/University of Colorado, 1989), and a volume of poetry, *Change of Territory* (1983). He is the translator of *The Collected Poems of Léopold Sédar Senghor* (University Press of Virginia, 1990) and has received fellowships in poetry and fiction from the National Endowment for the Arts and the New York Arts Foundation. His work has appeared in many journals and anthologies, including *Men on Men 2: Best New Gay Fiction; Poets for Life: 76 Poets Respond to AIDS*; and *In the Life*.

GUY-MARK FOSTER was born in Logan, West Virginia, in 1959. His prose and poetry have appeared in the *James White Review*, the *Pyramid Periodical*, and the collection of short stories *Shadows of Love*. He currently lives in Brooklyn.

DAVID FRECHETTE is a native New Yorker whose film, music, and gay culture articles have appeared in the *City Sun, Essence*, the *Advocate, Right On!*, and *Black Film Review*. His poetry has appeared in the *Pyramid Periodical* and *RFD*. A founding member of Other Countries, he is currently working on a short story collection.

CHARLES HENRY FULLER is a free-lance writer based in Cambridge, Massachusetts. His essays and literary criticism have appeared nationally in *Gay Community News, Windy City Times*, and *Seattle Gay News*. His work has been anthologized in *Gay Life*. He is the author of an unpublished novel, *Cakewalk*, and is currently at work on a second.

CALVIN GLENN is a creative writing major at Dartmouth College. He serves as secretary for the gay and lesbian organization on campus. "In My Own Space" is his first published piece.

D. RUBIN GREEN is an actor, writer, musician, and teacher now living in Brooklyn. His poetry has previously appeared in the *Other Countries Journal*. He has performed at numerous New York and regional theaters as well as in various film, radio, and television works. He is a graduate of Yale University.

CHARLES HARPE, thirty-seven, resides in Philadelphia. A graduate of Syracuse and Drexel Universities, he has combined his writing pursuits with a career in nonprofit administration, and has held positions with several mental health, arts, and AIDS service organizations. His work for the stage has been produced by the Bushfire Theatre of the Performing Arts and was featured on National Public Radio. His essays, commentaries, and reviews have been published in the *Philadelphia New Observer* and the *Real News*.

CRAIG G. HARRIS is a journalist, fiction writer, and poet who has been published in the *Advocate, Blackheart 3, Black/Out, Central Park, Changing Men, Gay Community News*, the *New York Native, Out/Week*, the *Philadelphia Tribune, RFD*, the *Washington Blade*, and numerous other periodicals. His work is a part of several anthologies including *Gay Life; In the Life; New Men, New Minds*; and *Tongues Untied*.

ESSEX HEMPHILL is the author of *Earth Life* and *Conditions*. He is the recipient of fellowships in literature from the D.C. Commission for the Arts and the National Endowment for the Arts. His work is featured in the black gay films *Looking for Langston* and *Tongues Untied*, and he narrated the black gay AIDS documentary *Out of the Shadows*. His work is anthologized in: *Tongues Untied; In the Life; New Men, New Minds; Gay and Lesbian Poetry in Our Time; Art Against Apartheid; Men and Intimacy; The Poet Upstairs; Natives, Tourists and Other Mysteries;* and *High Risk*. His essays have appeared in *High Performance, Gay Community News, Out/Week,* and the *Advocate*.

REGINALD T. JACKSON is a playwright and director. He is the founder and artistic director of the Rainbow Repertory Theatre (which produces original works by lesbians and gay men of color in New York City). He is a board member of Other Countries, a black gay literary collective. He currently lives in Brooklyn where he dedicates his life to the work at hand, and his heart to his man — Greg.

CARY ALAN JOHNSON is an author, activist, and Africanist. His work has appeared in magazines, anthologies, and on stages and screens throughout the United States, in Africa, and in Europe. Brooklyn is his home.

ISAAC JULIEN is a founding member of Britain's internationally known Sankofa Film and Video Collective. His film works include *The Passion of Remembrance,* produced with Sankofa member Maureen Blackwood; *This Is Not An AIDS Advertisement;* and the critically acclaimed *Looking for Langston.* His forthcoming film, *Young Soul Rebels,* is concerned with color differences, interracial couples, and homosexuality.

JOHN KEENE, JR., was born in 1965 and raised in St. Louis, Missouri. He attended Harvard University, where he studied literature and writing with Carlos Fuentes and Ishmael Reed. He is the recipient of a 1990 Fellowship in Fiction from the Artists Foundation/Massachusetts Cultural Council. He is a member of the Dark Room Writers Collective and the Union of Writers of African Peoples. He is presently working on a cycle of stories exploring the lives of African Americans based in Boston.

KOBENA MERCER was a member of the Gay Black Group in London in the early 1980s. He has written and lectured widely on issues of race, sexuality, and representation. His essays have appeared in *Screen, 10-8,* and *New Formations.* After working at the British Film Institute, he is presently assistant professor in art history at the University of California at Santa Cruz.

ALAN E. MILLER lives in Oakland, California. A native of Chicago and an Amherst College graduate, his writing has appeared in *Gay Community News, Outlook, Black American Literature Forum,* and *MAWA Review.* He likes to think himself a free spirit.

CHARLES I. NERO received his Ph.D. in Speech Communication and Afro-American Studies from Indiana University in Bloomington in 1990. He received an M.A. from Wake Forest University and a B.A. from Xavier University in New Orleans. He has taught at Valdosta State College, Indiana University, and Ithaca College. Currently, he is working on a study of the Haitian Revolution and a history of African American gay performance aesthetics. He lives in Gainesville, Florida, with his lover of seven years.

ROGER V. PAMPLIN, JR., was born in Chicago in 1960. He was the first of three children and the only boy. Roger attended Mendel Catholic High School, where he excelled in academics, wrestling, and track, and as a result, he was awarded a track and academic scholarship to Chicago State University. In 1979, Roger married and entered the military, during which time his two children, Courtney and Roger III, were born. He was divorced in 1985 and immediately began a promising bodybuilding and film career. Roger contracted AIDS in July 1987 and succumbed to the disease three years later.

CHARLES R.P. POUNCY is the past editor of the *Pyramid Periodical*. His work has appeared in the *Other Countries Journal*, and his play *Kids* was produced in 1989 by the Rainbow Repertory Theatre Company in New York City. He is a graduate of Fordham University and the Cornell Law School. He currently lives and practices in New York City.

ROBERT F. REID-PHARR is a writer, scholar, and activist living in Brooklyn. He is currently compiling a book-length bibliography of writings by and about gay men of African descent and doing research for a manuscript on gender ideology in nineteenth-century African American nationalism.

CRAIG REYNOLDS, a native Washingtonian, has had poetry published in *Changing Men, Turnstile,* and *Black American Literature Forum*. His work has also appeared in *In the Life* and in Howard University's *New Directions*. He has read at the International Monetary Fund and the National Theater.

MARLON RIGGS graduated with honors from Harvard College in 1978 and received his master's degree from U.C. Berkeley's Graduate School of Journalism in 1981. He is the producer, director, and writer of the prize-winning documentary *Ethnic Notions*, which received a National Emmy Award, and the producer, director, and editor of the black gay documentary *Tongues Untied*. A native of Texas, Riggs presently resides in Oakland, California, and is a faculty member at the Graduate School of Journalism at U.C. Berkeley. His work-in-progress, *Color Adjustment*, is a sequel to *Ethnic Notions*, and is supported by grants from the Rockefeller Foundation, the Corporation for Public Broadcasting, and the American Film Institute's Independent Filmmaker Program, among others.

ASSOTO SAINT is the author of *Risin' to the Love We Need, New Love Song, Nuclear Lovers,* and other theatrical pieces that deal with the lives of gay African Americans. His most recent poetry collection is *Stations*. He is the recipient of the 1990 James Baldwin Award from the Black Gay and Lesbian Leadership Forum. He was awarded a 1990 Fellowship in Poetry from the New York Foundation for the Arts.

RON SIMMONS, Ph.D., is a native of Brooklyn. He has been a free-lance writer, photographer, and media producer for nearly twenty years. His productions include *New Directions for the Black Church; Hunger in the Nation's Capital; Think: Howard;* and *NCBLG: The First Decade*. He was a cast member, still photographer, and the Washington, D.C., field producer for the award-winning film *Tongues Untied*. Dr. Simmons is currently an assistant professor in the Department of Radio, TV, and Film at Howard University.

BOBBY (Robert G.) SMITH, a native of Seattle, Washington, now makes his home in Los Angeles, where he has been active in gay politics and health education for the past several years. He founded the Black Gay Men's Coalition for Human Rights and is a founding member of the Minority AIDS Project. He is a health educator for the National Task Force on AIDS Prevention and serves as a counselor for the Gay and Lesbian Community Services Center. He writes in his spare time.

ADRIAN STANFORD was a native of Philadelphia. He was the author of a chapbook of poems entitled *Black and Queer* and published by Good Gay Poets Press of Boston in 1977. Mr. Stanford befell an early and unfortunate demise in 1981. To his credit, *Black and Queer* is considered to be the first collection of homoerotic poetry published by a black gay man. The selections of Stanford's work appearing in this anthology are from *Black and Queer*.

LAMONT B. STEPTOE is a poet, photographer, and publisher and the author of three books: *Crimson River, American Morning/Mourning,* and *Small Steps and Toes,* a collaboration with poet Bob Small. Steptoe is the founder of Whirlwind Press, which recently published South African poet-in-exile Dennis Brutus's *Airs and Tributes.* Born and raised in Pittsburgh, Steptoe has read at the Library of Congress, the National Library of Nicaragua, the University of Pennsylvania, the Philadelphia Afro-American Historical and Cultural Museum, the Walt Whitman Poetry Center, and Giovanni's Room. His work has appeared in *Black/Out, Asphodel, Paper Air, Arabella,* and the *Painted Bride Quarterly.*

VEGA is a graphic artist, poet, and photographer. Born in New York in the fifties, under the sign of Virgo, in September of 1989 he published *Men of Color: An Essay on the Black Male Couple.* His latest work, *A Warm December,* will be released in the summer of 1991.

DONALD WOODS is a poet, singer, and arts worker living in Brooklyn. Woods's work as a writer began with involvement in the Blackheart Collective, a group of black gay men who published a series of journals and presented readings. He was a student of Audre Lorde, and peer group experiences such as Other Countries, a black gay men's writing workshop, provided the critical support that helped develop his craft. His work — poetry and prose — has appeared in *Art & Artists; New York Native; Blackheart III; Ikon: Art Against Apartheid; In the Life;* and the *Other Countries Journal.* In June of 1989, with support from Art Matters, Inc., Woods self-published a portfolio of his poetry entitled *The Space.*

WRATH is a poet, performance artist, and Philadelphian presently residing in Los Angeles. In 1989, a chapbook of his work entitled *The Horrors of Humanity* was released. His work has been called "powerful and savage." A fellow poet has likened a reading by Wrath as tantamount to "being mugged by poetry."

Other books of interest from
ALYSON PUBLICATIONS

IN THE LIFE, edited by Joseph Beam, $9.00. When writer and activist Joseph Beam became frustrated that so little gay literature spoke to him as a black gay man, he did something about it: The result was *In the Life,* an anthology which takes its name from a black slang expression for "gay." Here, thirty-three writers and artists explore what it means to be doubly different — black and gay — in modern America. Their stories, essays, poetry, and artwork voice the concerns and aspirations of an often silent minority.

AS WE ARE, by Don Clark, $8.00. This book, from the author of *Loving Someone Gay* and *Living Gay,* examines our gay identity in the AIDS era. Clark explores the growth and maturation of the gay community in recent years. By breaking down our ability to love and care for one another into its components, Clark creates a clear picture of where we have been, where we are going, and he emphasizes the importance of being *As We Are.*

THE ADVOCATE ADVISER, by Pat Califia, $9.00. The Miss Manners of gay culture tackles subjects ranging from the ethics of zoophilia to the etiquette of a holy union ceremony. Along the way she covers interracial relationships, in-law problems, and the problems facing gay parents. No other gay columnist so successfully combines useful advice, an unorthodox perspective, and a wicked sense of humor.

THE ALYSON ALMANAC, $9.00. How did your representatives in Congress vote on gay issues? What are the best gay and lesbian books, movies, and plays? When was the first gay and lesbian March on Washington? With what king did Julius Caesar have a sexual relationship? You'll find all this, and more, in this unique and entertaining reference work.

CERTAIN VOICES, edited by Darryl Pilcher, $9.00. This new collection of gay male fiction showcases both new writers and already-known names such as Michael Nava, Lev Raphael, and Larry Duplechan. The eighteen stories address a wide spectrum of concerns: AIDS, and our perspectives on it; homophobia; relationships with children; and, of course, being in and out of love.

BI ANY OTHER NAME, edited by Loraine Hutchins and Lani Kaahumanu, $12.00. Hear the voices of over seventy women and men from all walks of life describe their lives as bisexuals. They tell their stories — personal, political, spiritual, historical — in prose, poetry, art, and essays. These are individuals who have fought prejudice from both the gay and straight communities and who have begun only recently to share their experiences. This ground-breaking anthology is an important step in the process of forming a community of their own.

LAVENDER LISTS, by Lynne Yamaguchi Fletcher and Adrien Saks, $9.00. Here are more entertaining and informative new lists about our culture: 8 button slogans of the 1960s, 16 couples and how they met, 10 openly gay cops, 9 massive anti-gay purges, and much more.

COMING OUT RIGHT, by Wes Muchmore and William Hanson, $8.00. Every gay man can recall the first time he stepped into a gay bar. That difficult step often represents the transition from a life of secrecy and isolation into a world of unknowns. The transition will be easier for men who have this recently updated book. Here, many facets of gay life are spelled out for the newcomer, including: coming out at work; gay health and the AIDS crisis; and the unique problems faced by men who are coming out when they're under 18 or over 30.

COMING ALONG FINE, by Wes Muchmore and William Hanson, $7.00. What are the tricks to making a long-term gay relationship work? How can you minimize the problems of gay travel abroad? Is it realistic to think about starting your own gay business? Here is an informative, often opinionated, and always entertaining look at these and other questions facing today's gay man.

DADDY'S ROOMMATE, by Michael Willhoite, cloth, $15.00. This is the first book written for the children of gay men. In thirty-two pages a young boy, his father, and the father's lover take part in activities familiar to all kinds of families: cleaning the house, shopping, playing games, fighting, and making up. The drawings, by popular caricaturist Michael Willhoite, are simple and colorful, and the binding is sturdy — perfect for children aged two to five.

THE TWO OF US, by Larry J. Uhrig, $7.00. Any two people trying to build a fulfilling relationship today face some major hurdles. A gay or lesbian couple faces even more potential problems. Here, Larry Uhrig, pastor of the Metropolitan Community Church in Washington, D.C., draws on his experience counseling gay couples to provide a practical handbook about how to make a gay relationship work.

EIGHT DAYS A WEEK, by Larry Duplechan, $7.00. Johnnie Ray Rousseau is a 22-year-old black gay pop singer whose day starts at 11 p.m. Keith Keller is a white banker with a 10 o'clock bedtime — and muscles to die for. This story of their love affair is one of the most engrossing — and funniest — you'll ever read.

FROM FEMALE TO MALE, by Louis Graydon Sullivan, $9.00. On Monday, September 21, 1936, the San Francisco *Chronicle* announced the shocking news on its front page: "'Jack Bee' Was Woman." And so ended the forty-year secret of "Jack Bee," who was born Virginia Mugarrieta in San Francisco in 1869. This well-researched book chronicles the life of a popular journalist who spent most of her life posing as a man. *From Female to Male* covers Garland's impoverished childhood in San Francisco, her well-publicized life in Stockton, California, and her travels to the Philippines during the Spanish-American War.

GAY AND GRAY, by Raymond M. Berger, $8.00. There are over a million gay men in the U.S. over age 65, yet they are among the most invisible of all minorities. Here, working from questionnaires and case histories, Raymond Berger looks at the special circumstances of this group. Some, he finds, express resentment at the physical inroads of age, yet others testify that with age has come greater freedom from public opinion and increased happiness.

HOT LIVING, edited by John Preston, $9.00. The AIDS crisis has closed off some forms of sexual activity for health-conscious gay men, but it has also encouraged many men to look for new forms of sexual expression. Here, over a dozen of today's most popular gay writers erotically describe those new possibilities.

THE GAY BOOK OF LISTS, by Leigh Rutledge, $8.00. Rutledge has compiled a fascinating and informative collection of lists. His subject matter ranges from history (6 gay popes) to politics (9 perfectly disgusting reactions to AIDS) to entertainment (12 examples of gays on network television) to humor (9 Victorian "cures" for masturbation). Learning about gay culture and history has never been so much fun.

THE GAY FIRESIDE COMPANION, by Leigh Rutledge, $9.00. Leigh Rutledge, author of *The Gay Book of Lists* and *Unnatural Quotations,* has written fact-filled articles on scores of subjects: unusual gay historic sites in the U.S.; fascinating mothers of famous gay men; footnote gay people in history; public opinion polls on homosexuality over the last twenty years; a day-by-day, year-by-year history of the AIDS epidemic.

THE CARAVAGGIO SHAWL, by Samuel M. Steward, $9.00. Gertrude Stein and Alice B. Toklas step out of the literary haut monde and into the Parisian underworld to track down a murderer and art thief. While Gertrude and Alice dig for clues in literary salons and art exhibitions, Johnny McAndrews, a gay American writer, takes us on a wild and wicked romp through the decadent side of Parisian life.

GAYS IN UNIFORM, edited by Kate Dyer, $7.00. Why doesn't the Pentagon want you to read this book? When two studies by a research arm of the Pentagon concluded that there was no justification for keeping gay people out of the military, the generals deep-sixed the reports. Those reports are now available, in book form, to the public at large. Find out for yourself what the Pentagon doesn't want you to know about gays in the military.

MATLOVICH, by Mike Hippler, $9.00. Air Force Sergeant Leonard Matlovich appeared on the cover of *Time* magazine when he was discharged for being gay — and decided to fight back. This courageous activist did not fit the usual gay stereotype, and his outspoken, generally conservative views created controversy over his role as a community leader. Mike Hippler has written, with Matlovich's cooperation, the definitive biography of this gay hero.

HOW WOULD YOU FEEL IF YOUR DAD WAS GAY?, by Ann Heron and Meredith Maran; illustrated by George Martins, cloth, $15.00. When Jasmine announces in class that her dad is gay, her brother complains that she had no right to reveal a fact that he wanted to keep secret. This, and other concerns facing the children of lesbian and gay parents, are addressed in the context of real-life situations. This is the first book to provide role models for children in these nontraditional families and to give insight into the unique problems they face.

LIFETIME GUARANTEE, by Alice Bloch, $7.00. In this personal journal of a woman faced with the impending death of her sister from cancer, Alice Bloch goes beyond her specific experiences to a moving exploration of the themes of survival, support, and affirmation of life.

DECADE DANCE, by Michael Lassell, $8.00. Lassell's gritty, passionate poems capture the piercing losses and gentle victories of gay men during the plague years of the eighties. Lassell's steely but soft characters look you straight in the eye to tell you their — your — story. Remembrances of friends lost, lovers found, and the slow dawning "idea of me." This powerful collection will prove to be a touchstone for a generation of gay men who must make sense of those desperate years.

WORLDS APART, edited by Camilla Decarnin, Eric Garber, Lyn Paleo, $8.00. The world of science fiction allows writers to freely explore alternative sexualities. These eleven stories take full advantage of that opportunity with characters ranging from a black lesbian vampire to a gay psychodroid. Here are adventure, romance, and excitement — and perhaps some genuine alternatives for our future.

BOYS' TOWN, by Art Bosch, $8.00. Join Scout DeYoung and Nash Aquilon in *Boys' Town*, West Hollywood, as they search for lasting love in these "times of disposable *everything*." Their lives have ridiculous elements, like the burglar who steals their porn and rearranges the furniture, and also the harsh realities of AIDS and gay-bashing. But through it all, they succeed in creating an extended gay family and a warm, loving place to call home.

COWBOY BLUES, by Stephen Lewis, $7.00. Jake Lieberman is a gay detective in the typical California tradition. When a 45-year-old cowboy comes into his office to report that his younger partner is missing, Jake's first impulse is to gently explain to the guy that he's been dumped. But soon his investigation shows that Andy Jones's disappearance is only part of a much wider scheme. The only question is: Will Jake live to uncover it all?

BETTER ANGEL, by Richard Meeker, $7.00. The touching story of a young man's gay awakening in the years between the World Wars. Kurt Gray is a shy, bookish boy growing up in a small town in Michigan. Even at the age of thirteen he knows that somehow he is different. Gradually he recognizes his desire for a man's companionship and love. As a talented composer, breaking into New York's musical world, he finds the love he's sought.

QUATREFOIL, by James Barr. Introduction by Samuel Steward, $8.00. When this novel was first published in 1950, it presented two of the first positive, nonstereotyped gay characters to be found in American fiction. As a novel it is still as thrilling as ever; on top of that, it provides a vivid picture of life in our recent, but often-forgotten, past.

CHINA HOUSE, by Vincent Lardo, $7.00. Scott Evans inherits an elegant mansion near the New England town of Salem. He enlists the help of Howard Roth, a psychologist who specializes in the supernatural, and they soon find that in China House anything can happen. This gay gothic novel has everything: romance, intrigue, a young heir obsessed by the death of his identical twin brother, and a father–son relationship that's closer than most.

THE HUSTLER, by John Henry Mackay, $8.00. Gunther is fifteen when he arrives alone in the Berlin of the 1920s. Soon he discovers the boys of Friedrich Street, and the men who stroll by and speak with them — and one man in particular, the young Hermann Graff, who falls hopelessly in love with Gunther. Mackay wrote *The Hustler* in 1926. Today, this first English translation combines a poignant love story with a colorful portrayal of the gay subculture that thrived in Berlin sixty years ago.

ONE TEENAGER IN TEN, edited by Ann Heron, $4.00. One teenager in ten is gay. Here, twenty-six young people from around the country discuss their experiences: coming out to themselves, to parents, and friends; trying to pass as straight; running away; incest; trouble with the law; making initial contacts with the gay community; religious concerns; and more. Their words will provide encouragement for other teenagers facing similar experiences.

KAIROS, by Zalmon O. Sherwood, $7.00. In 1985, a young Episcopal priest found that his search for human justice and human warmth had brought him to a collision course with the traditional expectations of his church. Here, Zal Sherwood describes his *kairos* — the moment he decided to come out and expose the discrimination he experienced as a gay priest. He offers a personal look at a public man's courage.

LAVENDER COUCH, by Marny Hall, $8.00. What can you realistically expect to accomplish by seeing a therapist? How can you choose a therapist who's right for you? What should you consider when discussing fees? When is it time to get out of therapy? These are a few of the questions addressed here, in the first book that specifically addresses the concerns of gay men and lesbians who are considering therapy. Dr. Hall's advice will be invaluable both for individuals already in therapy, and those who are contemplating it.

IN THE LAND OF ALEXANDER, by Keith Hale, $9.00. Find out how modern-day Alexanders live the gay life. This travel book, by the author of the popular novel *Cody*, gives profiles of gay life in European countries unfamiliar to most gay men. Hale's sharp historical and cultural insights combine with useful travel tips to provide a perfect complement to the traditional travel guidebook.

LOVESEX, by Max Exander, $7.00. Through entries in his diary, Max Exander gives a vivid account of his six-month odyssey toward establishing a lasting gay relationship which incorporates safer sex and discards stereotypical ideas about two men in love with each other.

THE LITTLE DEATH, by Michael Nava, $8.00. As a public defender, Henry Rios finds himself losing the idealism he had as a law student. Then a man he has befriended — and loved — dies under suspicious circumstances. As he investigates the murder, Rios finds the solution as subtle as the law itself.

LONG TIME PASSING, edited by Marcy Adelman, $8.00. Here, in their own words, women talk about age-related concerns: the fear of losing a lover; the experience of being a lesbian in the 1940s and '50s; the issues of loneliness and community. Most contributors are older lesbians, but several younger voices are represented.

CHANGING PITCHES, by Steve Kluger, $8.00. Scotty Mackay is an American League pitcher who, at thirty-six, has to hit the comeback trail to save his all-star career. All goes well until he gets teamed up with a young catcher he detests: pretty-boy Jason Cornell. Jason has lots of teeth, poses for underwear ads, and has blue eyes ... and Scotty's favorite color is blue. By August, Scotty's got a major-league problem on his hands.

MACHO SLUTS, by Pat Califia, $10.00. Pat Califia, the prolific lesbian author, has put together a stunning collection of her best erotic short fiction. She explores sexual fantasy and adventure in previously taboo territory — incest, sex with a thirteen-year-old girl, a lesbian's encounter with two cops, a gay man who loves to dominate dominant men, as well as various S/M and "vanilla" scenes.

THE MEN WITH THE PINK TRIANGLE, by Heinz Heger, $8.00. For decades, history ignored the Nazi persecution of gay people. Only with the rise of the gay movement in the 1970s did historians finally recognize that gay people, like Jews and others deemed "undesirable," suffered enormously at the hands of the Nazi regime. Of the few who survived the concentration camps, only one ever came forward to tell his story. His true account of those nightmarish years provides an important introduction to a long-forgotten chapter of gay history.

OUT OF ALL TIME, by Terry Boughner, $7.00. Historian Terry Boughner scans the centuries and picks out scores of the past's most celebrated gay, lesbian, and bisexual personalities. From ancient Egypt to the twentieth century, from Alcibiades to Willa Cather, we discover a part of history that has too often been censored or ignored. Each chapter is imaginatively illustrated by *Washington Blade* caricaturist Michael Willhoite.

REFLECTIONS OF A ROCK LOBSTER, by Aaron Fricke, $7.00. Guess who's coming to the prom! In the spring of 1980, Aaron Fricke made national news by taking a male date to his high school prom. Yet for the first sixteen years of his life, Fricke had closely guarded the secret of his homosexuality. Here, told with insight and humor, is his story about growing up gay, about realizing that he was different, and about how he ultimately developed a positive gay identity in spite of the prejudice around him.

REVELATIONS, edited by Wayne Curtis, $8.00. For most gay men, one critical moment stands out as a special time in the coming-out process. It may be a special friendship, or a sexual episode, or a book or movie that communicates the right message at the right time. In *Revelations*, twenty-two men of varying ages and backgrounds give an account of this moment of truth. These tales of self-discovery will strike a chord of recognition in every gay reader.

TALK BACK!, by Lesbian and Gay Media Advocates, $4.00. When were you last offended by a homophobic story in the news media? Now there's something you can do about poor press coverage of gay and lesbian lives. Based on their own experience, the authors of *Talk Back!* tell how an individual or a group can do something about anti-gay bias in the media.

SHADOWS OF LOVE, edited by Charles Jurrist, $9.00. In this new short-story anthology, editor Charles Jurrist displays the rich diversity of gay male writing in contemporary America. Among the sixteen authors represented in this collection are several previously unpublished writers, as well as the often-unheard voices of racial and ethnic minorities. These stories present fresh and unusual perspectives on the modern gay experience.

THE BEST MAN, by Paul Reidinger, $8.00. Ross is an attractive, blond-haired, well-built law student at Stanford ... and he's made it quite obvious to David that he'd like them to spend more time together. That's the good news. The bad news is that Ross is already involved with David's best friend Katherine. What's a boy to do?

SOMEWHERE IN THE NIGHT, by Jeffrey N. McMahan, $8.00. Here are eight eerie tales of suspense and the supernatural by a newfound talent. Jeffrey N. McMahan weaves horribly realistic stories that contain just the right mix of horror, humor, and eroticism: a gruesome Halloween party, a vampire whose conscience bothers him, and a suburbanite with a killer lawn.

TREASURES ON EARTH, by Carter Wilson, $9.00. First published in cloth by Knopf in 1981, *Treasures on Earth* tells the "shadow history" of the historic 1911 expedition that led to the discovery of Machu Picchu in the Peruvian Andes. While the explorers search greedily for the "lost" city and the acclaim that will certainly follow, Willie Hickler, the expedition's photographer (and Wilson's central and fictional character), searches for love with Ernesto Mena, the expedition's handsome Peruvian guide.

LUCKY IN LOVE, by Don Sakers, $6.00. Frank Beale's best friend moves away and at first he's at loose ends. Then he accepts the job of manager of the high school basketball team — and strikes up a special friendship with the star player — and things start looking up fast.

THE GOLDDIGGERS, by Paul Monette, $9.00. Three men and one woman come together in Crook House, a grand old mansion left over from Hollywood's most glorious days. A hilarious murder, hidden treasure, and an exploding gay relationship await them. Their adventures call up America's favorite fantasies of fortune, fame, and living happily ever after.

FINALE, edited by Michael Nava, $9.00. Eight carefully crafted stories of mystery and suspense by both well-known authors and newfound talent: An anniversary party ends abruptly when a guest is found in the bathroom with his throat slashed; a frustrated writer plans the murder of a successful novelist; a young man's hauntingly familiar dreams lead him into a forgotten past.

ULRICHS, by Hubert Kennedy, $9.00. Karl Heinrich Ulrichs became the first man in modern times to publicly speak out in favor of homosexual rights when he declared to a convention of German jurists in 1867 that he himself was an "Urning." He was also an activist and writer in an age when that meant standing alone. Here, in the first complete biography of this early pioneer, Hubert Kennedy describes the life and ideas of the man who laid the foundation for today's gay movement.

UNNATURAL QUOTATIONS, by Leigh W. Rutledge, $9.00. The author of *The Gay Book of Lists* has put together an entertaining collection of quotations by, for, or about gay men and lesbians. Hundreds of figures — both past and present, homophilic and homophobic — are represented here. Well illustrated and indexed for handy reference, *Unnatural Quotations* promises the same excitement generated by *The Gay Book of Lists*.

SAFESTUD, by Max Exander, $8.00. Max Exander's first reaction to the idea of safe sex is disappointment. But with time, and with a little help from friends, he finds that the change from his old habits can be invigorating in unexpected ways.

THE TROUBLE WITH HARRY HAY, by Stuart Timmons, cloth, $20.00. This complete biography of Harry Hay, known as the father of gay liberation, sweeps through forty years of the gay movement and nearly eighty years of a colorful and original American life. Hay went from a pampered childhood, through a Hollywood acting career and a stint in the Communist Party before starting his life's work in 1950 when he founded the Mattachine Society, the forerunner of today's gay movement.

SUPPORT YOUR LOCAL BOOKSTORE

Most of the books described above are available at your nearest gay or feminist bookstore, and many of them will be available at other bookstores. If you can't get these books locally, order by mail using this form.

Enclosed is $_____ for the following books. (Add $1.00 postage when ordering just one book. If you order two or more, we'll pay the postage.)

1. _____

2. _____

3. _____

name: _____ address: _____

city: _____ state: _____ zip: _____

ALYSON PUBLICATIONS
Dept. H-46, 40 Plympton St., Boston, MA 02118

After December 31, 1992, please write for current catalog.